ALAN N. SUSSMAN is an attorney practicing law in Kingston, New York, with the firm of Ricken, Goldman, Sussman and Blythe. Additionally, he is Associate Adjunct Professor at the New York University School of Law where he teaches a course on juvenile justice. Previously, Mr. Sussman served as staff attorney for the Juvenile Rights Division of the New York City Legal Aid Society and as "Ombudsman" for children in institutions under the authority of the New York State Division for Youth. He is the author of *The Rights of Young People*, co-author of *Reporting Child Abuse and Neglect: Guidelines for Legislation*, and served as editor of the monthly ACLU publication, *Children's Rights Report*.

MARTIN GUGGENHEIM is Clinical Professor of Law and Director of the Juvenile Rights Clinic at the New York University School of Law. Previously, Mr. Guggenheim served as staff attorney and Acting Director of the Juvenile Rights Project of the American Civil Liberties Union and as staff attorney for the Juvenile Rights Division of the New York City Legal Aid Society. Mr. Guggenheim has litigated many important cases concerning juvenile justice and parents' rights. He is the author of numerous legal articles on juvenile law.

Also in this Series

AN AMERICAN
CIVIL LIBERTIES
UNION HANDBOOK

THE RIGHTS OF PARENTS

THE BASIC ACLU GUIDE TO THE RIGHTS OF PARENTS

Alan Sussman
and
Martin Guggenheim

General Editor of this series:
Norman Dorsen, *President, ACLU*

AVON
PUBLISHERS OF BARD, CAMELOT AND DISCUS BOOKS

THE RIGHTS OF PARENTS is an original publication of Avon Books. This work has never before appeared in book form.

AVON BOOKS
A division of
The Hearst Corporation
959 Eighth Avenue
New York, New York 10019

First Avon Printing, December, 1980

AVON TRADEMARK REG. U.S. PAT. OFF. AND IN
OTHER COUNTRIES, MARCA REGISTRADA, HECHO EN
U.S.A.

Printed in the U.S.A.

To Anna Sarah Sussman
and
Jamie, Courtney and Lesley Guggenheim

Acknowledgments

We would like to thank those who helped in the preparation of this work: Linda Whaley and Mary Ann Bollen for typing the manuscript; Mary Clark, Julia Weiss, Jill Sarnoff, and George Henry, who conducted research; New York University School of Law for providing research funds for students; Richard Crouch for reviewing the manuscript; and Mindy Brown and Denise Guggenheim for permitting us to be less than dedicated parents during the preparation of this book.

The model laws found in Appendix B are reprinted with permission from the National Commissioners on Uniform State Laws.

Contents

Preface

This guide sets forth your rights under present law and offers suggestions on how you can protect your rights. It is one of a continuing series of handbooks published in cooperation with the American Civil Liberties Union.

The hope surrounding these publications is that Americans informed of their rights will be encouraged to exercise them. Through their exercise, rights are given life. If they are rarely used, they may be forgotten and violations may become routine.

This guide offers no assurances that your rights will be respected. The laws may change and, in some of the subjects covered in these pages, they change quite rapidly. An effort has been made to note those parts of the law where movement is taking place, but it is not always possible to predict accurately when the law *will* change.

Even if the laws remain the same, interpretations of them by courts and administrative officials often vary. In a federal system such as ours, there is a built-in problem of the differences between state and federal law, not to speak of the confusion of the differences from state to state. In addition, there are wide variations in the ways in which particular courts and administrative officials will interpret the same law at any given moment.

If you encounter what you consider to be a specific abuse of your rights you should seek legal assistance. There are a number of agencies that may help you, among them ACLU affiliate offices, but bear in mind that the ACLU is a limited-purpose organization. In many communities, there are federally funded legal service offices which provide assistance to poor persons who cannot afford the costs of legal representation. In general, the rights that the ACLU defends are freedom of inquiry and expression; due process of law; equal protection of the laws; and privacy. The authors in this series have discussed other rights in these books (even though they sometimes fall outside the ACLU's usual concern) in order to provide as much guidance as possible.

These books have been planned as guides for the people directly affected: therefore the question and answer format. (In some areas there are more detailed works available for "experts.") These guides seek to raise the largest issues and inform the non-specialist of the basic law on the subject. The authors of the books are themselves specialists who understand the need for information at "street level."

No attorney can be an expert in every part of the law. If you encounter a specific legal problem in an area discussed in one of these handbooks, show the book to your attorney. Of course, he or she will not be able to rely *exclusively* on the handbook to provide you with adequate representation. But if your attorney hasn't had a great deal of experience in the specific area, the handbook can provide helpful suggestions on how to proceed.

Norman Dorsen, President
American Civil Liberties Union

The principal purpose of this handbook, and others in this series, is to inform individuals of their legal rights. The authors from time to time suggest what the law should be, but the author's personal views are not necessarily those of the ACLU. For the ACLU's position on the issues discussed in this handbook, the reader should write to Librarian, ACLU, 132 West 43rd Street, New York, N.Y. 10036.

Introduction

This book deals with a topic that concerns everyone with children: the rights of parents. To our knowledge, they have never been explained before. This is probably because the rights possessed by parents have no single source in law. Some derive from laws enacted by state legislatures, others from opinions written by federal and state courts, and some from the customs and traditions of western civilization itself. In this brief book we try to synthesize and make some sense of the many aspects and diverse declarations of the legal status of parents.

While the scope of a topic like this is potentially limitless, we have confined our research to issues such as the rights and limits of parents to control their children, the power of parents to determine the proper medical care and education of their children, and the special legal status of certain types of parents such as adoptive parents, foster parents, and grandparents.

Although the book touches upon aspects of marriage and divorce, these topics are covered only insofar as they affect the parental relationship (such as custody or visitation).

Surprisingly, only a small portion of the contents of this book deals with the rights of parents *as opposed to the rights of children*. These surface primarily in the discussion of medical care and, to a lesser extent, in questions concerning child abuse and neglect. The major part of the book's focus is on the rights of parents *as opposed to the power of the state*.

Through most of the history of the United States, the state played virtually no role in the upbringing of children; parents had a free hand in the custody and raising of their children. Until the past century, the only limit imposed by the state was the duty of parents to support and discipline their offspring. An important exception existed with respect to poor children, who frequently were apprenticed or bound out for work without much concern for the prerogatives of their parents. For the vast bulk of families, however, the state evinced little concern about the goings-on within the home. Parental rights, likened to property rights, were almost absolute.

With the advent of the industrial revolution and concern about child welfare, the power of the state to take children from poverty-stricken, "idle," and neglectful parents grew at the expense of the rights of parents. The state, considering itself the protector of children, bestowed upon itself the legal power to do with them whatever it considered "best," even over the wishes of parents. Today, this power has become more sophisticated, somewhat less arbitrary, and in many cases entirely appropriate, but it is without question pervasive and complex.

Today state involvement in the raising of children is a fact of life. All states, except one, require parents to send their children to school for a certain number of hours each day. Additionally, compulsory-vaccination laws and child-labor laws, which restrict the ability of children to work, are universal. And after the medical "discovery" of the battered-child syndrome in 1962, significant numbers of families were brought before the courts on grounds that the parents were raising their children in a harmful manner. At one time these laws would have been considered an unwarranted intrusion into the affairs of parents. That day has long passed.

In large measure, the contents of this book attempt to define the legal positions of parents when the state chooses to direct or dictate certain aspects of child-raising that were traditionally reserved for parents.

It is our belief that the family deserves legal protection from unreasonable intrusion by the state. It is one of the last bastions of privacy in our society. But the state constantly seeks to interfere in family life. Thus, in championing parental rights, we have no intention of diminishing the rights of children; rather, we hope to make parents aware of the rights they possess to protect themselves and their children from unnecessary and illegal action of the state. In short, we hope this short book serves to guard one of the most precious rights possessed by any person: the right to bear and raise children.

I

General Principles: Parental Rights and Family Integrity

Do parents have rights? If so, where do they come from?
The answer to the first question is yes. The answer to the second question is more complex.

The U.S. Constitution makes no mention whatsoever of either parents or families, but the legal rights of parents to bear children, raise their offspring, and guide their family according to their own beliefs are firmly rooted in the first ten amendments to the Constitution (otherwise known as the Bill of Rights). The rights of parents and the integrity of the family are therefore regarded as part of the highest law of the land.

The reason that parental and familial rights are accorded such high legal priority, even though they are not specifically articulated in the Constitution, is that our culture has always afforded a great deal of respect to the parent-child relationship, and almost all western legal codes have accepted the proposition that until children come of age, major decisions regarding their custody and control are left to the discretion of parents.

In our system of government, the Supreme Court has the responsibility of telling us what the Constitution means and how its brief but succinct statements of fundamental law may be applied to situations which the framers of that document did not foresee and could not have foreseen at the time of its creation. Naturally, as interpreted by the Supreme Court, the meaning of the Constitution is subject to change, since the members of the Court itself change over the years, and because ideas or policies con-

1

sidered acceptable in one era (for instance, school segregation) are unacceptable in another time.

But one notion—the primacy of parental rights—has remained fairly constant since the Court first considered the issue about fifty years ago.

What this means is that the state's power to regulate the lawful prerogatives of parents over their children or to intrude into the realm of family life is severely limited by the Constitution.

In 1923, for example, the Supreme Court struck down a Nebraska law that prohibited the teaching of a foreign language in state-run schools because "the right of parents . . . to instruct their children" is protected by the due-process clause of the Fourteenth Amendment to the Constitution.[1] Eleven years later, in a 1934 opinion, the Court wrote, "It is cardinal with us that the custody, care and nurture of the child reside first in the parents, whose primary function and freedom include preparation for obligations the state can neither supply nor hinder."[2] And as recently as 1972, the Court reaffirmed its position by stating: "The history and culture of western civilization reflect a strong tradition of parental concern for the nurture and upbringing of their children. This primary role of the parents in the upbringing of their children is now established beyond debate as an enduring American tradition."[3]

Of course, these declarations have a rather general scope. The Supreme Court and other federal and state courts have made more specific rulings that delineate the rights (and limitations) of parents in matters of religion, education, medical care, custody, visitation, adoption, foster care, illegitimate children, and child neglect, to mention a few. In addition, hundreds of state statutes define the legal rights and duties of parents in various areas of family and social life. In the chapters to follow, these topics will be discussed in some detail.

How important are family and parental rights considered to be in the American legal system?

They are held in very high esteem. It might even be said that they command the highest respect of all personal rights protected by the Constitution.

Generally, the Bill of Rights protects a person's right

to property and liberty. How, then, do parental rights compare to these well-established rights? To cite only two of many illustrations, in 1953 the Supreme Court said that the custody rights of parents are "far more precious . . . than property rights." [4] And in 1972, the Court stated, "It is plain that the interest of a parent in the companionship, care, custody, and management of his or her children comes to this Court with a momentum for respect lacking when appeal is made to liberties which derive merely from shifting economic arrangements." [5]

What about the *family* itself? Are there such things as family rights?

Yes. They have come to be known as rights of "family integrity," and they are grounded in the Constitutional guarantee of privacy and liberty.

Interestingly, like the words "parent" and "family," the term "privacy" is not mentioned in the Constitution. Nevertheless, the Supreme Court has determined that personal privacy exists among the "penumbra" of rights protected by the Constitution.

An essential element of the growth of the right of privacy has been the right of *family* privacy. In fact, the right of privacy was first secured in a 1965 case involving privacy within the family. In that case, the issue before the Supreme Court was the power of the state to prohibit the sale of birth-control devices. The Court overruled a Connecticut law that banned their distribution on the grounds that a state has no right to pass laws that interfere with marital privacy. In a concurring opinion, Justice Goldberg wrote:

> Certainly the safeguarding of the home does not follow merely from the sanctity of property rights. The home derives its preeminence as the seat of family life. And the integrity of that life is something so fundamental that it has been found to draw to its protection the principles of more than one explicitly granted Constitutional right. . . . The entire fabric of the Constitution and the purposes that clearly underlie its specific guarantees demonstrate that the rights to marital privacy and to marry and

raise a family are of similar order and magnitude as the fundamental rights specifically protected.[6]

What are the practical effects of the rights of parents and the rights of family integrity?

They are much more than mere platitudes. They have meaning and value in almost every circumstance when the power of the government to "reach" into family life is called into question. The rights of parents and the rights of family integrity, in short, serve as a Constitutional barrier to protect parents from unreasonable or unnecessary intrusion by the state into family life.

For example, not long ago, the city of East Cleveland, Ohio, enacted an ordinance that made it illegal for a house to board residents who were not members of a single family. The city defined "family" in very narrow terms as a husband, wife, and unmarried children. Under this law, a woman was convicted of a crime because she lived with her son and two grandchildren, who came to live with her after their mother's death. The Supreme Court overturned the woman's conviction and declared East Cleveland's ordinance unconstitutional as an unreasonable invasion into family life. The woman had a right to live with her grandchildren, the Court ruled, and the city had no power to interfere with that right.[7] "This Court has long recognized," it stated, "that freedom of personal choice in matters of marriage and family life is one of the liberties of the Fourteenth Amendment." Referring to a number of the same cases mentioned above, the Court added: "A host of cases . . . have consistently acknowledged a 'private realm of family life' which the state cannot enter." The Court concluded:

> Our decisions establish that the Constitution protects the sanctity of the family precisely because the institution of the family is deeply rooted in this Nation's history and tradition. It is through the family that we inculcate and pass down many of our most cherished values, moral and cultural. Ours is by no means a tradition limited to respect for the bonds uniting the members of the nuclear family. The tradition of uncles, aunts, cousins, and especially grandparents sharing a household along with parents and children has

roots equally venerable and equally deserving of constitutional recognition. . . . The Constitution prevents East Cleveland from standardizing its children—and its adults—by forcing all to live in certain narrowly defined family patterns.

To cite a second example, in the realm of child neglect, a federal court recently ruled that an Alabama law was unconstitutional because it gave the state power to remove children from the parents' custody without a prior hearing and when there was no evidence of harm to the child. Referring to the right of family integrity, the court stated:

> There is no question that the family members will suffer a grievous loss if the state severs the parent-child relationship, an interest, we have held, that is part of the liberty concept of the Fourteenth Amendment. . . . Normally, before intrusion into the affairs of the family is allowed, the state should have reliable evidence that a child is in need of protective care." [8]

(For a fuller discussion of the rights of parents in child-neglect cases, see Chapter V.)

And in the area of foster care, a judge of the Supreme Court recently reaffirmed the primary rights of natural parents and their children by declaring:

> One of the liberties protected by the Due Process Clause . . . is the freedom to "establish a home and bring up children." . . . If a State were to attempt to force the breakup of a natural family, over the objections of the parents and their children, without some showing of unfitness and for the sole reason that to do so was thought to be in the children's best interest, I should have little doubt that the state would have intruded impermissibly on "the private realm of family life which the State cannot enter." [9]

(For a fuller discussion of the rights of parents and foster parents, see Chapter IX.)

Do parents have the right to name their children?
Yes. No person or governmental agency can deprive parents of this right.[10] (Even if the parents are themselves

minors, they have the right to name their child over the objections of the child's grandparents.)

A recent case from Hawaii illustrates this point. There, a baby was born in 1977 to a married couple with differing names; the mother's last name was Jech, and the father's was Befurt. They decided to name the child Adrian Jebef, the last name being composed of the first few letters of each parent's surname. This choice upset Hawaii officials, who said state law required them to register the child's *father's* surname on the birth certificate. The parents sued and a federal court agreed with them. The court found the state law unconstitutional because it contravened the parents' right to choose a name for their own child. The court concluded, "a proper interpretation of Anglo-American political and legal history and precedent leads to the conclusion that parents have a common law right to give their child any name they wish, and that the Fourteenth Amendment protects this right from arbitrary state action." [11]

Parents also have the right, with court approval, to change the name they previously gave their child. One parent alone, however, may not change the name of a child over the other parent's objection, except under exceptional circumstances.[12] The conflict between one parent's desire to change a child's name and the other parent's refusal usually occurs after a divorce and one parent's subsequent remarriage. (This topic is discussed more fully in Chapter VII.)

Do parents have the right to custody of their children?
Yes. By virtue of being biological parents, the mother and father are automatic legal custodians of their child.[13]

The only way that they can be denied custody is if their rights are terminated by a court or if the child is adopted by others. (See Chapters VI and X.) Custody may also be temporarily suspended if parents voluntarily relinquish their children to foster or institutional care or if they are found guilty of neglectful or abusive treatment and their children are temporarily removed against their will. (See Chapter V.)

(Of course, if parents separate or divorce, custody may be delivered to one or the other parent by mutual agreement or by court order. In that event, the noncustodial parent will likely find his or her custodial rights reduced to periodical visitation privileges. See Chapter VII.)

Parents' rights to the custody of their children cannot be defeated by the state or by nonparents except for compelling reasons in which the health or welfare of the children is in danger.[14] (See Chapter VI.) Therefore, if one parent dies, the other automatically assumes custody, even if the surviving parent was not granted custody in a prior agreement or decree.[15]

In a case decided by the Supreme Court of California, custody of a child was awarded to the mother (the father had died) rather than to the foster parents with whom the child had lived for some time.[16] The court relied upon a California law that stated that no court could award custody to a person other than a child's parent unless it reached a conclusion that custody to the parent would be detrimental to the child and that the award to the nonparent was required to serve the best interests of the child.[17]

Even more recent is the Supreme Court ruling quoted above.[18]

Do parents have a right to control and discipline their children?

Yes. An inseparable part of the parental right to custody of their children is the right to discipline their behavior and control their actions. (The right to control a child is also part of the reciprocal duty to provide support for children.)

The right to control a child is also part of a duty imposed by the state. All states have disobedient-child laws—also called Children in Need of Supervision (CHINS) or Persons in Need of Supervision (PINS) statutes—which permit juvenile courts to exercise jurisdiction over children who are not being adequately supervised by their parents. In many cases, parents themselves bring their children to court because they seek the aid of the state in forcing obedience of their children.

As a drastic but not uncommon consequence of these CHINS or PINS cases, a child may be taken from the control of his or her parents by court order. As stated by a Massachusetts court:

While the State defers to the parents with respect to most decisions on family matters, it has an interest in insuring the existence of harmonious relations between family members, and between the family unit and the rest of the public society. To protect this interest, the State may properly require that unemancipated children obey the reasonable and lawful commands of their parents, and it may impose criminal penalties on the children if they persistently disobey such commands. The State is not powerless to prevent or control situations which threaten the proper functioning of a family unit as an important segment of the total society. It may properly extend the protection of its laws in aid of the head of a family unit whose reasonable and lawful commands are being disobeyed by children who are bound to obey them.[19]

Are there limits to the right of parents to control and discipline their children?

Yes. While parents have the right to discipline and control their children, they may do so only by reasonable means. Thus, parents may spank their children but not injure or abuse them. They may require their children to be home by a certain hour, but they may not keep them locked in their room for a long period of time. They may deprive their children of an occasional meal as punishment, but they may not subject them to malnutrition. In short, the right to control and discipline children ends where child abuse and neglect begin. (For a fuller discussion of the limits of parental control, see Chapters IV and V.)

A second limit of parental control should be discussed briefly. Actually, it has nothing to do with limits imposed by the law, but with the diminishing practical power of parental control as children reach maturity. For example, a parent's right to determine the religious instruction of his or her child remains intact, but if a fifteen-year-old refuses to go to church, or say prayers, there is little or no legal recourse for the parent. Parents may impose family-created sanctions, such as withdrawal of an allowance, vacation, or other privileges, but no parent would find help from the police or a court of law in imposing his or her religious demands on a child who simply refuses to obey. On the other hand, if the child refused other parental demands which are also required by state law, such as the duty to refrain from criminal conduct or the duty to obtain an education, parents may seek recourse in the legal structure pursuant to the disobedient-child laws mentioned in the previous question and answer.

Do parents have the right to determine the education of their children?

Yes. Actually, parents have a legal *duty* to educate their children, as prescribed by law in almost every state.[20] However, the *type* of education a child receives (public school, religious school, boarding school, and sometimes at-home instruction) is in the province of parental rights.[21] (For a fuller discussion, see Chapter II.)

Do parents have the right to determine the religion and religious training of their children?

Absolutely. This right is grounded securely in the right of family privacy and integrity, discussed earlier, and protected by the First Amendment, which guarantees free exercise of religion.[22] The right of parents to have their children raised in the faith of their choice is so strong that in some states it will be determinative even if a child is under the care of a guardian, foster parent, or state institution.[23]

Parental rights to determine the religious training of their children may be truncated by a court if the practice of the religion seriously endangers the health of the child (such as a religion which prescribes the handling of dangerous snakes) or requires a child to violate child-labor laws.[24] But even in these cases, no court will prohibit the teachings or beliefs of a particular religion; its concern would be only in certain *activities* that might harm a child.

Do parents have the right to determine what medical care their children will receive?

Yes. With a few exceptions in the area of sex-related medical treatment (i.e., venereal disease, contraception, and abortion), parents have the right to make decisions regarding almost every aspect of their children's medical needs. These include matters of surgery, choice of doctors and hospital, yearly checkups, and daily medication.

Except in emergencies, the law requires all patients to give their consent to treatment before it may be received. But the law considers minors *incapable* of giving their consent; only a child's parent or lawful guardian may provide the necessary consent. Therefore, no medical treatment or care may be administered upon a child without his or her parent's consent.[25] Similarly, the right of a child to *refuse* certain medical treatment is a right which belongs to the parents, not the child.[26] (A fuller discussion of medical care, including important exceptions to this principle, is found in Chapter III.)

Like many other aspects of parental rights (food, shelter, education, and control), the right to provide medical care is also a legal *duty*. Parents are charged with seeing that the basic, minimal medical needs of their children are met. Thus, failure to treat a serious wound or refusal to permit a doctor to treat a serious disease or impairment may result in a judicial finding of child neglect so that the child may be properly treated. (For more on child neglect, see Chapter V.)

What if the parents' religious beliefs dictate that their child may not receive certain medical treatments?

In this conflict of rights (a parent's right of religious freedom vs. a child's right to adequate medical care), courts will almost always favor the right of the child. Thus, parents whose religious beliefs forbid them to accept blood transfusions, for example, have the right to refuse medically necessary transfusions for *themselves*, but not for their children.

Cases have arisen in which doctors have recommended operations, including blood transfusions, in order to save the life of a child, but the parents refused consent for religious reasons. Doctors in these situations usually apply to juvenile courts for an order temporarily suspending the parents' control over their children, for the duration of the medical treatment, and appointing a special guardian who may then consent to the operation and transfusion.[27]

What if two parents disagree between themselves about the choice of religion or education for their children?

Generally, courts will refrain from entertaining cases such as these. With the exception of divorce and child-custody cases, courts are reluctant to settle family disputes, especially those that involve only philosophical differences between members of an intact family.

Two cases illustrate this point quite clearly. In 1936, the highest court in New York heard a dispute between parents regarding the education of their child. The issue did not involve custody (the parents lived together) nor did either parent claim that the child's health or welfare was in danger. The question was simply what school the child should attend. The court dismissed the entire case, ruling in favor of neither parent, saying,

> The Court cannot regulate by its processes the internal affairs of the home. Dispute between parents when it does not involve anything immoral or harmful to the welfare of the child is beyond the reach of the law. The vast majority of matters concerning the upbringing of children must be left to the conscience, patience, and self-restraint of father and mother. No end of difficulties would arise should judges try to tell parents how to bring up their children. Only when moral, mental and physical conditions are so bad, as seriously to affect the health or morals of children, should the courts be called upon to act.[28]

The Supreme Court of Alabama voiced similar sentiments in 1958 when it heard a dispute in which a father wanted his seven-year-old daughter to attend a religious school of his own faith, while the mother, who was of a different faith, wanted her daughter to attend public school. In the words of the court:

> As we see it, the decisive question presented is whether a court has inherent jurisdiction to resolve a family dispute between parents as to the school their minor child should attend, when there is no question concerning the custody of the child. . . . It seems to us, if we should hold that [we have] jurisdiction in this case, such holding will open the gates for all sorts

of varieties of intimate family disputes concerning the
upbringing of children.

The court, of course, refused to entertain the case and
thereby abstained from making a decision in favor of the
father or the mother. One reason it gave was that if it
did order the child to attend one school or the other, it
would be giving legal preference to a particular religious
belief contrary to the First Amendment of the Constitution. The other reason was based on practical wisdom.
The court concluded:

> It may well be suggested that a court of equity
> ought to interfere to prevent such a direful conse-
> quence as divorce or separation, rather than await the
> disruption of the marital relationship. Our answer to
> this is that intervention, rather than preventing or
> healing a disruption, would quite likely serve as the
> spark to a smoldering fire. A mandatory court decree
> supporting the position of one parent against the other
> would hardly be a composing situation for the unsuc-
> cessful parent to be confronted with daily. One spouse
> could scarcely be expected to entertain a tender, affec-
> tionate regard for the other spouse who brings him
> or her under restraint. The judicial mind and con-
> science is repelled by the thought of disruption of
> the sacred marital relationship, and usually voices the
> hope that the breach may somehow be healed by
> mutual understanding between the parents them-
> selves.[29]

**Do parents have the right to feed, clothe, and shelter
their children as they see fit?**
Yes, so long as they provide at least the minimal level
of care necessary for the proper health and safety of their
children. If parents fail to provide adequate levels of food,
clothing, and shelter for their children, and are financially
able to do so, it may result in a court order of child
neglect, and the children may be removed from their home.
(See Chapter V.)

So long as parents provide the necessities of life adequately, they may choose whatever *type* of food, clothing,
or shelter they desire. Thus, no one may prohibit parents
from raising their children, for example, on a vegetarian

diet, so long as the child receives adequate nutrition, nor may any state agency prohibit parents from dressing their children in unorthodox clothing, so long as it protects them from the elements.

Do parents have the right to refuse permission for their child's adoption by others?

Yes. Part of the fundamental right of custody is the right *not* to have children raised and controlled by others.

A child may be adopted in only one of two ways. First, parents may consent to have their children adopted by others. This consent must be entirely voluntary and without coercion. Moreover, both parents, if available, must provide their consent.

Second, under extenuating circumstances, children may be freed for adoption without parental consent if the parents have been found, by a court of law, to have abandoned their children or to have failed to provide for them for a certain length of time. (For the rights of parents whose children are being taken away from them, see Chapter VI.)

Do parents have the right to prohibit their children from getting married?

Yes. In almost all states, children may not marry without their parents' consent if they are under the age of eighteen. (Children under fourteen or sixteen normally need permission of their parents *and* a judge before they may marry.) Generally, parental consent to marry means the prior, written consent of both parents, if alive.

Do parents have the right to prevent their children's enlistment in the armed forces?

Yes, so long as their children are under the age of eighteen. Children eighteen and older, however, may enlist without parental consent.

Do parents have the right to receive prior notice of legal proceedings against their children?

Yes. Anyone taking legal action against a dependent child must notify the child and his or her parents before the matter may be heard or determined by a court of law. This includes petitions in juvenile court to determine juvenile delinquency and summonses and complaints in civil courts for monetary damages.

Does one parent have any greater right than the other to determine the custody, control, name, religion, or education of children?

Neither parent has any greater legal standing than the other to determine issues that are in the realm of parental rights and powers over their children.

The early English law gave sole power to the father to make serious decisions about the upbringing of children. But this rule has received little support in this country and has been abolished in England as well.[30] Generally, authority between parents living together is considered equal.[31]

Even upon separation or divorce, in all but a few states, the mother has no greater legal rights to custody than the father, and if the parents cannot agree between themselves, a court will decide the question of custody in accord with what it thinks will promote the "best interests" of the children.

Once custody is determined, however, whether by agreement or court decree, the custodial parent will have greater legal rights than the noncustodial parent in determining issues such as residence, religion, medical care, education, and food and clothing for the child.[32] (See Chapter VII.)

Can parents be forced to testify in court against their children?

Probably. Many states protect husbands and wives from having to testify against each other, but few, if any, have any legal prohibition against forcing parents to testify against their children.

Two cases will illustrate this point. In the first, a well-known civil rights lawyer was summoned before a federal grand jury to disclose the address of his daughter. He refused, claiming a "parent-child privilege." He was threatened with contempt of court for refusing to provide the information and the matter went to court. The judge denied the lawyer's claim, stating:

> (The father) invokes the "parent-child privilege." But there is no such thing. All of us, whether parents

or children, may empathize of the imaginable prospect of being asked to incriminate those close to us. However, that is not necessarily the situation here and it would not in any event justify enforcement of the novel privilege now asserted.[33]

In the second case, the mother of a sixteen-year old was called before a grand jury because the prosecutor wanted to find out whether or not her son, who was suspected of committing an act of arson, had made any admissions to her. An appellate court ruled that the legislature had not created a "parent-child privilege," but

communications made by a minor child to his parents within the context of the family relationship may, under some circumstances, be within the "private realm of family life which the state cannot enter." . . . It would be difficult to think of a situation which more strikingly embodies the intimate and confidential relationship which exists among family members than that in which a troubled young person, perhaps beset with remorse and guilt, turns for counsel and guidance to his mother and father. There is nothing more natural, more consistent with our concept of the parental role, than that a child may rely on his parents for help and advice.[34]

The court did not rule that the mother in this case was free from her obligation to answer questions from the grand jury, but it did suggest that some of her communications with her son may be "privileged" and therefore nondisclosable in the interest of family privacy. (Recently, this opinion was approved by a judge of a Westchester, New York County Court which held that "the confidences extended between a parent and child are just as sacrosanct as between a doctor and a patient or a priest and a penitent.")[35]

Are there any situations when parental rights over their children come to an end and are no longer enforceable?

Yes. This can come about in one of three ways.

First, parental rights come to an end automatically when a child reaches the age of majority, which is eighteen in most states. At this point, the child is no longer a minor and becomes an adult. Thus, his or her parents no longer have any legal power to enforce their rights mentioned in this chapter.

Second, parents may be divested of their legal rights over their minor children if a court rules that their parental rights are to be terminated. This may come about if they have abandoned or seriously neglected their children or failed to uphold certain minimal standards of parenthood. After parental rights are terminated, children may be adopted by others without their natural parents' consent. (See Chapter VI.)

Third, parents may lose some or all of their rights if their minor children become emancipated. Emancipation is a complicated and much-misunderstood concept, but generally it means that even though a child is still a minor, he or she may be considered an adult (emancipated) for some specific purpose. Thus, a child entertainer may become emancipated for the purpose of signing a binding contract, or children who live by themselves and earn their own living may be considered emancipated for the purpose of relieving themselves from parental control —and the duty of parental support. Children become emancipated for *all* purposes (and are thereby treated as legal adults even though they are still under age eighteen) if they marry, enlist in the armed forces, or in some states, if they become parents themselves. (See Chapter IV.)

Is it lawful for landlords to refuse to rent apartments to families with children?

It may be. No definitive judicial ruling on this point has been made, but most courts that have considered the question have allowed landlords to discriminate against parents with young children.[36] On the other hand, some states have passed laws prohibiting this type of discrimination.[37]

May an employer refuse to hire employees with preschool children?

Yes, if there are actual conflicting family obligations that are demonstrably relevant to job performance. But an employer's refusal to hire women with preschool children, while at the same time hiring *men* similarly situated, would be illegal and unconstitutional.[38]

May employers require pregnant women employees to take maternity leaves long before the expected birth?

No. The United States Supreme Court has held that "overly restrictive maternity-leave regulations" penalize women for deciding to bear children. This is impermissible because the Constitution protects freedom of personal choice in matters of marriage and family life. In the case decided by the Supreme Court, the employer required maternity leaves five months before the expected birth.[39] Less-restrictive mandatory maternity leaves may be lawful if the employer has valid job-related justifications, for the required leave.

May an employer refuse to pay disability benefits due to pregnancy?

Yes. The Supreme Court has ruled that employers may withhold certain medical coverage, including disability due to pregnancy, without running afoul of the Constitution as long as the exclusions are not designed to discriminate on the basis of sex.[40] Employees can attempt to have these benefits covered by plans, but employers are not required by law to include them.

NOTES

1. Meyer v. Nebraska, 262 U.S. 390 400 (1923).
2. Prince v. Massachusetts, 321 U.S. 158 (1944).
3. Wisconsin v. Yoder, 406 U.S. 205 233 (1972).
4. May v. Anderson, 354 U.S. 528 (1953).
5. Stanley v. Illinois, 405 U.S. 645 (1972).
6. Griswold v. Connecticut, 381 U.S. 479 (1965).
7. Moore v. City of East Cleveland, Ohio, 431 U.S. 494 (1977).
8. Roe v. Conn, 417 F.Supp. 769 (M.D. Ala. 1976).
9. Justice Stewart concurring in Smith v. Organization of Foster Families for Equality and Reform, 431 U.S. 816 (1977).
10. Daily v. Minnick, 117 Iowa 563, 91 N.W. 913 (1902); Eaton v. Libbey, 165 Mass. 218, 42 N.E. 1127 (1896).
11. Jech v. Burch, 466 F. Supp. 714 (D. Hawaii, 1979).
12. Kay v. Bell, 950 Ohio App. 520, 121 N.E.2d 206 (1953).
13. *See, e.g.,* Stanley v. Illinois, 405 U.S. 645 (1972); Skeadas v. Sklaroff, 84 R.I. 206, 122 A.2d 444 (1956).

14. People *ex rel.* O'Connell v. Turner, 55 Ill, 280 (1870); Skeadas v. Sklaroff, *supra* note 13.

15. *See, e.g.,* Leclerc v. Leclerc, 85 N.H. 121, 155 A. 249 (1931); N.Y. Dom. Rel. Law §81.

16. *In re* B.G., 11 Cal.3d 679, 523 P.2d 244 (1974).

17. CAL. CIV. CODE §4600.

18. See discussion at note 9, *supra.*

19. Commonwealth v. Brashear, 270 N.E.2d 389 (S. Ct. Mass. 1971).

20. *See, e.g.,* State v. Garber, 197 Kan. 567, 419 P.2d 896 (1966), *cert. denied* 389 U.S. 51 (1967).

21. Wisconsin v. Yoder, 406 U.S. 205 (1972); Pierce v. Society of Sisters, 268 U.S. 510 (1925).

22. Knowlton v. Baumhover, 182 Iowa 691, 166 N.W. 202 (1918); People *ex rel.* Portnoy v. Strasser, 303 N.Y. 539, 104 N.E.2d 895 (1952).

23. N.Y. Const. Art. 6, §32; Wilder v. Sugarman, 385 F. Supp. 1013 (S.D. N.Y. 1974).

24. Prince v. Massachusetts, *supra* note 2.

25. *See, e.g.,* Lacey v. Laird, 166 Ohio St. 12, 139 N.E.2d 25 (1956).

26. Friedrichsen v. Niemotka, 71 N.J. Super. 398, 177 A.2d 58 (1962).

27. *See, e.g.,* Wallace v. Labrenz, 411 Ill. 618, 104 N.E.2d 769 (1952), *cert. denied* 344 U.S. 824 (1952); N.Y. Soc. Serv. L. §383-b; *In re* Cirero, N.Y. Sup. Ct. Sept. 11, 1979 *in* 5 F.L.R.2941.

28. People *ex rel.* Sisson v. Sisson, 271 N.Y. 285, 2 N.E.2d 660 (1936).

29. Kilgrow v. Kilgrow, 107 So.2d 885 (Ala. 1958).

30. *See, generally,* 59 AM. JUR.2d *Parent and Child* §§22, 28.

31. *See, e.g.,* N.Y. DOM. REL. LAW §70; Donahue v. Donahue, 142 N.J. Eq. 701, 61 A.2d 243 (1948).

32. *See, e.g.,* Boerger v. Boerger, 26 N.J. Super. 90, 97 A.2d 419 (1953); Miller v. Hedrick, 158 Cal. App.2d 281, 322 P.2d 231 (1958); Goodman v. Goodman, 180 Neb. 83, 141 N.W.2d 445 (1966); Zande v. Zande, 3 N.C. App. 149, 164 S.E.2d 523 (1968).

33. *In re* Kinoy, 362 F. Supp. 400, 406 (S.D. N.Y. 1970).

34. *In re* A. and M., 61 A.D.2d 426, 403 N.Y.S.2d 375, (2nd Dept. 1978).

35. People v. Fitzgerald, No. 76–43 (Nat. L.J. Nov. 9, 1979, p. 7).

36. *See, e.g.,* Riley v. Stoves, 22 Ariz. App. 223, 526 P.2d 747 (1974), Marina Point, Ltd. v. Wolfson, Calif. Ct. App., Sept. 26, 1979, 5 F.L.R. 2954.

37. *See, e.g.,* DEL. CODE ANN. tit. 25, §6506.
38. Phillips v. Martin Marietta Corp., 400 U.S. 542 (1971).
39. Cleveland Board of Education v. LaFleur, 414 U.S. 632 (1974).
40. General Electric Co. v. Gilbert, 429 U.S. 125 (1976); Geduldig v. Aiello, 417 U.S. 484 (1974).

II

Education of Children

Must parents send their children to school?

Not necessarily. In every state, children are entitled to a free, public education. And in every state but one (Mississippi), there are compulsory-education laws which require children to obtain an education for a certain length of time, usually from age five or six to sixteen or seventeen. But compulsory *education* is not necessarily the same as compulsory *school*.

In many states, the compulsory-education law requires only that children receive a minimal, adequate education. This may be met through school or home instruction. If it can be demonstrated that the home instruction provided to children is acceptable, compliance with the compulsory-education laws may be satisfied. It is not easy, however, for parents to prove that home instruction is adequate; the burden is on the parents to establish that they have provided an acceptable course of instruction for their children.[1] In some jurisdictions, home instruction may be allowed as an alternative to public or private schooling only if the instruction is approved in advance by the school superintendent.[2]

Is home instruction always an alternative to school?

No. Some states require attendance at some actual school, either public or private. Other states require that all teachers be certified or at least possess a minimal background in education. Even in some jurisdictions that require schooling, however, home instruction may be approved if a court finds that home instruction constitutes a private school within the meaning of the compulsory-

20

education law.[3] Among the factors the court will take into account are the competency of the teacher, the adequacy of the subjects taught, the regularity of sessions, and number of the hours taught per week.

Can parents be required to send their children to *public* schools?

No. As discussed in Chapter I, one of the rights inherent in parenthood is the right to "control the detail and upbringing" of children.[4] Thus, while a state may require that all children be minimally educated, it may not require that parents send their children only to a public school.

Of course, the state may provide *free* education at public schools only, thereby rendering the choice of any other school more costly. (The only circumstance in which the state will be obligated to pay for a child's private schooling occurs when a child is placed there *by* the public school system in order to receive an appropriate, special education.)

Can parents be punished for violating compulsory-education laws?

Yes. Parents can be criminally prosecuted or they can be charged with neglecting their children.

To be found guilty of a *crime,* the state must prove that the parents actually assisted or abetted the child's non-attendance of school or instruction.

To be found *neglectful,* the state need only prove that the parents should have known that their children were not receiving instruction or that they were negligent by not making certain that their children attended school. If parents are found to have neglected their children, the children could be placed under supervision by a child welfare agency or, if the facts were extreme, parents could lose custody of their children to the state. (The consequences of child neglect are discussed more fully in Chapter V.)

Are compulsory-education laws valid even when they interfere with the religious beliefs of parents?

In most cases, yes.[5] In 1972, however, the United States Supreme Court recognized a very limited exception to a state law that required parents to send their children to school until they reach sixteen. The Supreme Court ruled that Amish parents have a constitutional right to remove their children from school at the age of fourteen to let them work at home with their families; to rule otherwise, the Court believed, would violate the constitutional right of the Amish people to maintain their traditional way of life.[6] It is not clear, however, whether this opinion may be applied to other situations.

Are some children exempt from compulsory-education laws?

Yes. In most states, children whose mental or physical conditions prevent them from attending regular public-school classes are excluded from compulsory-education laws. Since the passage of the Education for All Handicapped Children Act of 1975,[7] however, all states are obligated to accommodate handicapped children and provide them with a free education. This law does not *require* parents of handicapped children to avail themselves of free education, but they now have the right if they wish to exercise it.

May school officials ask personal questions of students that infringe upon family privacy?

Probably not. There is, of course, much information a school may gather through students about their personal history that serves a legitimate administrative or educational purpose. But there are limits to such inquiries.

In recent years, tests and surveys seeking psychological or sociological information of students have become popular among school administrators. Some tests, especially those which attempt to identify neglected children or predict drug abuse, ask extremely personal questions of students, including inquiries about their family and home life. In the only court case dealing with this problem, a federal court ruled that a survey designed to point out potential drug abusers had to be suspended following objection by parents who felt that the survey interfered with the privacy rights of both their children and themselves. Some of the questions in the survey that the federal court found objectionable were whether a student's parents "hugged and kissed him good night when he was small," whether they told the student "how much they loved him," whether they "seemed to know what the student's needs are," and whether the student "feels that he is loved by his parents." [8]

Do parents have a right to prevent corporal punishment of their children in public schools?

Probably not. The Supreme Court has ruled that corporal punishment is constitutional even over the objection of parents.[9] But just because corporal punishment is permissible does not mean that states or school districts *must* use it. States, cities, and local school districts are free to formulate their own policies concerning the use of corporal punishment, including its prohibition.

Corporal punishment is illegal by state law in New Jersey, Massachusetts, Maine, and temporarily in Hawaii. In Maryland, the decision is left to local school dstricts. New York City, Chicago, Baltimore, Washington, D.C., Pittsburgh (for kindergarten through seventh grade), and Oakland, California, have banned corporal punishment in all public schools in those municipalities.

Even in states that permit corporal punishment, many of them (thirty, in fact) have rules and regulations limiting its use to some degree. Some states limit *who* may legally strike children. Some permit classroom teachers, others authorize only administrators, and in still others only certified personnel are allowed to punish students. Some states regulate *in whose presence* a student may be corporally punished: some prohibit it in front of other students, and some states require that another adult or the school principal must be present. Some states specify *where*, on the body, a student may not be struck, prohibiting blows on the face and head. And some states require *permission* from the school principal before a student may be corporally punished. One state in which corporal punishment is permitted (California) requires prior written approval of a student's parent or guardian before it may be administered.

Even with limits such as those described above, the fact remains that the Supreme Court's authorization of corporal punishment, coupled with compulsory-education laws, results in parents' loss of control over their "right" to prevent their children being struck by other adults, at least during the time their children are in public schools.

If a child is suspended or expelled from school, do his or her parents have any rights?

Yes. According to a United States Supreme Court decision, students are entitled to a hearing before or as soon as possible after suspension.[10] Both the student and his or her parents are entitled to be notified of the suspension and of their right to appear at a hearing. The Supreme Court did not say how soon the hearing must be held, but states have imposed certain time limits.

In California, for example, a student may be suspended by a teacher for the remainder of a school day and one day more. Principals may suspend a student up to five days. Within twenty-four hours of the suspension, the child's parents must be notified, and both the student and the parents must be told the reason for suspension. Within three days of the suspension, the parents must also be told that they have a right to attend a meeting with the teacher and principal to discuss their child's problem. The parents may bring a representative to the meeting (a lawyer or anyone else) if they wish. If the principal does not reinstate the child after this meeting, the student must be allowed to return to classes no later than five days after the original suspension. A student may be kept from school longer than this only if the school decides to have a formal hearing to decide if the student will be expelled. This hearing is held before a Discipline Hearing Panel, and the decision to expel a student can be made only by the School Board. Parents must be notified of an expulsion hearing at least ten days before the hearing by written letter. The letter must explain when and where the hearing will be, what the facts are, and what rules the student is accused of breaking. Parents may attend the hearing, bring a representative (a lawyer or nonlawyer) with them, look at their child's records, ask questions of the witnesses who testify against their child, and bring witnesses to testify on the child's behalf. If a child is expelled, the parents may appeal the decision to the County Board of Education and ultimately to the courts.[11]

In New York, teachers, deans, vice-principals, and staff members have no authority to suspend students; the power to suspend rests solely with superintendents, boards of education, and principals. *Before* students may be suspended, they are entitled to notice of the charges against them and an opportunity to refute the charges or explain their conduct, unless the student's conduct constitutes an emergency. (And in that case, the notice and opportunity to be heard must follow as soon as possible.) Parents, too, must be notified of a student's suspension, by telephone and written notice. Upon request, the parents must be given an opportunity for a conference with the principal and the right to ask questions of the person who made the complaint against the student. During suspension, students are entitled to alternate, at-home instruction.[12] If the suspension is to last longer than five days, students and their parents have a right to a more formal hearing, including notice of the hearing, representation by an attorney or lay advocate, the right to present witnesses and evidence, the right to cross-examine witnesses against them, the right to have the hearing tape-recorded, the right to have an impartial hearing officer, and the right to a written decision. The decision is forwarded to the superintendent, who then decides if the student should be suspended for more than five days. Principals have no power to suspend a student for more than five days. The superintendent's decision may be appealed to the board of education, to the state commissioner of education, and ultimately to the courts.[13]

Do parents have a right to sue a school district for money damages if the school fails to teach their child basic educational skills?

Generally, lawsuits against schools for the miseducation of children have not been successful.[14] Courts have been reluctant to decide in favor of parents in "educational malpractice" cases even when children have spent years in the school system, advancing from one grade to another, without learning how to read or write.

One reason courts have offered for refusing to find schools liable is that it is difficult to assess the degree to which the school is directly at fault for a student's inability to read or write. Another reason is that any decision in the parents' favor would result in a rash of lawsuits in which parents could claim that every educational problem their children encountered was the school's fault. In dis-

missing a case of this type, a court in California ruled that
if schools were held liable to claims of disaffected students
and parents, "the ultimate consequences, in terms of public time and money, would burden them—and society—
beyond calculation." [15]

**What are the rights of students who are pregnant or
students who are parents?**

This topic is discussed in Chapter XII, "Minor Parents."

**Does the state have to provide a free education for a
handicapped child?**

Yes. If a state provides free public education for some
students, it must do so for *all* students, whether or not
they are handicapped. Pursuant to the Education for All
Handicapped Children Act of 1975, all state education
systems receiving federal funds are prohibited by law from
discriminating against handicapped children in their
schools. The purpose of the Act is "to assure that all
handicapped children have available to them . . . a free
and appropriate education which emphasizes special education and related services designed to meet their unique
needs." [16]

The Act covers all students and potential students aged
three to twenty-one. The scope of the Act covers all handicapped children within this age bracket, no matter what
the disability and no matter how severe. Disabilities include (but are not limited to) children who are blind,
deaf, mentally retarded, emotionally disturbed, children
who have physical handicaps, cerebral palsy, epilepsy, and
learning disabilities.

The Act includes vocational as well as academic schooling, which means that vocational-training centers as well
as traditional schools must be opened to handicapped students.[17]

**Do parents have any rights regarding the education of
their handicapped children?**

Yes, the Act referred to above grants parents of handicapped children many rights—more rights, in fact, than
enjoyed by parents of nonhandicapped children.

First, parents have the right to be involved in planning
what is called their child's Individualized Education Pro-

gram (IEP). Parents must approve their plans *before* they become effective. This right remains intact whether the student is in elementary, junior, high, or vocational school.

Second, parents have the right to be notified in writing before any action is taken to change a child's IEP. Parents must give their consent for any change in the program. Similarly, parents have the right to request changes in the IEP, and if the request is denied, the reasons for the denial must be given to them in writing.

Third, if the parent and school cannot agree on the best type of IEP for a child, they have the right to a due-process hearing before an impartial hearing officer. The hearing officer may not be employed by the school district or involved in the education of the child whose case is the subject of the hearing. At the hearing, parents also have the right to a lawyer or a lay advocate, the right to state their own case, the right to have witnesses on their own behalf, the right to cross-examine witnesses for the school, and the right to obtain a record of the hearing and the decision.

Fourth, if parents are unsatisfied with the results of the due-process hearing, they have the right to appeal the decision to the state department of education or department of special education.

Fifth, if the decision of the state department of education or special education does not seem fair, parents have the right to appeal further to the courts.

Sixth, parents have a right to review and copy all records relating to the identification, evaluation, placement, and development of an educational program for their child. If parents believe that some information is incorrect, they have the right to request its removal from their child's file. If removed, it cannot be used for further planning or placement of the child.

Seventh, parents have the right to have their children educated in what is known as the "least restrictive environment," which means that their children may be placed in separate or special classes *only* when it is clearly impossible to arrange placement in a regular class. Of course, if a parent wants a special class, this may be discussed in the original plans for a child's IEP, which includes parental involvement.

Do parents have the right to inspect their child's school file?

Yes. A federal law was enacted in 1974 which gives every parent access to their children's educational records.[18] This law covers all public and private schools that receive funds through the Office of Education. Virtually every public school receives these funds.

What if the parents are divorced or separated? Who has access to a child's files?

Both parents always have access, whether they are living together or not.[19] Therefore, after a divorce or child-custody dispute, the custodial parent cannot prevent the noncustodial parent from inspecting the child's school file.

How do parents request access to their child's school records?

The request may be made orally or in writing. The request should be to examine the *complete* record. A school must respond to the request within a "reasonable" period of time, and never longer than forty-five days.[20] It is usually best to make a request in writing, sent by registered or certified mail, with a copy of the letter kept by the parent. This way there always will be proof that a request was made.

Once a request for inspection has been made, may a school remove or destroy any part of the child's record if it thinks it should not be disclosed?

No.[21]

How does a parent actually go about inspecting these records?

The right of access entitles parents to personally inspect all records, regardless of their location. While school officials cannot deny a parent's actual inspection, they can insist that an official be present during the inspection. A parent has no right to remove documents from the file, but he or she may copy their contents on paper. Schools are not required to give parents photocopies of the files (except under circumstances described in the following answer), but many schools permit photocopying on the premises, for a small fee. A school may *not* charge a parent for staff time spent searching or retrieving records.[22]

Is there any material in a child's school file which may *not* be disclosed to a parent?

Yes. Some items in a file may be withheld from parents, such as notes made by teachers or school officials for their own use only, records of school security police if they are kept solely for law-enforcement purposes and if they are not revealed to anyone other than law-enforcement officials, personnel records of school employees, and records of a school where a student has applied but never attended.[23]

If information is found in a student's file which a parent thinks is untrue, what can be done about it?

Federal law allows a parent to challenge information discovered in a student's record. Parents may request that the school remove or correct what they believe to be incorrect information. Within a short time the school must either agree with the request or refuse. If the school refuses, the parent has a right to request a hearing on the matter.[24] (Naturally, the request to correct or remove information and the request for a hearing, if necessary, should be in writing so they can be used as evidence later on, if the school claims it was never notified.)

What rights do parents have at the hearing to correct or remove information?

First, the hearing must be held within a reasonable time following the request, and parents must be given reasonable notice before the hearing as to when it will be held.

Second, the hearing must be conducted before an unbiased hearing officer who acts as judge, but the hearing officer may be an employee of the school. Obviously, a teacher who inserted the challenged information into the file is not unbiased, and he or she could not serve as the hearing officer.

Third, certain procedural rights are guaranteed parents, such as the opportunity to present evidence and the right to be represented by anyone the parent chooses, including a lawyer.

Fourth, parents have a right to a reasonably prompt decision by the hearing officer, which must be stated *in writing*, explaining the reasons for the decision, and based solely on the evidence presented at the hearing.

If, as a result of the hearing, the hearing officer decides that information in the student's file is inaccurate or misleading, the permanent record will be corrected or expunged.[25]

What if the hearing officer decides that information in the record should not be removed or corrected—do parents have any further recourse?

Yes. Parents may still place a statement into the student's file explaining why they think the record is unfair or incorrect. This statement becomes part of the record and must be included any time the record is disclosed to anyone else.[25]

What should parents do if the school fails to comply with any of the rights regarding student records mentioned above?

A letter of complaint should be sent to Washington detailing the facts of the situation, including names, dates, and places necessary to document the violation. The letter should be sent to: The Family Educational Rights and Privacy Act Office, Department of Health, Education & Welfare, 330 Independence Avenue S.W., Washington, D.C. 20201. The names and addresses of the parent and student and the name and address of the school should be included. As usual, a copy should be kept for a parent's own records.

The federal agency will then notify the school and request an explanation from them. If the agency believes that the law has been violated, it will direct the school to comply.[27] If the school fails to comply or demonstrates a history of noncompliance in this area, the federal agency is empowered to seek an order terminating all federal funds to the school district.[28]

Can the school ever disclose information in a student's file to a person other than the student's parents, *without* the parent's consent?

Yes, but only under very limited circumstances.

First, a school may disclose the contents of a student's file to the student himself once he attains the age of eighteen or attends postsecondary school.[29] When the child is below eighteen or not attending a postsecondary school, he cannot view the contents of his own school file without his parents' consent.

Second, a school may disclose information to school officials in the district attended by the student, to school officials in a district to which the student intends to transfer, to various state and national education agencies, to student financial-aid officials, to courts, and to appropriate persons when the student's health or safety demands the transfer of certain information.[30]

May parents permit schools to disclose information in their child's file to another person or institution?

Yes, so long as the parents' permission is in writing, signed, and dated. The parents' consent must also specify which records are to be disclosed—such as medical records, academic transcripts, etc.—the purpose of the disclosure, and the individual or organization to whom the disclosure is to be made.[31] Such permission may be necessary if a parent wishes information to be communicated to an attorney, relative, friend, social worker, youth advocate, or civil-rights or civil-liberties organization.

NOTES

1. *In re* Shinn, 195 Cal. App.2d 683, 16 Cal. Rptr. 165 (1961); *see, e.g.,* People v. Levison, 404 Ill. 574, 90 N.E. 2d (1950); *But see contra,* Op. Atty. Gen. N.Car., Aug. 9, 1979.
2. *See, e.g.,* Commonwealth v. Renfrew, 332 Mass. 492, 126 N.E.2d 109 (1955).
3. *See, e.g.,* People v. Levison, *supra* note 1.
4. Pierce v. Society of Sisters, 268 U.S. 510 (1925).
5. *See, e.g.,* State v. Garber, 197 Kan. 567, 419 P.2d 896, 1966, *cert. denied and appeal dismissed* 389 U.S. 51 (1967); State *ex rel.* Shoreline School Dist. v. Superior Court for King County, 55 Wash.2d 177, 346 P.2d 999, *cert. denied* 363 U.S. 814 (1960).
6. Wisconsin v. Yoder, 406 U.S. 205 (1972).
7. 20 U.S.C. §§1401 *et. seq.*

8. Merriken v. Cressman, 364 F. Supp. 913 (E.D. Pa. 1973).
9. Ingraham v. Wright, 430 U.S. 651 (1977).
10. Goss v. Lopez, 419 U.S. 565 (1965).
11. Cal. Ed. Code §48900, *et. seq.*
12. N.Y. EDUC. LAW §3214; Turner v. Kowalski, 49 A.D.2d 943, 374 N.Y.S.2d 133 (2nd Dept. 1975).
13. N.Y. EDUC. LAW §3214.
14. *See, e.g.,* Donohue v. Copiague Union Free School, 64 A.D.2d 29, 407 N.Y.S.2d 874 (1978); *aff'd.* 47 N.Y.2d 440, 418 N.Y.S.2d 375 (1979); Peter W. v. San Francisco Unified School Dist., 60 Cal. App.3d 814, 131 Cal. Rptr. 854 (1976).
15. Peter W. v. San Francisco Unified School Dist., *supra* note 14.
16. *See* n. 7, *supra.*
17. 20 U.S.C. §§1242 *et seq.*
18. 20 U.S.C. §1232(g).
19. 45 C.F.R. §99.3.
20. 45 C.F.R. §99.11.
21. 45 C.F.R. §99.13.
22. 45 C.F.R. §99.8.
23. 45 C.F.R. §§99.3, 99.12.
24. 45 C.F.R. §99.20.
25. 45 C.F.R. §§99.20(c), 99.21(b).
26. 45 C.F.R. §99.21(c)(d).
27. 45 C.F.R. §99.63.
28. 45 C.F.R. §99.64.
29. 45 C.F.R. §99.3.
30. 45 C.F.R. §§99.31; 99.34.
31. 45 C.F.R. §99.30.

III

Medical Care of Children

Can children receive medical care or treatment without their parents' consent?

In general, no. But there are a number of exceptions to this rule which will be discussed in the following questions and answers.

Generally, children below the age of majority are deemed legally incapable of consenting to medical care or treatment on their own behalf. The "age of majority" is a legal term used to describe the legal age at which a person becomes an adult, which is eighteen in most states.

No doctor, surgeon, nurse, or other medical professional may treat a patient of *any* age without his or her consent. Technically, if a physician operates upon or even touches a patient without this consent, the physician may be liable for assault or battery. Since children are legally deemed incapable of giving consent to their own medical care, no medical professional may treat them even if they *do* consent.

Therefore, only a child's parents (or guardians) may provide the necessary consent for medical treatment of a child; without it, a doctor or medical professional who provides treatment will risk liability to the child or his parent.[1]

What are the exceptions to the rule that medical care may be given children only with their parents' consent?

In all states, a child may be treated even without his parent's consent in the case of an *emergency*.

Children who are *emancipated* may be treated on their own consent alone.

In some states, children who are deemed *mature minors* also may be treated upon their own request.

Finally, special types of medical care, such as treatment for venereal disease, prenatal care, or an abortion, may be obtained by a child without parental consent under certain circumstances.

These exceptions will be discussed more fully below.

What is a "Medical emergency"?

An emergency is a situation in which medical care is required immediately and the parents or guardians of the child cannot be reached in time to provide consent. To qualify as an emergency, the degree of harm which might result if treatment is not provided is high; the child's life or health must be in danger.[2]

What does "emancipation" mean?

A child becomes emancipated in most states when he or she enlists in the United States Armed Forces, marries, or is declared emancipated by a court. Emancipated minors, even if they are below the age of majority, may receive medical care and treatment without the consent of their parents.[3] In some states a female child is considered emancipated for the purpose of consenting to medical care if she is pregnant or has given birth to a child, whether she is married or single.[4]

What is a "mature minor"?

A mature minor is a legal term that is not easily defined. Generally, it means a child intelligent enough to understand and appreciate the nature and consequences of a specific medical treatment for his or her own benefit.[5] Factors to be considered in determining whether a child might qualify as a mature minor are his or her age, intellectual maturity, and the expected benefits of the proposed treatment. If a physician or medical professional believes that a child is a mature minor, as defined above, he or she may provide medical treatment without first obtaining the consent of the child's parents.

However, the mature-minor doctrine is not recognized in all states.

What other special conditions permit a child to consent to medical treatment without parental consent?

In almost all states, minors can consent to treatment for venereal diseases (VD) without their parents' consent or knowledge.[6] This is because most state legislatures have decided that requiring parental consent might inhibit children from seeking treatment of these communicable diseases and that the health of the community, which would be endangered if VD were not treated, is of greater importance than the right of parents to consent to medical treatment for their children.

In many states, a minor's addiction to alcohol or other drugs also may be treated without parental consent, for the same reason.[7]

In many states, treatment for VD and drug and alcohol addiction is provided without cost to the patient.

In almost all states, minor females who are pregnant may receive medical care for themselves and their unborn children without first securing their parents' permission.[8] Again, this appears to be a policy decision of state lawmakers that it is better to be certain that young mothers and their unborn children receive proper prenatal care, than to insist on parental consent when a pregnant female's fear of parental disapproval might prevent her from seeking treatment.

Can a child have an abortion without the consent of her parents?

Yes. A more complete understanding of the answer requires a brief historical account of legislation and litigation concerning this issue.

When the U.S. Supreme Court ruled in 1973 that states could not prohibit abortions if performed through the second trimester (twenty-four weeks) of a woman's pregnancy,[9] the question of whether the decision applied to *unmarried minor* females remained unanswered. Many states began to pass laws covering this situation, some of which made it impossible for unmarried minor females to obtain an abortion without obtaining prior parental consent.

In 1976, the Supreme Court had a chance to review a law of this sort when it struck down a Missouri statute that made it a crime for a physician to perform an abortion on an unmarried minor without her parents' permission.[10] The Missouri law was so strict that it gave parents an absolute veto over their daughter's decision. It was this fact—that a minor female had no recourse whatsoever if her parents withheld permission—that made the law constitutionally unacceptable to the Supreme Court. The Court said: "Any independent interest a parent may have in the termination of their daughter's pregnancy is no more weighty than the right of privacy of the competent minor mature enough to have become pregnant."

Thus, as of 1976, it could be said that parental consent was not required before a minor could seek and obtain an abortion.

In 1979, the Supreme Court reviewed another law, this time from Massachusetts, which required prior parental consent, but also provided that if consent was denied, the minor female had a right to seek approval from a court, which had the power, after a hearing, to overrule her parents' decision if it believed that termination of the child's pregnancy was in her best interest. Under the Massachusetts law, the minor's parents had a right to be present at the hearing and offer their reasons for denying consent.

The Supreme Court ruled that this law also was unconstitutional for two main reasons. First, because the law permitted a court to deny the child's right to an abortion even if she was mature and fully competent to make an independent decision; second, because it required parental consultation in all cases and left no room for a child to seek court permission without first notifying her parents.[11]

The Supreme Court differentiated a child's decision to terminate a pregnancy from other types of medical decisions for which parental consent is required. The Court noted that the pregnant minor's options are much more limited than, say, a minor unable to obtain parental consent to marry. "A minor not permitted to marry before the age of majority," the Court stated, "is required simply to postpone her decision. . . . A pregnant adolescent, however, cannot preserve for long the possibility of aborting, which effectively expires in a matter of weeks from the onset of pregnancy." The Court continued:

Moreover, the potentially severe detriment facing a pregnant woman is not mitigated by her minority. Indeed, considering her probable education, employment skills, financial resources, and emotional maturity, unwanted motherhood may be exceptionally burdensome for a minor. . . . In sum, there are few situations in which denying a minor the right to make an important decision will have consequences so grave and indelible.

Thus, as of 1979, it is still the case that parental consent is not required before a minor may seek and obtain an abortion.

It is noteworthy that in finding the Massachusetts parental-consent law unconstitutional, the Supreme Court did something extremely rare: it discussed what type of law *might* be constitutional, if a state chose to enact it. The Court suggested that a law that required a pregnant minor to obtain either parental consent *or* permission from a local court or an administrative agency might not be unconstitutional. Permission from the local court or agency would be granted if the minor could show that she was mature enough to make decisions in consultation with her physician without parental involvement, or the court or agency could grant permission if it believed that the abortion would be in the child's best interest. The proceeding before the court or agency would be quick, anonymous, and carried on without the knowledge or involvement of the child's parents. However, no such law has come before the Supreme Court for constitutional review, and if and when it did, there is no guarantee that the Court, at that time, would adhere to its own suggestions offered in 1979. *In any event, until further pronouncements from the Supreme Court, laws requiring parental consent for abortions are unconstitutional.*

Do parents have the right to *force* their minor daughter to terminate her pregnancy if she opposes?

No. The same right of a minor child that permits her to obtain an abortion without parental consent also guarantees the right of a child *not* to abort if she so desires.[12] The right to abort or not belongs solely to the person who is pregnant.

Do children have the right to seek and obtain birth-control devices without prior parental consent?

Yes, although the answer for *prescription* birth-control pill devices may not be as certain.

Generally, over-the-counter birth-control devices (condoms, vaginal foams) are available to anyone who wishes to buy them, regardless of age. Laws in some states making it illegal to sell nonprescription birth-control devices to minors were struck down a few years ago by the United States Supreme Court because they violated a minor's right to privacy. The Court held that "In a field that by definition concerns the most intimate of human activities and relationships, decisions whether to accomplish or to prevent conception are among the most private and sensitive . . . Restrictions on the distribution of contraceptives clearly burden the freedom to make such decisions." [13] If a drugstore (or any store) is permitted to sell nonprescription birth-control devices to minors, they have no legal duty to inform the parents of a minor who purchases them.

Moreover, in a number of states, local welfare departments are required or permitted to distribute birth-control information and devices to minors of childbearing age without the consent of their parents. [14] In fact, the 1974 amendment to the federal Aid and Services to Needy Families with Children Act (which used to be known as Aid to Dependent Children) declares that states must offer family-planning services and supplies to eligible persons of childbearing age, including minors, without regard to marital status or age. [15] It is likely that states will not be permitted to require the written consent of a minor's parents before such services and supplies may be furnished. [16]

As for prescription birth-control devices (pills, diaphragms, intrauterine devices), the law is less clear. In some states, the law permits doctors to provide birth-control information and prescribe contraceptives to patients of any age without parental consent. [17] But most states simply have no laws governing this issue, and the question remains whether treatment for contraception falls into the general rule that prior parental consent is required for all medical care for children, or whether sex-related medical treatment (including prescription birth-control devices) qualifies as an exception based on the child's right to privacy.

Recently, a federal appeals court decided a case involving minors who were prescribed birth-control devices by a state-sponsored clinic. A group of parents sued, not to stop the clinic from dispensing birth-control devices, but to require the clinic to *inform* the parents that their children were being treated. The court ruled against the parents, saying that a state may provide information and devices relating to birth control to persons of any age without giving notice to anyone.[18]

Do parents have the right to place their children in mental hospitals?

Yes, if the mental hospital's medical staff concludes that the child is in need of care and treatment. The United States Supreme Court recently held that extensive pre-commitment procedures, such as a court hearing at which the child would be represented by an attorney or representative who would be in a position to oppose the planned placement, are not constitutionally required.[19]

While the decision has been considered by many to be a blow against the due-process rights of children, it conforms to the general theory stated at the outset of this chapter that parents have the right and power to determine the need and type of medical care for their children. According to Chief Justice Burger, who wrote the opinion of the Supreme Court:

> Our jurisprudence historically has reflected Western Civilization concepts of the family as a unit with broad parental authority over minor children. Our cases have consistently followed that course; our constitutional system long ago rejected any notion that a child is "the mere creature of the state" and on the contrary, asserted that parents generally "have the right, coupled with the high duty, to recognize and prepare [their children] for additional obligations." Surely, this includes a "high duty" to recognize symptoms of illness and to seek and follow medical advice. The law's concept of the family rests

on a presumption that parents possess what a child lacks in maturity, experience and capacity for judgment required for making life's difficult decisions. More important, historically, it has recognized that the natural bonds of affection lead parents to act in the best interests of their children. . . .

Most children, even in adolescence, simply are not able to make sound judgments concerning many decisions including their need for medical care and treatment. Parents can and must make those judgments.

The Supreme Court did require, however, that in addition to a child's parents, a hospital staff physician must decide that a child is in need of medical care and that the physician's decision must be "independent"; that is, free from parental influence and based on all sources of information that are traditionally relied upon by physicians, including consultation with behavioral specialists. The Court also required that some kind of preadmission inquiry must be made by a "neutral factfinder" to carefully probe the child's background, using all available sources, including parents, schools, and social agencies. The investigation must also include an interview with the child. Finally, the Court ruled that once a child is committed, his or her continuing need for commitment must be reviewed periodically by a "similarly independent procedure."

It should be noted that because the Court ruled that court hearings are not constitutionally required, this does not mean that states are prohibited from establishing procedures more strict than those set forth by the Court. For example, some states require that parents may commit children only if the child is under a certain age, such as thirteen or fifteen, and that if children over this age are to be committed by their parents, they must give their own consent.[20] Other states require that children may be committed by their parents, but if they are over a certain age they may obtain their own release.[21] Still others require the consent of parents and *two* physicians before a child may be committed.[22] Michigan law states that if a child objects, he or she must receive a hearing within thirty days of commitment.[23]

Do parents have a right to refuse medical treatment for their children based on religious grounds?

Yes, but the right is not unlimited by any means.

The general rule is that a parent has the right to seek a certain kind of medical treatment for his or her child or to refuse treatment altogether, based on religious reasons. This is partly because a parent has the constitutional right to raise a child free from outside interference by the state and partly because the Constitution forbids the state to interfere with a person's religious beliefs and practices.

But, as stated at the beginning of this answer, there are certain limits to parental rights even when coupled with religious freedom. For example, parents have no choice to prevent their children from being immunized against a communicable disease such as smallpox if the law requires immunization. This has been recognized as part of the reasonable exercise of the state's "police power" in protecting society from disease and epidemic.[24] This power may not be disregarded by parents who do not wish to have their children immunized, whether the objection is based on religious grounds or not.

In addition, the parental prerogative to determine proper medical care is limited if it would endanger the life of a child. Thus, if there is an imminent danger to the life of a child if surgery is not performed, a parent's objection to surgery on religious grounds will not be honored.[25] While adults have the right to refuse medical treatment for themselves, for religious or personal reasons, they do not have the right to make life-threatening decisions for their children. As stated by the Supreme Court in another context, "Parents may be free to become martyrs themselves. But it does not follow that they are free to make martyrs of their children before they have reached the age of full and legal discretion when they can make that choice for themselves." [26]

What about necessary but *nonemergency* medical treatment? Do parents have the right to refuse this on religious grounds?

There is no clear answer to this question. This is partly because it is difficult to determine what threatens a life and what does not. For example, a medical procedure may not be necessary to save the life of a child now, but if the treatment is postponed the condition might later worsen and pose a fatal danger. Moreover, a particular operation or treatment may not be necessary to save the life of a child, but it may be considered so necessary for the child to lead a normal or healthy life that a court would order it to be undertaken, even over the objections of a child's parents.

A few illustrations will demonstrate the different approaches courts have taken on this conflict. In 1942, a Washington court refused to order the amputation of a child's deformed arm when medical testimony indicated that the operation was dangerous, even though it would enable the child to lead a normal life.[27] In 1955, a New York court refused to order corrective surgery of a boy's harelip and cleft palate even though the operation involved little risk and could become more difficult with time.[28] In the second case, the parents objected to the operation for religious reasons, but the court based a major part of its decision on the right of the child, then fourteen years of age, to make up his own mind as the years went on.

But opposite decisions are also reached. In a 1970 New York case, the mother of a boy whose face was disfigured objected to cosmetic surgery, since it would involve blood transfusions to which she objected on religious grounds. Despite the fact that an operation was not necessary to preserve the life or health of the child, the court ordered surgery, since without it the boy would be unable to lead a normal, useful life.[29] And in 1972, an Iowa court ordered the surgical removal of tonsils and adenoids of a child over the religious objections of the father, who preferred medication as the treatment. The court reasoned that it had the duty to preserve the health of a child even though there was no evidence of an immediate threat to his life or limb.[30]

Can the state require children to become inoculated or vaccinated against communicable diseases as a requirement for enrollment in school?
    Yes.[31]

Do parents, with the consent of physicians, have the right to turn off life-support devices sustaining children who are comatose and who have no realistic chance of living without artificial support?

Yes, if they obtain court approval.

In the highly publicized case of Karen Ann Quinlan, in which a minor existed only in sleep-wake cycles with no signs of consciousness, a court granted her parents the authority to disconnect life-support systems upon a finding by physicians that there was no reasonable possibility that the child would ever emerge from her comatose state.[32] (In cases where there is any chance of regaining cognition, it is virtually certain that courts would not authorize disconnecting life-support systems.)

Do parents have the authority to have their children sterilized?

Probably not. Although parents have the right, as well as the duty, to care for their children's health and to do whatever is necessary for their well-being, their authority is not absolute and may be limited by courts. If sterilization is to be performed at all, it may be accomplished only in accord with state law and with approval by a court; parents do not possess this extraordinary power by themselves.[33]

Courts generally do not grant parents permission to have their children sterilized unless there is a compelling reason, such as very severe mental or physical retardation. For example, a federal court in Connecticut ruled that parents do not have the right to take such a drastic step, and based its decision on the Supreme Court's ruling that neither a parent nor the state may veto a child's decision to decide whether to bear or beget a child. Thus, for the same reason that parents have no power to prohibit their daughter from obtaining an abortion, they have no power to sterilize their children. But the court took note of a Connecticut law that permitted parents to seek medical authorization for sterilization of inmates in state institutions for the mentally incompetent, and concluded that the same right should be granted to parents of non-institutionalized retarded children. "If the state may . . . decide to sterilize some individuals to avoid incomprehensible pregnancy," the court said, "it makes shamefully limited sense to contend that the same right should be denied to others in the same situation." [34]

Do parents have a right to be informed about medical treatment delivered to their children?

No one is certain about the answer to this question— least of all, doctors.

If a parent takes a child to a doctor for treatment and the child is quite young, the answer is that the parent has a right to be told virtually everything. Parents are charged with providing adequate medical care for their children. They must also pay for the medical services their children receive. Therefore, they have a right to know what type of treatment and care their children are given. This includes the severity of the malady, the type of medication, and all other relevant aspects of a child's medical or hospital care.

As a child reaches adolescence, however, the question becomes more complex. This is because in every state, laws ensure that communications between a doctor and patient are considered "privileged"; [35] that is, information communicated to or discovered by a physician (or nurse, dentist, surgeon, etc.) cannot be disclosed by the physician to anyone other than the patient, unless the patient consents. Medical ethics uphold the same standard. [36] When a patient is an infant or a small child, there is no question that the "privilege" between doctor and patient includes the parent. But as a child matures the rights of parents to be informed about treatment given their children is less secure, because the "privilege" may belong to the patient only.

In most states, for example, if a child seeks treatment for venereal disease, information regarding the patient's name cannot be revealed to anyone, including his or her parents. [37] Some states take the same view for treatment of a child's drug or alcohol addiction. [38] Also, many physicians regard sex-related health care so private that they consider it unethical to disclose information to a child's parents.

With regard to general medical treatment, a number of states take a middle position and permit physicians to use their own best judgment in advising parents that their child is seeking treatment. [39] A Minnesota law permits doctors to inform parents when failure to inform them may jeopardize the health of the child, and in Kentucky, disclosure to parents is permitted when it would be beneficial to the minor's health.[40] In Maryland, physicians may disclose information to parents only if failure to do so would be detrimental to the health of the child and only after making reasonable efforts to persuade the child to consent to disclosure.[41] In California, the law protects the rights of the child by stating that a physician may contact the parents only if the child says where they live.[42]

As a final note, parents should be aware that the doctor-patient privilege, whether it attaches to the child or the adult, cannot be invoked in cases of suspected child abuse or neglect. Thus, doctors are free—in fact, doctors are *required*—to report their suspicions of abuse or neglect of children in their care. (See Chapter V.)

NOTES

1. *See, e.g.,* Bonner v. Moran, 126 F.2d 121 (D.C. Cir. 1941); Lacey v. Laird, 166 Ohio St. 12, 139 N.E.2d 25 (1956).
2. *See, e.g.,* N.Y. PUB. HEALTH LAW §2504(3).
3. Rothe v. Hall, 352 Mo. 926, 180 S.W.2d 7 (1944).
4. *See, e.g.,* N.Y. PUB HEALTH LAW §2054(1).
5. *See, e.g.,* Gulf & S.I.R. Co. v. Sullivan, 155 Miss. 1, 119 So. 501 (1928).
6. *See, e.g.,* N.Y. PUB. HEALTH LAW §2305(2); PA. STAT. ANN. tit. 35, §10104; MINN. STAT. ANN. §144.343; MAINE REV. STAT. ANN. tit. 32, §3154.
7. *See, e.g.,* MASS. GEN. LAWS ANN. ch. 112, §12E; COLO. REV. STAT. §13–22–102; CAL. CIV. CODE §34.7; 21 U.S.C. §1175.
8. *See, e.g.,* CAL. CIV. CODE §34.5; N.J. STAT. ANN. §9: 17A–1; N.Y. PUB HEALTH L. §2504.
9. Roe v. Wade, 410 U.S. 113 (1973).
10. Planned Parenthood v. Danforth, 428 U.S. 52 (1976).
11. Bellotti v. Baird, 443 U.S. 622 61 L. Ed.2d 797 (1979).
12. *See, e.g., In re* Smith, 16 Md. App. 209, 295 A.2d 238 (1972).
13. Carey v. Population Services Int'l, 431 U.S. 678 (1977).
14. *See, e.g.,* N.Y. SOC. SERV. LAW §350(1)(e).
15. 42 U.S.C. §602(s) (15) (a) (1974); C.F.R. Sec. 220.21.
16. T.H. v. Jones, 425 F. Supp, 873 (D. Utah 1975); *see also* discussion of parental consent for abortions in this chapter.

17. *See, e.g.,* Cal. Senate Bill No. 395 ch. 6 (1975); COLO. REV. STAT. §13–22–105 (1973); MD. ANN. CODE art. 43, §135(a)(3).
18. Doe v. Irwin, —— F.2d —— (6th Cir. 1980), reversing 441 F. Supp. 1247 (E.D. Mich. 1977).
19. Parham v. J.L. 442 U.S. 584, 61 L. Ed.2d 101 (1979); Pennsylvania Sec'y of Pub. Welfare v. Institutionalized Juveniles, —— U.S. ——, 61 L. Ed.2d 142 (1979).
20. *See, e.g.,* WASH. REV. CODE §72.23.070(2); W. VA. CODE §27–4–1(b).
21. *See, e.g.,* IDAHO CODE §66–318, 320; N.Y. MENTAL HYG. LAW §31.13.
22. MISS. CODE ANN. §41–21–103(c).
23. MICH. STAT. ANN. §14.800(415)(2).
24. *See, e.g.,* Jacobson v. Massachusetts, 197 U.S. 11 (1905).
25. Jehovah's Witnesses in State of Washington v. King County Hospital, 278 F. Supp. 488 (W.D. Wash. 1967), *aff'd.* 390 U.S. 598 (1968).
26. Prince v. Massachusetts, 321 U.S. 158 (1943), *cited in* Jehovah's Witnesses, *supra* note 25.
27. *In re* Hudson, 13 Wash.2d 673, 126 P.2d 765 (1942).
28. Matter of Seiferth, 309 N.Y. 80, 127 N.E.2d 820 (1955); *see also, In re* Green, 448 Pa. 338, 292 A.2d 387 (1972); 452 Pa. 373, 307 A.2d 279 (1973).
29. *In re* Sampson, 65 Misc.2d 658, 317 N.Y.S.2d 641 (Fam. Ct., Ulster Co. 1970); *aff'd.* 37 A.D.2d 668, 323 N.Y.S.2d 253 (3rd Dept. 1971); *aff'd. per curiam* 29 N.Y.2d 900, 328 N.Y.S.2d 686 (1972).
30. *In re* Karwath, 199 N.W.2d 147 (Iowa 1972).
31. *See, e.g.,* Jacobsen v. Massachusetts, *supra* n. 24; N.Y. PUB. HEALTH L. §2164; Viemeister v. White, 179 N.Y. 235, 72 N.E. 97 (1904).
32. *In re* Quinlan, 70 N.J. 10, 355 A.2d 647 (1976).
33. *See, e.g.,* L. v H., 163 Ind. App. 636, 325 N.E.2d 501 (Ind. App. 1975), *cert. denied* 425 U.S. 936 (1976).
34. Ruby v. Massey, 452 F. Supp. 361 (D.Conn. 1978).
35. *See, e.g.,* Cal. Ev. Code, §§917, 992; N.Y. C.P.L.R. §4504.
36. American Medical Association, Principles of Medical Ethics §9.
37. *See* n. 6, *supra.*
38. *See* n. 7, *supra.*
39. *See, e.g.,* KAN. STAT. ANN. §65–2892. N.J. STAT. ANN. §9:17A 5.
40. MINN. STAT. ANN. §144.346; KY. REV. STAT. §214.185.
41. MD. STAT. ANN. art. 43, §135(c) (Supp. 1973).
42. CAL. CIV. CODE §43.6.

IV

Control and Discipline
of Children

It is a deeply ingrained tenet of law and custom that parents have the right—and sometimes the duty—to control and discipline their children. This can be traced to the biblical dictate that children must honor and obey their parents. But it is also justified by strictly practical notions that the safety of children and their proper training for responsible adulthood demands constant parental guidance and sometimes less-than-pleasant learning experiences. Therefore, reasonable forms of punishment (including spanking), withholding certain privileges, verbal reprimand, and demands of reasonable obedience are proper parental prerogatives.

Even though parents have the power to administer discipline and exercise control over their children, the law jealously protects the rights of children as well, and the state will not tolerate forms of parental behavior that endanger the health or safety of a child. Simply stated, there are bounds beyond which parental discipline may not be carried, and reliance upon parental rights will not justify child abuse or neglect.

Along with the parental right to discipline children is the concomitant duty to support them. Parents who fail to support their children may be found guilty of child neglect and might have them taken away by the state. The legal duty to support one's children is so strong that it survives the dissolution of a family by separation or divorce, and exists until children reach a certain age, usually eighteen or twenty-one or until they become emancipated.

Since parents have the duty to support their children, they also have the right to collect money damages for injury *to* their children caused by the negligence or intentional acts of others. Parents are liable for the acts *of* their children, however, only under certain circumstances.

These issues will be discussed in greater detail in this chapter.

Do parents have the right to control and discipline their children?

Most certainly. The right to control and discipline children is one of the central aspects of the constitutional right of family integrity (see Chapter I). The law respects the right of parents to make reasonable demands upon their children and to expect obedience in return.[1] But this is more than a right; the law imposes a reciprocal obligation upon parents to control and protect their children and to use their disciplinary power in a manner which will promote the long-range education and welfare of their offspring.

No less an authority than the Supreme Court stated, in 1968, "Constitutional interpretation has consistently recognized that the parents' claim to authority in their own household to direct the rearing of their children is basic to the structure of our society."[2] And as recently as 1979, it asserted that the rights of children cannot be equated with those of adults for three reasons: because (1) children are vulnerable; (2) children are unable to make decisions in an informed, mature manner; and (3) because of "the importance of the parental role in child rearing."[3]

But neither the Supreme Court nor anyone else has told parents how to *enforce* the rights that are theirs. Thus, parental power over children, especially adolescents, may be more elusive than real.

The "right" of parents to control their children's reading habits might illustrate this point. A federal law was enacted a few years ago which gave parents the right to order commercial mailing establishments to remove the names of their children from lists for the delivery of pornographic mail.[4] Moreover, most states have laws prohibiting adult book dealers from selling pornographic literature to minors. But no law in any state grants parents the power to control their children's choice of reading materials—including pornographic literature—*after* it comes into their hands. Parents may forbid their children to bring objectionable literature into their home, or enforce their disapproval through normal parental pressure, but in no case would parents have the right to enforce their power by invoking coercive *state* intervention in situations such as this. The same could probably be said of the "right" of parents to force their adolescent children to attend church, to accompany them on a vacation or attend private rather than public school.

For example, in one of the few cases of its kind, a Minnesota Juvenile Court was called upon to decide a dispute between a fifteen-year-old girl whose dating patterns so distressed her parents that they demanded her company with them on a four-year sailing trip around the world. The daughter refused and asked the court to let her decide for herself where she would reside and whom she would date. The court rather uncomfortably backed up parental control but added:

> For children to become functional adults, as they mature, they must increasingly be listened to before (parental) authority is exercised. If they are not, the family unit becomes disfunctional, as here.

The judge then concluded that even though the sailing trip was the parents' "first preference as to their daughter's upbringing," the trip would be an "emotional disaster for the child." The court therefore permitted the parents to implement their second choice; placement of their daughter with a relative in another state.[5]

Do parents have the right to corporally punish their children?

Yes, so long as the punishment inflicted is reasonable and does not injure or harm the child. Thus, while parents have a right to spank their children, this form of punishment may be legally impermissible if administered in an excessive or abusive manner.

Where is the line drawn between "reasonable" or "permissible" discipline and "excessive" or "abusive" punishment?

This is a difficult question to answer, since every case

is determined by its own facts. Ultimately, it is up to a judge or a jury to decide if harsh discipline constitutes unreasonable or excessive force or not.

Historically, parents in the United States have had a great deal of latitude in punishing their children. The first known laws enacted by the colonists in 1654 permitted— in fact, required—corporal punishment of "disrespectful and disobedient children."[6] Whipping was considered an appropriate punishment at that time.

Today, parents have less authority over their children than in the seventeenth century, at least with regard to the degree of force used upon them. When a child's health or welfare is endangered or harmed, the state has the power to intervene in the otherwise private realm of family life and come to the aid of the child.

Corporal punishment and other forms of discipline are permitted, in the words of the courts, so long as the chastisement is "moderate and reasonable," in light of the age and condition of the child and other surrounding circumstances.[7] On the other hand, if punishment is inflicted with a "malicious desire to cause pain" or if it causes injury to the child, it will be deemed unreasonable and the parent may be subject to penal or civil sanctions imposed by law.[8]

The age of the child is often a factor in determining reasonableness. For example, a spanking of moderate force might be reasonable if inflicted upon a four-year-old as punishment for running into a busy street. But a spanking with similar force upon a mere infant for any reason might be considered abusive—and therefore illegal—since an infant's threshold for injury is very low. Similarly, the nature of the penalty of the child may determine whether or not a particular punishment is reasonable. It might be reasonable to forbid a twelve-year-old to be out of the home past 7:00 P.M., but it would be unreasonable—and probably considered abusive—to lock the child in a closet to make sure he stays home.

The law considers parents sufficiently intelligent to distinguish between ordinary discipline and abuse. As stated in 1978 by a Maryland court,

> parents of ordinary intelligence are aware that they do not subject themselves to the [child abuse] statutes

by merely engaging in corporal discipline for the purpose of punishment or correction. Only when the line is crossed and physical injury is intentionally and maliciously or cruelly inflicted does criminal responsibility attach.[9]

That same year, a New York court ruled that since there is no precise standard of the use of corporal punishment, courts must look at all circumstances of the case to see if the parents exceeded the "balance of moderation" and were "cruel and merciless." [10] In the case it was deciding, the court found the conduct of a father, who had beaten his thirteen-year-old daughter with a wooden shingle, leaving severe bruises on her buttocks and arms, to be "unreasonable, excessive and dangerous" to the child's physical, mental, and emotional well-being.

Therefore, if parental demands become unreasonable or parental discipline becomes abusive, the law imposes a limit on the rights of parents and it will not hesitate— through its authorized agencies such as child-welfare departments or, when necessary, the courts—to intrude into the otherwise protected area of family privacy for the purpose of protecting a child. When such intervention occurs, the law may require the parents to obtain some type of help for their problem, it may temporarily remove children from their custody or it may hold the parent responsible for the commission of a crime.[11]

May parents ever call upon the police or go to court to enforce their discipline upon disobedient children?

Yes. All states have "disobedient-child" laws which permit parents to bring their children into court for failing to obey their reasonable commands. These laws—also known as Persons In Need of Supervision (PINS), Children In Need of Supervision (CINS) or Minors in Need of Supervision (MINS) Laws—are not criminal statutes, since they do not apply to children who have committed criminal or even delinquent acts. They are aimed solely at children whose behavior is disobedient or disruptive and poses a danger to themselves or others. Those who justify these laws say that their chief purpose is to provide help for children or to prevent them from committing delinquent or criminal acts in the future.[12]

The California disobedent-child law is typical. It defines a person in need of supervision as "Any person under the age of 18 years who persistently or habitually refuses to obey the reasonable and proper orders or directions of his parents, guardian [or] custodian . . . or who is beyond the control of such person." [13] New York defines a PINS child as anyone under sixteen who does not attend school as required by law or "who is incorrigible, ungovernable or habitually disobedient and beyond the lawful control of parents or other lawful authority." [14]

Parents most often invoke these laws when their children have run away from home or constantly stay out of the home late at night or overnight without permission. If a child has run away from home, or is out overnight without permission, the parents may seek police assistance in locating and returning their child. The parents then may take the child to court and accuse him or her of disobedience. (Of course, they are under no legal obligation to do so if they find it more advisable to deal with their disobedient child at home.)

Cases involving children or minors in need of supervision are handled in juvenile or family courts, and the proceedings are usually confidential. Most courts will appoint an independent attorney to represent a child in such proceedings, and this attorney may well oppose the petition brought by the child's parents.

Since most CINS laws define disobedience as the habitual refusal to obey reasonable demands, parents may not be able to convince a court that their child is "guilty" if the child has exhibited only minor or infrequent disobedience or if the demands on the child were clearly unreasonable.[15]

If a court finds a child to be ungovernable or in need of supervision, it has a number of options: it may do nothing or merely give the child a warning; it may place the child on probation; or it may place the child in a foster home or an institution for disobedient children. Recently, under pressure from the federal government, states have begun to refrain from placing disobedient children in the same institutions as delinquent children and from sending them to large institutions.[16]

May a state or city prohibit children from being on the street at night even if they have their parents' permission?

Yes. Many communities in the United States have curfew laws or ordinances that restrict the right of minors to be on the street or in public places after a certain hour of the night. Some apply to all people under eighteen or under sixteen; some specify a certain hour after which a person under eighteen must be home and an earlier hour after which persons under sixteen or fourteen must be inside; some specify certain hours for weekdays and later hours for weekend evenings. Not all counties or towns have curfews. Some enacted curfews long ago and no longer enforce them. But even in localities where curfews exist and are enforced, parents may accompany their own children on the street and in public places at any hour without running afoul of the law.

Are curfews constitutional?

Some are and some are not. A number of courts have found curfew laws too broad, too vague, or simply unnecessary instrusions on parental prerogatives. Other courts have found them entirely permissible.

Curfew laws are penal laws. To be valid, a penal law must be clear enough to be understood by those subject to its provisions. Laws that do not meet this test are often found to violate the Fourteenth Amendment's guarantee of the due process of law because their terms are so vague that they do not provide adequate notice of the prohibited activity. In the past decade, a number of laws which prohibited "loitering" or "vagrancy" (by adults) have been declared void for reasons of vagueness, since these terms are incapable of precise definition.[17] Many curfew laws contain similar vague terms and are therefore subject to the same constitutional scrutiny. Laws in Hawaii and Oklahoma have been declared void for this reason.[18]

In other locations, curfew laws have been overturned for more substantive reasons. As early as 1898, a city ordinance in Graham, Texas, which made it unlawful for persons under twenty-one to be on the streets after 9:00 P.M., was struck down since it unlawfully usurped the rule and function of parents.[19] More recently, curfew laws in California and Florida were declared void since they violated the child's rights of liberty and freedom of travel.[20]

In overturning a Seattle curfew, the Supreme Court of Washington stated, "Prima facie, mere sauntering or loitering on a public way is lawful and the right of any man, woman or child." [21] The court then went on to cite a U.S. Supreme Court opinion that walking, strolling, wandering, and even loafing and loitering in public places "are historically part of the amenities of life as we have known them." [22]

A Portland curfew was struck down on the ground that it gave police the power to arrest a person on the suspicion that he had no lawful purpose for merely being somewhere, when the true standard for arrest should be probable cause that a crime has been committed. [23] Similarly, the Seattle curfew ordinance was found to exceed the lawful scope of police power by making no distinction between conduct calculated to harm and conduct that is essentially innocent. [24]

Not all curfew laws have been declared void when challenged: at least four have withstood recent constitutional attack. [25] In one of these cases, the United States Supreme Court refused to review the decision of a lower federal court which upheld a curfew ordinance on the ground that it was a reasonable means of furthering the following four legitimate state goals: 1) the protection of children from each other and from other persons on the street during the nighttime hours; 2) the enforcement of parental control and responsibility for their children; 3) the protection of the public from nocturnal mischief by minors; and 4) reduction in the incidence of juvenile criminal activity. [25.5]

SUPPORT

Do parents have the duty to support their children?

Yes. This duty exists in all states and is universally recognized as a moral and legal obligation of parenthood. This duty is set forth by statute in most states and recognized by case law in every jurisdiction. It is usually defined as the obligation to feed, clothe, and shelter children adequately and provide them with necessary medical care. [26]

The duty to support continues until the child reaches a

certain age set forth by law, usually eighteen or twenty-one. The duty may be curtailed earlier by the child's emancipation, marriage, or enlistment in the armed forces.

If the child is mentally or physically defective, however, the parental obligation to support may extend beyond the age of majority.[27]

Are parents obliged to support their children if they leave the parent's home agaginst the wishes of the parents?

No. Along with a child's right to support goes a responsibility to live his or her life according to the instructions of the supporting parents. Thus, if a child is old enough to leave home legally, and does so contrary to the desires of his or her parents, or, once away from home acts in a manner which runs counter to the strong desires of his or her parents, the parents may be free from the obligation to support their errant child.

In one reported case, a college student refused to live on campus in a dormitory pursuant to her father's instructions and moved into an apartment with a friend. The father demonstrated his disapproval of this arrangement by cutting off tuition payments to his daughter. She sued her father, claiming her right to receive support, but the court upheld the propriety of her father's action, stating:

> The father, in return for maintenance and support, may establish and impose reasonable regulations for his child . . . To hold otherwise would be to allow . . . a minor of employable age to deliberately flout the legitimate mandates of her father while requiring that the latter support her in her decision to place herself beyond his effective control.[28]

May parents be required to pay the expenses related to the confinement of their children as juvenile delinquents?

Yes. Many states have laws requiring parents to reimburse the state for the detention of children, and courts have found these laws valid.[29]

Are mothers and fathers equally responsible for child-support expenses?

It depends on the state. In states that have passed equal rights laws and where courts have construed relevant statutes in a way that prohibits discrimination on the basis of gender, mothers and fathers are proportionately responsible for the support of their children. In other words, in these states if the mother and father have identical income and expenses, they would be equally liable for support. If, however, the father earns all the income and the mother earns nothing, the father would be fully responsible for support.[30]

In states that have not enacted equal-rights laws or have not otherwise placed men and women on an equal legal footing, the father is usually primarily liable for the support of his minor children. This doctrine, which is derived from the common law, does not preclude the mother from being responsible for child support; but she would become liable only if the father is unable to pay the full amount. Generally, if the father can pay the full amount of support, even if the mother is able to pay *part* of the amount, the father may be obliged to pay child support in its entirety.

Such questions, however, normally surface only when parents are separated or divorced from each other.

Are stepparents obliged to support the children of their spouses?

Generally not. The rule in most states is that a stepparent is under no obligation to support the children of his or her spouse by a former marriage.[31] Some jurisdictions, however, have enacted statutes which do impose a duty of support on stepparents.[32] But in most of these states, the support obligation of the stepparent is limited to situations in which the stepchildren are receiving public assistance, are in danger of becoming public charges, or are wards of the state.[33] Generally, under stepparent-support laws, both stepmothers and stepfathers are included in the term "stepparents," [34] as is a person who marries the parent of an illegitimate child.[35]

Do parents have the right to receive the wages earned by their minor children?

Yes. Because parents are obliged to support their children the law provides that they are entitled to the services and income of their children in exchange. This rule, however, was designed in a different era and is not generally enforced today, and some states have passed laws restricting the parents' right to such money. In California, for example, the wages of a minor may be paid to a child unless his or her parents or guardians give the employer notice that the wages are claimed by them.[36] In New York and Idaho, what an employer pays to a child cannot be claimed unless the parents give written notice of a claim to their child's earnings within thirty days after the employment starts.[37]

Do parents have a right to be supported by their children?

Generally, the obligation to support one's parents is considered a moral duty but *not* a legal one. Some states have enacted laws requiring children to support their poor or indigent parents [38] or making them liable for the maintenance of a parent in a state institution.[39] But these laws are rarely enforced, except in circumstances discussed in the following question and answer.

Can children be legally obliged to support their parents if their parents are receiving public assistance?

Yes. Some state laws provide that if a person is receiving public assistance and has an adult child who is able to support him or her, the child can be ordered by a court to reimburse the state to help support the parent.[40] However, medical payments made by the state to poor parents are not chargeable to their adult children.[41]

If a minor becomes a public charge and is receiving public assistance, may the state obtain reimbursements from the parent?

No. If the child has disobeyed the parent's instructions and left the parental home without permission, the parent is not obliged to pay for the child's support even if it means the state will.[42]

May parents be sued by their children for raising them less than adequately?

Probably not. A few cases have been commenced in the past several years by children seeking to obtain damages from their parents for inadequate parenting. Thus far, none have been successful.[43]

EMANCIPATION FROM PARENTAL CONTROL

What does "emancipation" mean?

Emancipation is a legal term used to describe the condition whereby a child may be released from some or all of the disabilities of childhood and receive the rights and duties of adulthood even before reaching the age of majority. Emancipation also relinquishes parents from their parental rights and duties, including the right to the custody and control of their child, the right to receive the services and earnings, and the duty to support, maintain, protect, and educate their child.[44]

Are there degrees of emancipation?

Yes. Emancipation may be total, complete or partial. A *complete emancipation* occurs when there is an agreement or a court declares that parents have relinquished control and authority over their child, conferring on the child the right to his or her own earnings, and extinguishing the parents' legal duty to support and maintain the child.

Partial emancipation, on the other hand, results when a child is freed from some of his or her parents' control during all or part of the child's minority, or from all of the parents' control during part of the child's minority.[45] Under partial emancipation, a child may be allowed to keep his or her own earnings and still be entitled to receive some degree of parental support and maintenance.[46]

How does a child become emancipated?

The most common form of emancipation takes place automatically when a young person reaches the age of majority. Emancipation also takes place automatically when a child marries or joins the armed forces.[47] Generally, emancipation before these events occur can be granted only by a court of law.

There are some exceptions to this rule. Children may become emancipated in whole or in part by implication, consent, or agreement, even without permission or approval of a court. These possibilities will be discussed in the following questions and answers.

How, and under what conditions, will a court declare a child emancipated?

Historically, emancipation was a privilege granted to parents, not children.[48] A parent could—and still can—petition a court for a declaration of emancipation to be released from the legal obligation to support, maintain, and educate a child.

In determining whether a child is to be emancipated, a court will consider factors such as the age of the child, whether he or she lives at home,[49] and whether the child is free from the authority and control of his or her parents.[50] Most important, however, are financial considerations such as the child's employment and source of income,[51] his or her freedom to spend money without parental permission,[52] whether the child pays room and board if living at home,[53] whether the child pays his or her own debts,[54] and whether the parents have listed the child as a dependent for tax purposes.[55]

What conditions might constitute emancipation by implication, agreement, or some other means?

Generally, they are the same as those considered by a court; that is, if a child has left home and established an independent household, if a child has his or her own source of income, if a child manages his or her own affairs, and other similar conditions and circumstances. If the child and parent agree to the establishment of such conditions,[56] if the parents consent to such conditions, or acquiesce by not demanding that the circumstances change, if parents require their child to pay room and board, or if parents actually force their child out of the home and require that the child support himself,[57] complete or partial emancipation may be established without the benefit (or bother) of obtaining judicial approval.

What is the practical effect of emancipation?

An emancipated child (and parents of emancipated children) may be exempt from many of the rights and obligations discussed in this chapter. Depending on the purpose for which a child is emancipated, a parent may have no right to control an emancipated child nor any right to receive his or her services. Consequently, the parent of an emancipated child may have no right to collect damages for injury to the child nor, conversely, any liability for acts caused by the child. Similarly, parents of emancipated children may have no obligation to support or maintain them.

INJURIES TO CHILDREN

Do parents have the right to recover monetary damages if their child is injured by the negligence of another person?

Yes. This means that if a person other than a child's parent negligently causes injury to the child—say by hitting the child with a car—the child's parents have the right to sue and collect monetary damages from the driver. But an explanation of legal theory must be offered at this point.

The theory is that parents cannot sue the negligent person for the child's *actual* injury, since it was the child and not the parent who sustained the injury. But since parents have the duty to support their children, provide medical treatment, and the right to collect their earnings, they have the right to recover monetary damages for medical expenses and loss of the child's services and earnings (including future earnings).[58] Normally, parents may not recover punitive or exemplary damages.[59]

In some states, parents who actually witness the negligent injury of their child may recover damages for fright or emotional shock—but only if they were near the scene of the accident and the shock resulted from a direct emotional impact of observing the injury.[60]

Of course, the *child* may sue the negligent person for his or her own injuries.[61] And since minors cannot sue on their own, it is likely that the child's parents will act as the child's guardian and sue on his or her behalf. But monetary damages awarded for a child's injury belong to the child and not the parents.

Thus, there are usually *two* cases arising out of the same injury: first, the parents' case against the negligent person for medical expenses and loss of services and earnings; and second, the child's case against the negligent person for damages caused by the injury itself.

What about injuries to a child that result in death?

Curiously, in most states, parents have less legal recourse

to recover monetary damages for the death of their children than if their children were injured. This is because medical expenses will probably be less (or nonexistent, if death is instantaneous), and the common-law allows no recovery for loss of services or future earnings dating from the time of death.[62] (If the child does not die immediately, the parents can recover damages for medical expenses and loss of services from the time of the injury up to the time of death.)

But in states which have passed laws called "wrongful-death statutes," this common-law oddity no longer applies, and parents are permitted to sue the negligent person for causing the death of their child.[63] However, many states still deny parents the right to recover damages for their own anguish and suffering due to the loss of a child.[64]

May parents be held liable for *their own* negligence if they injure their own children?

The answer depends on whether the doctrine of "intra-family-tort immunity" is in effect in the state where the injury occurred. In states which honor the rule, parents would not be liable for injury to their children caused by their own negligence.

Generally, the "intrafamily-tort immunity" rule means that persons within a single family (parents and children, husbands and wives) are immune from suits brought by each other for negligent acts. The theory behind this rule is that families are regarded as a single entity, and a single entity cannot sue itself. Another theory supporting the rule has it that if the law permitted suits between members of the same family, the social order and domestic tranquillity would be unnecessarily disturbed. Practically speaking, the intrafamily-tort immunity rule has been supported on the ground that lawsuits between members of one family would permit fraudulent claims, since in most cases damages assessed against the negligent family member would be paid by his or her insurance company.

In the past two decades, however, the intrafamily-tort immunity rule has begun to crumble. Courts have abrogated the rule in at least nineteen states: (Alaska, Arizona, California, the District of Columbia, Hawaii, Illinois, Kentucky, Louisiana, Massachusetts, Michigan, Minnesota, New Hampshire, New Jersey, New York, North Dakota,

Pennsylvania, Vermont, Virginia, and Wisconsin).[65] In these states, parents may be held liable for their negligent or accidental actions which result in injuries to their children.

In abolishing the parent-child immunity rule, the California Supreme Court took note of the fact that even though parents have the right to discipline their children, they have no right to act negligently toward them. Most importantly, the court affirmed the doctrine that an injured person, regardless of age or family position, has a fundamental right to be compensated for injuries caused by another.[66] In New York, the highest court relied on the fact that automobile liability insurance is widespread and compulsory.[67] Thus, in cases arising out of automobile accidents, the true parties to intrafamily litigation are not the child and his parent but the injured child and an insurance company. In rebutting the argument that abolition of the immunity doctrine will foster collusion to defraud insurance companies or others, courts of many states have noted that the possibility of fraud exists in every liability case, not just those brought between members of a family.

Even in states where parent-child immunity exists, are there still situations in which parents may be held liable for acts causing harm or injury to their children?

Yes. Even where the intrafamily-tort immunity rule is in force, lawsuits are usually permitted on behalf of children against other members of their own family: 1) for damage to one's property (as distinguished from a personal injury);[68] 2) for personal injury resulting from a parent's willful or malicious action (as distinguished from negligent action);[69] 3) for matters involving cases against the estate of deceased parent;[70] 4) for claims against the employer of a parent for torts committed during the scope of a parent's employment;[71] and 5) for cases against parents in their business capacity.[72]

In discussing a child's right to recover for the malicious act of his parent, the California Supreme Court stated: "While it may seem repugnant to allow a minor to sue his parent, we think it more repugnant to leave a minor child without redress for the damages he has suffered by reason of his parent's willful or malicious misconduct." [73]

DAMAGE OR INJURY CAUSED BY CHILDREN

If a child injures another person or destroys another person's property, is the child's parent liable for the amount of damages?

Only under some circumstances. Generally, the mere fact of parenthood does not render a parent liable for the acts of his or her child. Thus, if a child is involved in an accident caused by his or her own carelessness or lack of judgment, his or her parents are probably not responsible for paying the damages resulting from that accident.[74]

But there are situations in which parents will be held liable for part or all of the damages caused by their children. For example, parents may be held liable for the acts of their children if it is shown that the child *worked* for the parent and was negligent while acting as an agent or employee of his or her employer-parent.[75] Thus, a Massachusetts court found a father liable for personal injuries caused to another by his child while riding a bicycle because at the time of the accident the child was a "servant" of his father, acting within the scope of his employment with his father's grocery business as a delivery boy.[76]

Also, parents may be held liable if they actually directed the child in causing damage to others, or if parents consented to or sponsored the child's actions.[77]

And in a few states, parents may be liable for the negligent acts of their children if parents are themselves negligent in failing to exercise proper control or supervision over their child, with knowledge that injury to another is a possible consequence of their child's conduct. As an example of this legal principle, a Florida court ruled that a parent may be liable to others by entrusting to a child a bicycle which, because of the child's young age, inexperience, and lack of judgment may be a source of danger to others. In this case, a woman was struck from behind by a five-year-old child riding a two-wheeled bicycle on a sidewalk. The child was riding without supervision only five days after the father had removed training wheels from the bike.[78]

Other exceptions to the general rule of nonliability of parents will be discussed below.

What if damages or injuries caused by a child are not the result of an accident but are *intentionally* inflicted?

There are two situations that may make parents liable for damages caused by the intentional or willful acts of their children.

First, parents may be found liable if they had knowledge of the destructive tendencies of their child beforehand, and did not exercise proper care or control to prevent such outbreaks.[79] If parents are found to have violated this "duty of care," they may be held responsible for the full amount of damages caused. Proving liability, however, is not an easy task. For example, in an Arizona case, a fourteen-year-old boy assaulted a woman and her two daughters with a hammer. The woman sued the boy's parents, but failed to establish a case because there was insufficient evidence to show that the parents knew that their son would commit the assault *or* that they should have known of their child's propensity for violence.[80] In another case, arising in California, a person was shot by a child who stationed himself on a hill and fired at passing motorists. The injured person sued the boy's parents and at the trial produced a psychiatrist who testified that the child was a paranoid schizophrenic and the symptoms should have been observed by his parents, alerting them that control should be exercised. The court disagreed and ruled that testimony by the psychiatrist alone was not sufficient to show that the parents were liable.[81]

Second, many states have recently passed laws making parents financially liable for intentional or willful acts of their children that cause damage or injury to others. These laws require parents to pay *regardless* of whether they knew or should have known of their children's propensity to cause damage. They have been enacted as a result of the much-publicized "wave" of juvenile crime, with the belief that parents will exercise greater control over their children's behavior if they know they are liable for damages caused by their children's intentional or illegal acts.

However, most of these laws also *limit* parental liability to a certain amount, specified by statute in each state, generally $500 or $1,000.[82] Thus, if the damage intentionally caused by the child is great, parents may be responsible only up to the lesser statutory amount.

If a parent leaves a gun or other dangerous instrument in a place where a child finds it and uses it to injure someone else, is the parent liable for the injury caused by the child?

Yes. A parent may be found liable for injury caused by a child's use of a gun, whether the parent actually gives the gun to an inexperienced child or leaves it in a place where the child is able to find it.[83]

In one case, parents were found guilty of negligence when their seven-year-old child shot his four-year-old brother with a pistol that was left in an unlocked automobile glove compartment.[84] In another case, a father had purchased a gun for his ten-year-old son and taught him never to point it at anyone and to use it only in the basement. However, the father was found negligent because he left it in an open cabinet where his son found it and accidentally shot his playmate while playing with the gun in the basement.[85]

On the other hand, if parents entrust a gun to a child who, for example, has a hunting license and has been schooled in the use of firearms, they might not be found liable for injuries caused by the child since they could have assumed that the child was a proper person to use the gun.[86]

If a parent permits a child to use a gun, may the parent be found *criminally* responsible?

In many states there are penal laws expressly prohibiting parents from giving to their children, or permitting them to use, pistols, B-B guns, air guns, and the like.[87] While a violation of these statutes may or may not have any bearing on a parent's *civil* liability (discussed in the previous questions), they may result in a fine and criminal record for the adults, if found guilty.

NOTES

1. Commonwealth v. Brasher, 270 N.E.2d 389 (Sup. Ct. Mass. 1971).
2. Ginsberg v. State of New York, 390 U.S. 629 (1968).
3. Bellotti v. Baird, 443 U.S. 622, 61 L. Ed.2d 797 (1979).
4. 39 U.S.C. §4009; Rowan v. United States Post Office, 397 U.S. 728 (1970).

5. *In re* L.A.G., Hennepin Co. Dist. Ct. (1972), in 24 Juv. Just. 34 (May, 1973).

6. Act of Colony of Massachusetts Bay of New England, 1654, Mass. Bay Records, Vol. III (1644–1657) at 355, *cited in* Commonwealth v. Brasher, *supra* note 1.

7. *See, e.g.,* People v. Green, 155 Mich. 524, 119 N.W. 1087 (1909); State v. Black, 360 Mo. 261, 227 S.W.2d 1006 (1950).

8. *See, e.g.,* Hinkel v. State, 127 Ind. 490, 26 N.E. 777 (1891); Neal v. State, 54 Ga. 281 (1875).

9. Bowers v. State, 283 Md. 115, 389 A.2d 341 (Ct. App. Md. 1978).

10. *In re* Shirley Roy, 418 N.Y.S.2d 913 (Fam. Ct. 1979).

11. *E.g.,* State v. Hunt, 2 Ariz. App. 6, 406 P.2d 208 (1965).

12. *See, e.g., In re* Presley, 47 Ill.2d 50, 264 N.E.2d 177 (1970).

13. CAL. WELF & INST. CODE §601.

14. N.Y. FAM. CT. ACT §712(b).

15. *See, e.g., In re* D.T.B., 18 Cal. App.3d 782, 98 Cal. Rptr. 146 (1971); *In re* O., 31 N.Y.2d 730, 290 N.E.2d 145 (1972).

16. *See* Juvenile Justice Delinquency and Prevention Act of 1974, P.L. 93–415, 88 Stat. 1109.

17. Papachristou v. City of Jacksonville, 405 U.S. 156, 92 S. Ct. 839 (1972); Ricks v. District of Columbia, 134 U.S. App. D.C. 201, 414 F.2d 1097, 1103–4, 1107 (D.C. Cir. 1968).

18. *In re* Doe, 54 Haw. 647, 513 P.2d 1385 (1973), striking down a Honolulu ordinance that prohibited a child under eighteen from loitering in public places between 10:00 P.M. and sunrise unless accompanied by a parent; Hays v. Municipal Court of Oklahoma City, 487 P.2d 974 (Okl. Crim. App. 1971), striking down an Oklahoma City ordinance that made it a crime for any person under sixteen to loaf or loiter on the streets between 9:00 P.M. and 6:00 A.M.

19. *Ex parte* McCarver, 46 S.W. 936 (Tex. Ct. Crim. App. 1898).

20. Alves v. Justice Court, 148 Cal. App.2d 419, 306 P.2d 601 (1957); W.J.W. v. State. 456 So.2d 48 (Fla. App. 1978).

21. City of Seattle v. Pullman, 82 Wash.2d 794, 514 P.2d 1059 (1973); *citing* Commonwealth v. Carpenter, 325 Mass. 519, 521, 91 N.E.2d 666, 667 (1950) (emphasis added).

22. City of Seattle v. Pullman, *supra* n. 21, at 1064, *citing* Papachristou v. City of Jacksonville, *supra* note 17, at 164.

23. City of Portland v. James, 444 P.2d 554 (Or. 1968).
24. City of Seattle v. Pullman, *supra* n. 21. *See also* People v. Chambers, 32 Ill. App.3d 444, 335 N.E.2d 612 (1975).
25. *In re* Nancy C., 28 Cal. App.3d 747, 105 Cal. Rptr. 113 (1972); Bykofsky v. Borough of Middletown, 401 F. Supp. 1242 (N.D. Pa. 1975); *aff'd.* 535 F.2d 1245 (3rd Cir. 1976), *cert. denied* 429 U.S. 964 (1976); *In re* Doe, 87 N.M. 466; People v. Chambers, 66 Ill.2d 36, 360 N.E.2d 55 (1976).
25.5 Bykofsky v. Borough of Middletown, *supra* n. 25.
26. State v. Moran, 99 Conn. 115, 121 A. 277 (1923).
27. Levy v. Levy, 245 Cal. App.2d 341, 53 Cal. Rptr. 790 (1966); Zandowich v. Sherwood, 19 Conn. Super. 89, 110 A.2d 290 (1954).
28. Roe v. Doe, 29 N.Y.2d 188, 272 N.E.2d 567 (1971); Parker v. Stage, 43 N.Y.2d 128, 371 N.E.2d 513 (1977).
29. *See, e.g.,* Jesmer v. Dundon, 29 N.Y.2d 5, 271 N.E.2d 905 (1971), *appeal dismissed* 404 U.S. 953; *In re* Shaieb, 250 Cal. App.2d 553, 58 Cal. Rptr. 631 (1967).
30. *See, e.g.,* Rand v. Rand, 374 A.2d 900 (Md. Ct. of App. 1977); Conway v. Dana, 456 Pa. 536, 318 A.2d 324 (1974); Carter v. Carter, 58 A.D.2d 438, 397 N.Y.S.2d 88 (2d Dept. 1977).
31. *See* 59 AM. JUR.2d, *Parent and Child* §§88, 91.
32. *See, e.g.,* N.Y. DOM. REL. LAW §§31, 32; WASH. REV. CODE §26.16.205.
33. *See, e.g.,* Chapin v. Superior Court of Kern County, 239 Cal. App.2d 851, 49 Cal. Rptr. 199 (1966); Baird v. Baird, 45 App. Div.2d 930, 357 N.Y.S.2d 327 (1974); *but see,* Hammond v. Sec. of H.E.W., U.S. Dist. Ct., D. Colo., Aug. 31, 1979 in 5 F.L.R. 2919.
34. Rann v. Rann, 54 Misc.2d 704, 283 N.Y.S.2d 426 (1967).
35. People *ex rel.* Coleman v. Fermoile, 236 A.D. 388, 259 N.Y.S. 564 (1932).
36. CAL. CIV. CODE §212.
37. N.Y. GEN. OBLIG. LAW §3-109; IDAHO CODE §32–1004.
38. *See, e.g.,* Ill. Stat. ch. 68 §§24–25.1; Ky. Rev. Stats. §405.080; *but see,* Woods v. Ashland Hosp. Co., 340 S.W. 2d 594.
39. *See, e.g.,* Moore v. Palen, 36 N.W.2d 540 (Minn. 1949).
40. *See, e.g.,* County of Alameda v. Aberle, 268 Cal. App.2d 424, 73 Cal. Rptr. 926 (1968); Maricopa County v. Douglas, 69 Ariz. 35, 208 P.2d 646 (1949); Mallatt v. Luihn, 206 Or. 678, 294 P.2d 871 (1956).
41. 42 U.S.C. §302(a)(11)(E).
42. Parker v. Stage, 43 N.Y.2d 128, 371 N.E.2d 513 (1977); Tucker v. Toia, 371 N.E.2d 449 (N.Y. 1977).

43. *See, e.g.,* Burnette v. Wahl, 588 P.2d 1105 (Or. 1978); Hansen v. Hansen, (Colo. Dist. Ct., Boulder County. 3/29/79) in 5 F.L.R. 2516.

44. 67 C.J.S. *Parent and Child* §2, p. 629; Matter of Bates v. Bates, 62 Misc.2d 498, 502, 310 N.Y.S.2d 26, 30 (Fam. Ct., Westchester County 1970).

45. *See* S. Katz, W. Schroeder, & L. Sidman, *Emancipating Our Children—Coming of Legal Age in America,* 7 FAM. L. Q. 211 (1973); Vaupel v. Bellach, 261 Iowa 376, 379–80, 154 N.W.2d 149, 150–51 (1967).

46. Turner v. Turner, 441 S.W.2d 105 (Ky. Ct. App. 1969).

47. *See, e.g.,* CAL. CIV. CODE §204; Allen v. Arthur, 139 Ind. App. 460, 220 N.E.2d 658 (1966); Iroquois Iron Co. v. Industrial Comm'n., 249 Ill. 106, 128 N.E. 289 (1920); *But see,* Argonaut Insurance Exchange v. Kates, 289 P.2d 801 (1955).

48. 39 AM. JUR. 702, §64; Matter of Bates v. Bates, 62 Misc.2d 498, 310 N.Y.S.2d 26 (Fam. Ct. 1970).

49. Fitzgerald v. Valdez, 77 N.M. 769, 427 P.2d 655 (1967).

50. Gillikin v. Burbage, 263 N.C. 317, 139 S.E.2d 753 (1965).

51. Schoenung v. Callet, 206 Wis. 52, 238 N.W. 852 (1931).

52. Lafkin v. Harvey, 131 Minn. 238, 154 N.W. 1097 (1915).

53. Wurth v. Wurth, 322 S.W.2d 745 (Mo. 1959).

54. Carricato v. Carricato, 384 S.W.2d 85 (Ky. Ct. App. 1964).

55. Wadoz v. United Nat'l. Indemnity Co., 274 Wis. 383, 80 N.W.2d 262 (1957).

56. Rounds Bros. v. McDaniel, 133 Ky. 669, 676, 118 S.W. 956, 958 (1909); Carricato v. Carricato, *supra* note 54.

57. Smith v. Gilbert, 80 Ark. 525, 98 S.W. 115 (1906).

58. Yordon v. Savage, 279 So.2d 844 (Fla. 1973).

59. *See, e.g.,* Hughey v. Ausborn, 249 S.C. 470, 154 S.E.2d 839 (1967); Mancino v. Webb, 274 A.2d 711 (Del., 1971). *See, contra,* Howell v. Howell, 162 N.C. 283, 78 S.E. 222 (1913).

60. *See, e.g.,* Dillon v. Legg, 68 Cal.2d 728, 69 Cal. Rptr. 72, 441 P.2d 912 (1968).

61. *See, e.g.,* Trevarton v. Trevarton, 151 Colo. 418, 378 P.2d 640 (1963).

62. Panama R. Co. v. Rock, 266 U.S. 209 (1924).

63. *See, e.g.,* CAL. CIV. PROC. CODE §377.

64. Krause v. Graham, 19 Cal.3d 59, 562 P.2d 1022, 137 Cal. Rptr. 863 (1977).

65. *See* Hebel v. Hebel, 435 P.2d 8 (Alaska 1967); Streenz v. Streenz, 106 Ariz. 86, 471 P.2d 282 (1970); Gibson v. Gibson, 3 Cal.3d 914, 479 P.2d 648 (1971); Tamashiro v. DeGama, 51 Haw. 484, 462 P.2d 1007 (1970);

Schenk v. Schenk, 100 Ill., App.2d 199, 241 N.E.2d 12 (1968); Rigdon v. Rigdon, 463 S.W.2d 631 (Ky. 1970); Rouley v. State Farm Mutual Auto Ins. Co., 235 F. Supp. 786 (W.D. La. 1964); Sileski v. Kelman, 281 Minn. 431, 161 N.W.2d 631 (1968); Briere v. Briere, 107 N.H. 434, 224 A.2d 588 (1966); France v. A.P.A. Transport Co., 56 N.J. 500, 267 A.2d 490 (1970); Gelbman v. Gelbman, 23 N.Y.2d 434, 245 N.E.2d 192 (1969); Nuelle v. Wells, 154 N.W.2d 364 (N.D. 1967); Goller v. White, 20 Wis.2d 402, 122 N.W.2d 193 (1963); Plumley v. Klein, 388 Mich. 1, 199 N.W.2d 169 (1972); Xaphes v. Mossey, 224 F. Supp. 578 (D. Vt. 1963); Falco v. Pados, 444 Pa. 372, 282 A.2d 351 (1971); Sorensen v. Sorensen, 339 N.E.2d 907 (Mass. 1975); Smith v. Kauffman, 212 Va. 181, 183 S.E.2d 190 (1971).

66. Gibson v. Gibson, *supra* note 65.

67. Gibson v. Gibson, *supra* note 65; Gelbman v. Gelbman, *supra* note 65.

68. Bradigan v. Bradigan, 9 N.Y.2d 472, 215 N.Y.S.2d 35, 174 N.E.2d 718 (1961) (dissent); Signs v. Signs, 156 Ohio St. 566, 103 N.E.2d 743 (1952).

69. Emery v. Emery, 45 Cal.2d 421, 289 P.2d 218 (1955); Cannon v. Cannon, 287 N.Y. 427, 40 N.E.2d 236 (1942); Mahnke v. Moore, 197 Md. 61, 77 A.2d 923 (1951).

70. Davis v. Smith, 253 F.2d 286 (3rd Cir. 1958); Dean v. Smith, 106 N.H. 314, 211 A.2d 410 (1965); Brennecke v. Kilpatrick, 336 S.W.2d 68 (Mo. 1968); Cannon v. Cannon, *supra* note 69.

71. Stapleton v. Stapleton, 85 Ga. App. 728, 70 S.E.2d 156 (1952); O'Connor v. Benson Coal Co., 301 Mass. 145, 16 N.E.2d 636 (1938); Chase v. New Haven Waste Material Co., 111 Conn., 377, 150 A.107 (1930); Briggs v. City of Philadelphia, 112 Pa.Super. 50, 170 A. 871 (1934).

72. Signs v. Signs, *supra* note 68; Borst v. Borst, 41 Wash.2d 642, 251 P.2d 149 (1952); Lusk v. Lusk, 113 W. Va. 17, 166 S.E. 538 (1932); Dunlap v. Dunlap, 84 N.H. 352, 150 A. 905 (1930); Worrell v. Worrell, 174 Va. 11, 4 S.E.2d 343 (1939).

73. Emery v. Emery, *supra* note 69, at 224.

74. Lastowski v. Norge Coin-O-Matic, 44 A.D.2d 127, 355 N.Y.S.2d 432 (1974); Parsons v. Smitty, 109 Ariz. 49, 504 P.2d 1272 (1972); Aetna Insurance Co. v. Richardell, 528 S.W.2d 280 (Tex. Civ. App. 1975); *see, contra,* Turner v. Bucher, 308 So.2d 270 (La. 1975).

75. Bradstreet v. Hall, 168 Ind. 192, 80 N.E. 145 (1907); Mirick v. Suchy, 74 Kan. 715, 87 P. 1141 (1906); Davis v. Littlefield, 97 S.C. 171, 81 S.E. 487 (1914).

76. Altoonian v. Muldonian, 277 Mass. 53, 177 N.E. 830 (1931).
77. *See e.g.*, Hupkins v. Droppers, 184 Wis. 400, 198 N.W. 738 (1924); Langford v. Shu, 258 N.C. 135, 128 S.E.2d 210 (1962); Guilbeau v. Guilbeau, 326 So.2d 654 (La. 1976).
78. Southern American Fire Ins. Co. v. Maxwell, 274 So.2d 579 (Fla. 1973), *cert. denied* 279 So.2d 32 (1973).
79. *See, e.g.*, Spector v. Neer, 262 So.2d 689 (Fla. 1972); Caldwell v. Zaher, 344 Mass. 590, 183 N.E.2d 706 (1962); Steinberg v. Cauhois, 249 A.D. 518, 593 N.Y.S. 147 (1937).
80. Parsons v. Smithey, 109 Ariz. 49, 504 P.2d 1272 (1973).
81. Reida v. Lund, 18 Cal. App.3d 698, 96 Cal. Rptr. 102 (1971).
82. *See, e.g.*, N.Y. GEN. OBLIG. LAW §3–112; Gen. Ins. Co. v. Faulkner, 259 N.C. 317, 130 S.E.2d 645 (1963); Landers v. Medford, 108 Ga. App. 525, 133 S.E.2d 403 (1963).
83. *See, e.g.*, Stoelting v. Hauck, 56 N.J. Super. 386, 153 A.2d 339 (1959).
84. Valence v. State, 280 So.2d 651; *cert, denied* 282 So.2d 517 (La. 1973).
85. Gerlat v. Christianson, 13 Wis.2d 31, 108 N.W.2d 194 (1961).
86. *See, e.g.*, Conley v. Long, 21 Misc.2d 759, 192 N.Y.S.2d 203 (1959).
87. *See, e.g.*, Fla. Stats. Ann. §§790.17, 790.22; Ohio Rev. Code, §2923.21. *See also,* Idaho Code, §18.3302 (crime to sell or give weapon to child without parent's consent.)

V

Child Abuse and Neglect

DEFINITIONS

What is child abuse?

No two states have laws that define child abuse exactly the same, but there are common aspects among all of them. Virtually every state law considers the infliction of *serious* physical injury upon a child by a parent or custodian to be child abuse. Most laws also include a parent's sexual *intercourse* with or sexual *molestation* of a child. Some laws are defined broadly and include conditions when a parent creates a *risk* of serious physical injury or inflicts *psychological* abuse. Still others consider the infliction of *any* injury to be abusive, whether it is "serious" or not.

A typical definition of child abuse is found in the California law. It makes it illegal for:

> Any person who, under circumstances likely to produce great bodily harm or death, willfully causes or permits any child to suffer, or inflicts thereon unjustifiable physical pain or mental suffering, or having the care or custody of any child, willfully causes or permits the person or health of such child to be injured . . . [or for] any person who, under circumstances or conditions other than those likely to produce great bodily harm, or death, willfully causes or permits any child to suffer, or inflicts thereon unjustifiable physical pain or mental suffering. . . .[1]

Can parents be found guilty of abuse even if there is no direct evidence that their child's injuries were inflicted by them?

Yes. Many—if not most—acts of child abuse occur in the home with no witnesses other than the parents themselves. Thus, most cases of child abuse hinge on circumstantial evidence, or evidence that proves guilt only by the circumstances of the case. Thus, if a child was injured in the home when the parents were there and medical evidence indicates that the injury was not accidental, the parents will probably be found guilty of child abuse.[2] As one court stated: "Proof of injuries as would ordinarily not be sustained or exist except by reasons of acts or omissions of parents shall be prima facie evidence." [3]

What is child neglect?

In most states, child neglect is more loosely defined than child abuse. Generally, it covers situations in which parents do *not* do something that should be done, thereby placing the health and safety of their children in danger.

Most states consider the failure of parents to supply their children with adequate food, shelter, clothing, and medical care to be child neglect. Leaving a child without adequate supervision for a certain length of time and abandonment are also considered acts of neglect in most states. Thus, if a child suffers from malnutrition because his parents do not feed him, or if he does not get proper medical attention for a wound or injury (regardless of how it was caused) because his parents fail to take him to a doctor, the parents may be charged with child neglect. Similarly, if parents leave their small children unattended overnight or longer and make no provisions for someone else to care for them, they may be accused of neglecting their children.

Many states include other categories of parental behavior as child neglect. In a number of states the failure to send a child to school is considered neglect, as is a parent's "moral unfitness," use of drugs, or excessive use of alcohol. A parent's conviction of a serious crime may also be deemed neglect in some states.

As stated at the beginning of this answer, child neglect is never defined as precisely as abuse. For example, some states define neglect as failure to provide a child with "proper" parental care or commission of an act which endangers a child's "morals." Naturally, these terms can mean a great number of things and they almost invite arbitrary and irrational enforcement. Not surprisingly, courts have relied upon these wide-ranging terms to find parents neglectful when they have exhibited only unusual behavior or actions with which a social agency or judge disagrees, without proof of actual harm or even impact on the "neglected" children. The constitutionality of laws containing vague definitions will be discussed later in this chapter.

Is the distinction between child abuse and neglect a clear one?

Not always. The difference between abuse and neglect is often hazy. Some states make no legal distinction between the two and call them both "child maltreatment" or "child dependency." Sometimes, the distinction depends on the degree or severity of harm inflicted on the child.

Up to what age of the child are parents liable for their abuse and neglect?

In forty-four states the age to which children may be found neglected or abused is eighteen. In the other states the cutoff age ranges from sixteen to twenty-one.

Can evidence of maltreatment of one child result in a finding of neglect or abuse of other children in the family, even if they were not specifically maltreated?

Yes. Evidence of parental neglect or abuse of one child may result in the automatic finding of abuse or neglect of other children in the same household even without any evidence of actual maltreatment of the other children.[4]

The theory behind this rule is that evidence of abuse or neglect of one child may indicate that other children in the same family are in extreme danger of harm, and that it is not necessary for parents to maltreat each child in succession in order for a court to intervene.

Does one have to be a *parent* to be charged with child abuse or neglect?

No. Most laws hold parents *and persons acting in the role of a parent* responsible for the abuse or neglect of children under their care. For example, New York's law extends responsibility to a parent "or other person legally responsible for [a child's] care," [5] and in Maryland, the law encompasses any parent "or other person who has the permanent or temporary care or custody or responsibility for the supervision of a minor child." [6]

Even in states where statutes refer only to "parents," courts have construed this as a reference to any person having the care and control of a child.[7]

This means that stepfathers or stepmothers may be charged with child maltreatment or uncles and aunts who regularly care for their nieces and nephews, or a parent's live-in boyfriend or girlfriend or even a baby-sitter may be liable for abusing or neglecting a child in his or her care.

Are child abuse and neglect crimes?

Child abuse, if it involves physical injury, is usually a criminal offense. (Intentionally caused injury to anyone is a crime, including injury to children). Sexual abuse of one's own child is also a crime, whether or not it causes physical injury. Child neglect may or may not be a crime, depending on what type of behavior is being considered. Since neglect encompasses a large scope of activity (and nonactivity), some acts would constitute criminal conduct while others, especially those involving nonintentional inadequacies of parenting, might not.

In any event, even when acts of child maltreatment rise to the level of criminal conduct, they are rarely treated as crimes. Exceptions to this statement would include acts resulting in death, serious injury, disfigurement, or sexual molestation. Generally, child abuse and neglect are dealt with as *civil* matters, in juvenile or family courts, which are civil, not criminal, courts. This is partly due to the fact that child maltreatment is difficult to prove in a criminal court—where the state must establish its case beyond a reasonable doubt—and partly because the emphasis in recent years has been focused less on punishing abusive and neglectful parents than providing help and assistance to children and their parents. Therefore, cases of child abuse and neglect, if they result in court cases, are usually prosecuted by social-welfare department lawyers in civil courts, not by district attorneys in criminal courts.

However, the use of the "civil" label does not mean that cases of child maltreatment are not taken seriously. They are prosecuted vigorously and the consequences are often grave. While findings of abuse or neglect do not usually result in jail terms, they may result in the temporary or permanent removal of children from their parents' custody.

How is abandonment defined?

Most state laws include abandonment as a condition of child neglect, but it is rarely defined. Most statutes simply state that children are deemed neglected if they are "abandoned" by their parents, guardians, or custodians. A few statutes are more specific. For example, in Arizona abandonment is defined as: "failure of a parent to provide reasonable support and maintain regular contact with the child, including the providing of normal supervision. Failure to maintain a normal parental relationship with the child without just cause for six months shall constitute prima facie evidence of abandonment." [8]

In all states, courts will decide whether the specific facts of each case constitutes abandonment or not.

Can parents be charged with neglect for leaving their child with a friend for a short period of time?

Probably not, if the person with whom the child is left is responsible and able to meet the needs of the child.[9]

Obviously, leaving a child with a baby-sitter for an evening is not abandonment, provided the sitter is of suitable age and discretion. But if the child suffered some injury due to the baby-sitter's own unfitness and the parents knew or should have known that the sitter was inadequate, or had previously mistreated children, then the parents might be deemed neglectful.

If the parents leave their child with a caretaker for a period of months and the caretaker is not licensed as a foster parent, the parents will be held to a fairly strict standard of knowledge about the caretaker's ability to handle children.

The question of abandonment and leaving a child in the care of another person might best be answered by referring to a recent Connecticut case. The welfare department claimed that a child was neglected because it was living with its grandaunt, rather than with its parents, but the child's mother was serving time in prison for armed robbery and the father worked full time. The juvenile court agreed with the welfare department and ruled that the child was "uncared-for." On appeal, however, the decision was reversed and the higher court ruled that the child was neither uncared-for nor abandoned. The court said that the welfare department's reasoning would result in the "undesirable consequence of discouraging biological parents from even temporarily entrusting their children to someone who could give them better care." [10]

Can parents be charged with neglect for failure to provide adequate medical care for their children?

Yes. This can come about in a number of ways.

First, parents can be found neglectful for not providing or seeking proper medical care when their children need treatment for illness, injury, or serious physical disorder. Second, they can be charged with neglect for taking a child from a doctor's care or from a hospital before necessary treatment is completed. Third, if parents have been told by doctors or other health professionals that an operation or particular medical treatment is necessary, they might be found neglectful for refusing such treatment. Child-neglect proceedings are frequently invoked to assure that children receive necessary medical treatment to which a parent is opposed but which has been prescribed by a doctor.[11]

For example, a case arose recently in Massachusetts in which the parents of a child suffering from lymphocytic leukemia were unwilling to submit the child to chemotherapy. The supreme court of that state considered the "primary right" of parents to raise children according to their own consciences, but ruled that parental rights do not give them life-and-death authority over their children. The court ordered treatment over the parents' objections because evidence showed that the disease was fatal if untreated, that chemotherapy was the only medical treatment offering a hope of cure, and that the risks of the treatment were minimal compared to the consequences of allowing the disease to go untreated. The court pointed to the power of the state to protect children and distinguished its decision in this case, where treatment was necessary to *save* a child's life, from other cases in which medical treatment has been sought merely to briefly *prolong* life.[12]

What if the necessary medical treatment is contrary to the parents' religious beliefs?

Although one's religious beliefs are protected by the First Amendment, courts will not permit a parent's religious beliefs to harm his or her child.

It is important, however, to bear in mind that the state must demonstrate a "compelling" interest to justify interference with parental discretion; this limits the type and degree of intervention which is legally permissible.

Thus, if a parent refuses consent, on religious grounds, to a medically necessary blood transfusion for his or her child, a court may declare the child to be neglected and authorize that the transfusion be administered. But in the absence of a finding that the parent neglected the child in any other way, no additional court order, such as removing the child from the parent's custody, would be constitutional.[13]

May parents be charged with neglect simply because their children suffer from a disability that requires special physical, mental, or educational services?

Probably not. A few states have laws permitting this to happen, but these laws were passed primarily to assure public funding for handicapped children. Since the passage of the Education for All Handicapped Children Act of 1975 (see Chapter II), however, it is likely that any state law would be found unconstitutional if it required handicapped children to be deemed "neglected," just so they may qualify for public funds.[14]

How is "psychological harm" defined?

Not all states include psychological harm as an aspect of abuse or neglect. Those that consider it part of the legal definition of child maltreatment do not define it very clearly. For example, New York includes in the definition of neglect a child whose mental or emotional condition has become impaired as a result of the parent's failure to exercise a minimum degree of care. The law defines "impairment of mental or emotional condition" in the following way:

'Impairment of emotional condition' includes a state of substantially diminished psychological or intellectual functioning in relation to, but not limited to, such factors as failure to thrive, control of aggressive or self-destructive impulses, ability to think and reason, or acting out of misbehavior, including incorrigibility, ingovernability or habitual truancy.[15]

Idaho permits a court to assume jurisdiction over a "child whose behavior indicates social or emotional maladjustment," which is defined as:

the condition of a child who has been denied proper parental love, or adequate affectionate parental association, and who behaves unnaturally and unrealistically in relation to normal situations, objects and other persons.[16]

The problem with extending traditional notions of abuse and neglect to include psychological harm is that it is very difficult to prove or, from the view of a parent who has been charged with psychological abuse or neglect, it is very difficult to *dis*prove. In short, no one can really say what psychological harm means. Chief Justice Burger of the Supreme Court recognized this problem when he concurred in a case involving the rights of people diagnosed mentally ill. He said, "there can be little responsible debate regarding the uncertainty of diagnosis in this field and the tentativeness of professional judgment." [17]

In child-maltreatment cases, the problem becomes even more difficult, because a judge must weigh the possible consequences of ruling that psychological harm exists— that is, removal of the child from its parents—against the probability of harm if the child remains at home. According to one expert: "No research has yet been done on the highly controversial question of whether custody by the [less than adequate] natural parent provides psychological benefits far outweighing any negative effects of discontinuity." [18]

Can parents be charged with neglect for not sending their child to school?

Yes. More precisely, if parents do not assure that their children receive adequate educational instruction, they may be charged with neglecting the needs of their children.[19] Examples of adequate substitute educational instruction are discussed in Chapter II of this book.

Can parents be charged with child abuse or neglect for "moral unfitness" such as excessive drinking, drug use, or sexual promiscuity?

In many states the answer is yes. Even though the state's power to interfere with parental discretion is derived from its power to protect children from harm, many child neglect laws focus on parental behavior alone, whether or not such behavior endangers children. The term "moral unfitness" or "immoral parental behavior" is found in nearly half of all state neglect statutes. Naturally, these terms are not (and cannot be) interpreted in any consistent fashion, and courts are applying them less vigorously today than in the past. Nevertheless, some child-neglect laws actually constitute an attempt by the state to regulate morality, and courts have found parents morally unfit (and therefore neglectful) because: a mother frequent[ed] taverns or had men visitors overnight; [20] the parents adhered to "extreme" religious practices, or lived in a communal setting; [21] or the parent was a lesbian, homosexual, or mother of an illegitimate child.[22] (For a discussion of the rights of unwed and homosexual and illegitimate parents, see Chapters VIII and XIII.)

More modern interpretations of those terms require that the alleged immorality be linked in some measure to proof of a real or imminent danger to the welfare of the child. For example, excessive drinking may not be sufficient grounds for a finding of neglect unless the parent's alcoholism actually renders him or her unable to care adequately for the child.

Can parents be charged with neglect because their failure to provide adequate care is due to their financial inability to do so?

It depends on the state. About one-quarter of the states have laws that provide an exemption to indigent parents from their duty to provide adequate food, shelter, clothing and medical care for children. But, if a family receives public assistance it is unlikely that they could rely on this

exemption if they were charged with child neglect for
failure to provide proper support for their children.[23]

Aren't some child-abuse and neglect laws quite vague?

Yes. This is because legislatures wish to give child-
protective agencies and courts a wide latitude in dealing
with cases of child maltreatment, so a child who is being
harmed or in severe danger of being harmed will not
escape detection and help simply because the *type* of harm
in a certain case was not specifically covered in a particular law. That is why definitions of maltreatment often
include phrases like "without proper parental care" or
"living under conditions injurious to a child's mental or
physical health or welfare." One court explained that the
term "neglect" has no fixed meaning, but "acquires con-
tent from the specific circumstances of each individual
case." [24]

A more significant question is whether the vagueness of
these laws makes them unconstitutional, for the reason
that they fail to give parents adequate warning of the type
of behavior or conditions that could lead to a ruling of
child neglect or abuse.

When courts have considered this question they have
generally ruled that even fairly vague child-maltreatment
laws are constitutional. For example, the Florida statute,
which reads,

> Whoever willfully or by culpable negligence, de-
> prives a child of or allows a child to be deprived of,
> necessary food, clothing, shelter or medical treatment,
> or who, knowing or by culpable negligence, permits
> the physical or mental health of the child to be ma-
> terially endangered, shall be quilty of a misde-
> meanor. . . .[25]

was found not vague and therefore constitutional by the
state supreme court.[26] And a Maryland law, which defines
abuse as "physical injury or injuries sustained by a child
as a result of cruel or inhuman treatment as a result of a
malicious act or acts, by any parent," [27] was found constitutional by an appellate court in that state as well.[28]

In fact, very few child-abuse and neglect laws have been
found unconstitutional for reasons of vagueness.[29] (This

has not necessarily been the case with similarly worded laws permitting the termination of parental rights. For a discussion of this issue, see Chapter VI.)

Even if most child-abuse and neglect laws are not un-constitutionally vague, do they violate the rights of parents to raise their children as they see fit?

No. Although the right to raise one's children free from state interference has been recognized by the Supreme Court to be one of the "basic civil rights of man" and "rights far more precious than property rights," [30] these rights are not without limitation. The state, through a legal power known in Latin as *parens patriae*, has the power and duty to protect the health and welfare of children who are being harmed by their parents. Some aspects of child-protective laws may unconstitutionally infringe on parents' rights (such as taking a child into protective custody without giving adequate due-process rights to parents, as will be discussed later in this chapter), but the basic power of the state to insist that parents raise their children according to minimal standards is constitutional. [31]

Nevertheless, parents are still entitled to the "fundamental" constitutional right to control the details of the upbringing of their children (see Chapter I) and recent decisions by federal courts have made it clear that the state must show a "compelling state interest" before it may interfere with family life. [32]

Between these two interests, there exists an unclear line of demarcation between state laws that are designed to protect children from real or imminent harm and those that reach unnecessarily into realms of family life where the state has no reason or justification to interfere.

Seen in this light, child neglect laws which authorize state intervention into family life because of the parents' "faults or habits"; [33] "immorality or depravity," [34] or "debauchery" [35] may well be subject to constitutional scrutiny. This is not necessarily because these phases are vague (although it could be argued that they are). Rather, laws with definitions such as these suggest that the state is more concerned with regulating parental "morality" than protecting children.

REPORTING AND INVESTIGATING CHILD ABUSE AND NEGLECT

Can parents be reported if someone suspects them of abusing or neglecting a child?

Yes. Every state has laws that create a mechanism for people to report their suspicions of child abuse and neglect. Some people are *required* by law to report their suspicions.

The theory behind reporting laws is that abused and neglected children are unable to ask for help. In addition, child abuse and neglect usually take place privately, in a home, with no witnesses other than the parents and children. Therefore, reporting laws are designed to bring cases of possible wrongdoing to the attention of public authorities who are in a position to help children and treat abusive and neglectful parents.

Who is required to report his or her suspicion of child abuse or neglect?

In some states only doctors are actually required to report their suspicion that a child under their care has been abused or neglected. In most states the list of required reporters is longer, including nurses, police officers, welfare workers, and sometimes teachers. Basically, most state laws require reporting from professionals who deal with children and are in a good position to detect certain symptoms of child abuse and neglect.

In New York, where the number of people required to report is probably the greatest in the country, the list includes physicians, surgeons, medical examiners, coroners, dentists, osteopaths, optometrists, chiropractors, podiatrists, resident interns, registered nurses, hospital personnel engaged in the treatment of patients, Christian Science practitioners, school teachers and officials, social-service workers, day-care workers, foster-care workers, mental-health professionals, police officers, and any other child-care worker.[36]

What happens if a person required to report child abuse or neglect does not report?

Most state laws provide that persons required to report their suspicions of child abuse or neglect may be criminally prosecuted if they fail to do so. In other words, if a person has reason to believe that a child has been abused or neglected *and* is required by law to report but makes no report, that person has committed a crime (usually a misdemeanor).

Naturally, these laws tend to make people report, even if there is some doubt in their minds whether a child has been maltreated. The prospect of facing a criminal penalty for failure to report makes it almost certain that someone will err on the side of reporting rather than not reporting. This is especially so among professionals who might find their licenses and careers in jeopardy if they are convicted of a crime.

Other than those required to report cases of child abuse and neglect, can anyone else report?

Yes. Most states encourage all people—regardless of their professional standing—to report their suspicions of child abuse and neglect. Therefore, reports from neighbors, family members, and even strangers will be accepted, even though people making these reports are not required to report.

To whom are such reports made?

Reports can be made to any official agency such as the police or the local department of welfare, but persons required to report are usually told to report to a specific office. Most states coordinate reports through civil agencies, such as a department of social welfare or a special child-protection unit of a social-service agency, but a few states (such as California) handle all reports through the police.

Are there centralized data banks containing reports of child abuse and neglect?

About three-fourths of all states maintain statewide central registers (some are computerized) with files containing all reports of child abuse and neglect. The amount of information kept in those registers varies from state to state but usually includes the name and address of the child, the nature of his or her alleged harm, the name and address of the parents or custodians, and the number of times, if any, that previous reports involving the same child or parents have been made.

At present, there is one national register of child abuse and neglect, but according to available information, names are not recorded; it is maintained for statistical purposes only.

Is information contained in these reports considered confidential?

Yes, in most states. This includes reports communicated to and stored in central registers as discussed in the paragraph above.

A 1974 regulation that guides the delivery of federal funds to states for child-abuse prevention and treatment programs requires states to pass laws making reports of child abuse and neglect confidential. These laws must make it a crime for any person to permit or encourage the dissemination of information on reports to anyone other than police and other agencies that investigate reports, courts, grand juries, state officials, researchers (if names are not released to them), persons authorized to take children into emergency protective custody, physicians who need to know if a child they are treating has been previously reported, the child in question, and the parents named in the report.[37]

The reason that there is great concern for the confidentiality of this information is that reports of abuse and neglect are just that—reports, and nothing more. They are not conclusive determinations nor judicial convictions. They are merely indications that someone is *suspected* of mistreating a child. The report may turn out to have been an honest mistake; it may have been made maliciously (by a jealous relative perhaps) or it may be accurate. But at the outset, it is just a report.

Does a parent have any legal recourse against a person who makes an inaccurate report?

There is usually no legal recourse available for the subject of a report (either the parent or the child) to take against the person who first made the report, even if it turns out to be untrue or mistaken. This is because every state has a law which *protects* makers of reports from liability in any subsequent civil or criminal suit that arises out of the report. In practical terms, this means that neither the parent nor the child mentioned in a report can sue the maker of the report for libel, slander, invasion of privacy, or loss of reputation even if the "suspected" abuse or neglect turns out not to be abuse or neglect at all.

There is one qualification to all this: the reporter is granted immunity only if the report is made in "good faith." Thus, a parent or child may have the right to sue a reporter whose report was made maliciously or with no foundation in fact whatsoever or if the report was made for the sole purpose of harming the reputation of the parent or child reported.

What happens after a report of child abuse or neglect is made?

After a report is made, whether it was made by a person required to report or by one permitted to report, and after the information is communicated to a central register (if one exists in that state), an *investigation* is launched by one or two individuals from the agency charged with administering reports in the location where the report was made—usually the state or county department of welfare or social services.

Generally, the investigation must start within a very short period of time. In New York, for example, the investigation must begin within twenty-four hours of receipt of the report.[38] Investigators will go to the home or place where the abuse or neglect allegedly occurred and speak with the parents or persons caring for the child. This will probably be the first time that the parents will be aware that a report concerning them has been made.

If investigators come to the home of the child, do the parents have to talk with them?

No. A person has the right to refuse to talk to anyone, even if the person conducting the investigation is a police officer.

On the other hand, it is likely that if the parent is non-cooperative with the investigators, the agency might assume the worst—that the parent has something to hide or cover up.

If parents are asked questions by those conducting the investigation, can the parents' answers be used againt them in court?

Yes. As strange as it may sound, a parent under investigation for child abuse or neglect has *fewer* rights regarding self-incrimination than a suspect under investigation for committing a crime. They even have fewer rights than suspected criminals regarding unreasonable searches of their homes.

In short, statements made by parents to investigators or social-welfare workers can be used against them in subsequent court hearings. Parents under investigation do not have to be given what are known as *Miranda* warnings by investigators or welfare workers. (That is, they do not have to be warned, prior to being asked questions, that they have a right to remain silent, that whatever they say may be used against them, that they have a right to an attorney, and that if they cannot afford an attorney, one will be provided for free). Moreover, social workers may enter and search welfare clients' apartments and homes even over the objection of their occupants.[39]

Do investigators have the right to speak with the child's doctor? Can a doctor testify in court against the parents?

The answer to both questions is yes. The doctor-patient "privilege," or confidentiality of communication, does not apply to parents of children who are suspected of being abused or neglected.[40]

What happens after the investigation?

It depends entirely on what the investigation reveals. The investigators will determine whether the allegations contained in the initial report are true or false. The conclusion of the investigators is not necessarily based upon what would be considered evidence in a courtroom; it is based solely upon the results of the investigation, whether performed thoroughly or not.

In most states, the investigation will result in an agency report that a child's maltreatment was or was not discovered. *However, the agency determination is not a legal decision. The conclusions of the investigators are purely administrative in nature; they cannot "convict" anyone of wrongdoing.*

Of course, if the agency conducting the investigation thinks it is appropriate, it has the power to take the parents to court by filing a petition charging them with child abuse or neglect. The court can then decide, after a hearing, if further action should be taken.

In many cases, even if the agency concludes that the report of abuse or neglect was true, it may decide *not* to go to court, but rather attempt to resolve the issue by offering services to the family. These may include therapy or counseling for the parents and/or the child, medical services such as visiting nurses, day-care or baby-sitting services, homemaker services, job training, new housing, or group counselling sessions with other parents. Sometimes the agency may suggest that the child be placed in temporary foster care.

Finally, the agency making the investigation may decide to do nothing further at all.

Are parents under any obligation to accept the services offered by the social-welfare agency?

No. Parents have an absolute right to refuse any offer of services they wish. This includes the right to resist offers of counseling and therapy for themselves or their children. It also includes the right to reject the suggestion that their child be placed in temporary foster care.

Sometimes, the agency may say to a parent, "You have the right to reject these services, but if you do, we will take you to court." However unethical it may be to make this threat in order to gain "voluntary" acceptance of their services, there is no question about the power of the agency to file a petition and ask a court to decide whether the parents have abused or neglected their children. If the court decides after a hearing that they did, then it has the power to *order* counseling or other services and even to *order* the placing of children in temporary foster care. Unlike services offered by the welfare agency, orders of the court cannot be rejected by the parents.

If, after investigating, the agency determines that the parents did abuse or neglect their child, can that decision be challenged?

In some states, agency determinations can be challenged by the parents.[41] In these states, parents have the right of access to information contained on the agency files, so that they may challenge it if they wish. Usually, the only information withheld from the parents is the name of the person who made the report in the first place. If the parents disagree with the agency's determination or any information in the report of the investigation, they have the right to an administrative hearing at which they may testify, produce witnesses on their own behalf, and cross-examine witnesses against them, for the purpose of having information they consider inaccurate either corrected or expunged.

REMOVING A CHILD FROM PARENTAL CUSTODY IN AN EMERGENCY

Is there any situation in which children may be taken from their parents without prior court approval?

Yes, when the child's life or safety is in immediate danger. Most state laws authorize police officers, doctors, or social-welfare agents to remove a child from his or her home (or, in the case of a doctor, to keep the child in a hospital) even if the parents object, if the person authorized by law believes that the child would die or be seriously injured if not removed. The theory behind these laws is that in emergency situations, a child's life and safety are more important than parental rights or legal procedures.

A statute typical of the ones referred to above is found in the Texas Family Code. It states:

> An authorized representative of the State Department of Public Welfare, a law-enforcement officer, or a juvenile probation officer may take possession of a child to protect him from an immediate danger to his health or physical safety and deliver him to any court having jurisdiction. . . . The child shall be delivered immediately to the court.[42]

New York's law is also fairly typical. It permits a peace officer, an employee of a department of social services, or an agent of the Society for the Prevention of Cruelty to Children to take a child into protective custody without a court order and without parental permission, but only if the child is in such a condition that staying in the home would present an imminent danger to the child's life or health *and* only if there is no time to apply for an order of removal from a family court.[43] Physicians are also permitted to keep a child in their custody if they believe that returning the child to the family would create an imminent danger to the child's life and health.

Taking a child from his or her home without the consent of the parents and before a hearing is commenced is an extremely drastic step. It is taken rarely—only when the child is truly in danger. Most child-abuse and neglect cases investigated by social-welfare agencies and most of those that reach the courts do not involve the emergency removal process described here.

If a child has been taken from his or her parents under an emergency removal law, may the parents contest this decision in court? If so, how soon after removal?

Emergency-removal statutes permit certain people to remove children believed to be in danger from their parents *prior* to a court hearing or a judicial termination. In all states, parents whose children were so removed are entitled to a court hearing shortly thereafter.

The time between the removal and the hearing varies from state to state, but all state laws require a hearing within a very short time. In New York, the hearing must be held "as soon as practicable," or, no later than three days of an application by a parent for a hearing.[44] In North Carolina, the hearing must be held no later than 5 days after the authorities have assumed custody of the child,[45] and in Texas, the statute says a hearing must be "immediate," [46] which was defined by a federal court to mean within 24 hours of removal.[47]

Do parents have a right to be notified of and to be present at a post-emergency removal hearing?

Yes. "Due process of law" requires that every effort be made to locate the parents of a child removed under emergency conditions. According to one federal court commenting on this point, the state is required to make "all reasonable efforts to serve upon (the parents) notice of this initial presentation to the court."[48] Once notified, parents have a right to be present at the post-emergency removal hearing, to speak in their own defense, to present evidence and witnesses in their favor, and to cross-examine witnesses against them.

At a hearing after an emergency removal, what must the state prove?

Not all state laws are the same, but generally the state must show that there was a valid reason for having removed the child in the first place and, if the state still does not want the child returned, that continued protection outside the home is necessary. One federal court recently ruled that the state must show at least a "danger of immediate harm or threatened harm to the child" to justify an emergency removal.[49] If the state does not meet its burden of proof, the child must be returned.

(Since the purpose of this hearing is not to prove that the parents are guilty of child neglect or abuse, nor to determine whether parental rights should be permanently terminated, but only to determine if there is reason to believe that harm was imminent and that it was essential to remove the child, the standard of proof is more akin to a finding of "probable cause" required in preliminary criminal procedures.)[50]

Can one who removes a child under emergency circumstances be sued later by parents for having exercised bad judgment?

No, so long as the person who removed the child was one who was authorized by law to do so, and the removal was carried out in "good faith." Just as all states provide immunity from prosecution for making reports, immunity is also granted people who are authorized to remove children under emergency conditions.[51] However, the initial removal must have been undertaken in "good faith" that the removal was necessary at the time; no person who removes a child without any reason or for malicious reasons will be immune from prosecution. Similarly, immunity will not shield someone who was not authorized by law to remove a child. Thus, if the law authorizes police officers and welfare employees only, anyone else who removes a child without parental permission will not be immune from prosecution.

Are all emergency removal statutes constitutional?

No. Some emergency removal laws contain overly broad or vague language. If a court determines that a statute's terms are too broad or vague, it may declare it unconstitutional.

Laws are designed to be enforced even-handedly. But if a statute authorizes people to take children into custody simply because their "welfare" or "best interest" requires it, too much discretion is given individuals—be they police officials, social workers, or judges—to decide who comes within the proper scope of the law. This, in turn, encourages arbitrary and discriminatory application and creates a risk that it will be enforced only against the disenfranchised, poor, and racial and cultural minorities.[52]

Another important constitutional defect in vague laws is that they fail to provide adequate notice to parents of what conduct may result in loss of custody of their children. Due process of law requires that any law must be clear enough so that reasonable people seeking to obey the law can understand what is expected of them.[53]

The problem of vagueness is considered more crucial in emergency-removal statutes than in definitions of neglect and abuse, because emergency-removal laws permit the swift removal of a child from his or her home—usually without a hearing—while determinations of neglect and abuse are made by judges after hearing evidence on all sides of the issue.

Recently, the Alabama statute authorizing emergency removal was found unconstitutionally vague. It permitted removal if the child was in "such a condition that its welfare requires that custody be immediately assumed." A federal court ruled that this statute violated parents' due-process rights, because no precise definition of terms was given.[54] (On the other hand, Texas' emergency-removal statute, quoted earlier, was challenged but found constitutionally permissible, since the standard that the child must be in physical danger was precise enough to give warning to the parents and meaning to the authorities.) [55]

COURT PROCEDURES

What happens if the parents are charged with neglect or abuse and taken to court?

This is a drastic but ever-present option available to the investigating agency and the possible consequences for the parents are very severe.

If an abuse or neglect case comes to court, a hearing will be held. The state will present evidence against the parents or custodians of the child in an attempt to prove that they mistreated their child, by showing that the child was harmed, deprived of adequate care, abandoned, or whatever the relevant definition of abuse or neglect in the state requires.

Parents have a *right* to a hearing. Unless parents wish to admit that their child is abused or neglected, a child cannot be declared by a court to be abused or neglected without a hearing.[56]

These hearings are usually held under civil rather than criminal laws and are held in family, juvenile, or children's courts rather than in criminal courts. Parents are usually referred to as *respondents* rather than *defendants*. The state prosecutes the case against the parents or on behalf of the child, but the state is usually represented by the attorney for the welfare or social-services agency rather than the district attorney. In most states, the hearing is closed to the public and is presided over by a judge, but in a few states judges may appoint *referees,* who make findings and recommendations.

How strong must the state's case be to prove abuse or neglect?

There is no overall rule regarding the standard of proof, or the strength with which the state must prove its case in all states.

About half the states require the charges to be proven by a "preponderance of the evidence" while about ten require proof by "clear and convincing evidence." Quite a few states have no exact standard at all, but simply follow normal rules of civil procedure.[57] The "preponderance" standard means that a finding of neglect or abuse cannot be sustained unless more evidence than not—a "preponderance"—proves the case. The "clear and convincing" standard is higher; that is, it requires more definite and positive proof by the state before neglect or abuse may be found. Both standards are less difficult for the state to meet than the burden required in criminal cases, namely, proof "beyond a reasonable doubt." But since child-maltreatment cases are civil, the criminal standard does not apply.

Do parents accused of neglecting or abusing their children have a right to a lawyer's help in defending themselves against the charges?

Yes. In many states, this right is secured by statute.[58] In the other states—where the legislatures have *not* granted to parents the right to counsel—most courts that have considered the question have held that due process requires the provision of free counsel to indigent parents in child-protective proceedings.[59]

(Children, too, are granted free legal representation in most states, even though they may be too young even to speak.[60] The attorney for the child is never the same as the attorney for the parent—the child's attorney is completely independent and may assume a stance contrary to the interests of the parent. A typical hearing therefore, may involve *three* separate attorneys: one for the state, one for the parents, and one for the child.)

At a hearing, may the court hear evidence or testimony by the child's doctor?

Yes. Normally, communications between a doctor and patient are confidential, and doctors may not testify about what was discussed or what a patient said during the course of treatment,[61] but this rule does not apply in child-protective proceedings, with regard to testimony and evidence concerning the child *and* the parents, for two reasons.

First, most states simply suspend the privilege in such proceedings as a matter of public policy in an effort to protect children.[62] Second, if a law has been broken—child abuse and neglect are both illegal—doctors are not required to honor the confidentiality of their communications.[63]

A few courts, however, have honored the privilege between a patient and psychotherapist, if the patient is a
parent seeking treatment according to a plan to help rectify
the problem causing child maltreatment.[64]

**At a hearing, may one parent be forced to testify against
the other?**

Generally, yes. This is so even in states which honor
the "marital privilege," which provides that one spouse
may not be examined against the other, without the other's
permission.[65] Just as in the case of doctor-patient communications, states have recognized that this rule may be
suspended in the overriding interest of protecting children and because the privilege is not meant to protect
people who have committed crimes.[66]

**If a court rules that a child is abused or neglected, do
the parents have a right to appeal the decision?**

Yes. Although less than half of the states mention the
right to appeal in their statutes, most if not all states permit parents to appeal adverse neglect and abuse decisions
to higher courts.[67]

CONSEQUENCES

**What can the state do to parents if a court rules that
they have abused or neglected their children?**

If a court decides that a child is neglected or abused, it
can order that the child be removed from the custody of
the parents for a specified period of time. If, within that
period of time, the parents do nothing to correct the
problem that resulted in the finding of neglect or abuse,
it is possible that the temporary separation will result in
a permanent termination of parental rights. (See next
chapter.)

Courts are not *required* to remove the child from the
custody of its parents, even if abuse or neglect is proven.
A less drastic sanction may be imposed, such as placing
parents on probation for a period of time and requiring
them to engage in a specific rehabilitative or educational
program while the child remains with them in their home.
For example, a court might require the parents to en-

gage in counseling, therapy, parent-training programs, the acceptance of periodic visits by homemakers, or the use of day-care centers.

As often happens, the court may order the child to be removed from the home and placed in temporary foster care *and* order the parents to participate in a rehabilitation program, which might include many of the services listed above. If, after a period of time, the parents make no use of court-ordered services or show no progress in their training or rehabilitation whatsoever, they may face court proceedings to terminate their parental rights.

While a few states have laws permitting a court to impose criminal sanctions after a ruling of abuse or neglect, criminal penalties are rarely imposed. Thus, as a result of having their children judged abused or neglected, parents will rarely be fined or imprisoned, but they do face the awesome possibility of having their children temporarily or permanently removed from their home.

NOTES

1. CAL. WELF. & INST. CODE §600 (West 1972).
2. *See, e.g.,* N.Y. FAM. CT. ACT §1046(a)(ii); Matter of J.R., 87 Misc.2d 900, 386 N.Y.S.2d 774 (Fam. Ct. 1976).
3. Matter of Roman, 94 Misc.2d 796, 405 N.Y.S.2d 899 (Fam. Ct. 1978).
4. *See, e.g.,* N.Y. FAM. CT. ACT §1046 a(i); *In re* Milton Edwards, 76 Misc.2d 781, 351 N.Y.S.2d 601 (Fam. Ct. 1972); *In re* Brooks, 379 N.E.2d 872 (Ill. App. 1979).
5. N.Y. FAM. CT. ACT §§1012(e), (f).
6. MD. ANN. CODE ART. 27, §35A.
7. *See, e.g.,* Bowers v. State, 283 Md. 115, 389 A.2d 350 (Ct. App. 1978); State v. Smith, 485 S.W.2d 461 (Mo. App. 1972).
8. ARIZ. REV. STAT. §§8–201(1); 8–546(A)(1).
9. *See, e.g.,* State v. Laemoa, 533 P.2d 370 (Or. App. 1975).
10. Welfare Commissioner v. Anonymous, 33 Conn. Sup. 100, 364 A.2d 250 (1977). *See also* Diernfeld v. People, 137 Colo. 238, 323 P.2d 628 (1958); *In re* Valdez, 29 Utah 2d 63, 504 P.2d 1372 (1973).
11. *See, e.g., In re* Seiferth, 309 N.Y. 80, 127 N.E.2d 820 (1956).
12. *In re* Custody of Minor, 379 N.E.2d 1053 (Mass. Sup. Ct. 1978 ; *but see, In re* Hofbauer, 405 N.Y.S.2d 799 (1979).

13. The constitutional infirmity in excessive or overboard state action of this sort is that it violates substantive due process of law. *See, e.g.*, N.Y. Soc. Serv. Law §383–b; Wallace v. Labrenz, 411 Ill. 618, 104 N.E.2d 769, *cert. denied* 344 U.S. 824 (1952).

14. Kruse v. Campbell, 431 F. Supp. 180 (E.D. Va. 1977); *vacated* 434 U.S. 808 (1977.)

15. N.Y. Fam. Ct. Act §1012(h).

16. Idaho Code Ann. §16–1625–26.

17. O'Connor v. Donaldson, 422 U.S. 563 (1975).

18. Okpaku, *Psychology: Impediment or Aid in Child Custody Cases?* 29 Rutgers L. Rev. 1117 at 1141 (1976); *see also,* Book Review of *Beyond the Best Interests of the Child,* 74 Colum. L. Rev. 996 (1974).

19. *See, e.g.*, N.Y. Fam. Ct. Act §1012(f)(i)(A).

20. *See, e.g., In re* Yardley, 260 Iowa 259, 149 N.W.2d 162 (1967); State v. Geer, 311 S.W.2d 49 (Mo. Ct. App. 1958).

21. *See, e.g., In re* Anonymous, 37 Misc.2d 411, 238 N.Y.S.2d 422 (Fam. Ct. 1962); *In re* Watson, 95 N.Y.S.2d 798 (Dom. Rel. Ct. 1950).

22. *See, e.g., In re Cager,* 251 Md. 473, 248 A.2d 384 (1968); *In re* C., 468 S.W.2d 689 (Mo. Ct. App. 1971).

23. *See, e.g.*, N.Y. Fam. Ct. Act §1012(f)(i)(A).

24. *In re* Brooks, 379 N.E.2d 872 (Ill. App. 1978).

25. Fla. Stat. §827.04(2).

26. State v. Joyce, 361 So.2d 406 (Fla. 1978).

27. Md. Ann. Code art. 27, §35A(b)(7)(A).

28. Bowers v. State, *supra* note 7.

29. *See, e.g.*, Campbell v. State. 240 So.2d 298 (Fla. 1970); People v. Vandiver, 51 Ill.2d 525, 283 N.E.2d 681 (1971); Hunter v. State, 360 N.E.2d 588 (Ind. 1977); State v. Fahy, 201 Kan. 366, 440 P.2d 566 (1968); State v. Kilroy, 73 Wis.2d 400, 243 N.W.2d 475 (1976).

30. Stanley v. Illinois, 405 U.S. 645, 651 (1972).

31. *See, e.g.*, State v. McMaster, 259 Or. 291, 486 P.2d 567 (1971).

32. *See, e.g.*, Alsager v. District Court, 406 F. Supp. 10 (S.D. Iowa 1975), *aff'd. in part* 545 F.2d 1137 (8th Cir. 1976); Roe v. Conn, 417 F. Supp. 769 (M.D. Ala. 1976).

33. *See, e.g.*, La. Rev. Stat. Ann. §13:1569.

34. *See, e.g.*, Tenn. Code Ann. §37–202.

35. *See, e.g.*, Mo. Ann. Code §3–801.

36. N.Y. Soc. Serv. Law §413.

37. 45 C.F.R. §1340.3–3(d)(5).

38. N.Y. Soc. Serv. Law §424.

39. Wyman v. James, 400 U.S. 309 (1971). *In re* Christopher B., 147 Cal. Rptr. 390 (Ct. of App. 1978).

40. *See, e.g.*, N.Y. FAM. CT. ACT §1046; MINN. STATS. ANN. §626.555.

41. *See, e.g.*, N.Y. SOC. SERV. LAW, §422(8).

42. TEX. FAM. CODE ANN. §17.01 (1978).

43. N.Y. Soc. Serv. Law, §417; Fam. Ct. Act, §§1022, 1024, 1026.

44. N.Y. Fam. Ct. Act. §§1027, 1028; Duchesne v. Sugarman, 566 F.2d 817 (2nd Cir. 1977).

45. *See* Newton v. Burgin, 363 F. Supp. 782 (W.D. N.Car. 1973), *aff'd.* 414 U.S. 1139 (1974).

46. TEX. FAM. CODE ANN., §17.01.

47. Sims v. State Dept. of Pub. Welf., 438 F. Supp. 1179 (S.D. Tex. 1977). This ruling has been reversed by the United States Supreme Court on jurisdictional grounds having nothing to do with the correctness or incorrectness of the court's decision on this point. Moore v. Sims, 422 U.S. 415, 61 L. Ed.2d. 321 (1979).

48. Roe v. Conn, *supra* note 32 at 778.

49. *Id.*

50. One court likened it to the "probable cause" hearing demanded by the Supreme Court in Gerstein v. Pugh, 420 U.S. 103 (1975). *See* Duchesne v. Sugarman, 566 F.2d 817, 828, n. 24 (2nd Cir. 1977).

51. *See, e.g.*, N.Y. SOC. SERV. LAW §415.

52. *See, e.g.*, Herndon v. Lowry, 301 U.S. 242 (1937); Papachristou v. City of Jacksonville, 415 U.S. 156 (1972).

53. *See, e.g.*, Grayned v. City of Rockford, 404 U.S. 104 (1972); Palmer v. Euclid, 402 U.S. 544 (1971).

54. Roe v. Conn, *supra* note 32.

55. See Sims v. Texas Dept. of Public Welfare, *supra* note 47. The Texas statute is quoted in the text to note 42, *supra.*

56. *In re* Christina T., 590 P.2d 189 (Okla. 1979).

57. *See* Katz, Howe & McGrath, *Child Neglect Laws In America*, 9 FAM. L.Q. 3, at 60 (1975).

58. Recognizing the constitutional requirement, several states have also enacted statutes providing for counsel. *See, e.g.*, CAL. CIV. CODE §237.5; COLO. REV. STATS. §19-1-106; CONN. GEN. STAT. §17–66B; MINN. STAT. §155; OHIO REV. CODE §2151.351.

59. Cleaver v. Wilcox, 499 F.2d 940 (9th Cir. 1974); Davis v. Page, 442 F. Supp. 258 (S.D. Fla. 1977); Smith v. Edmiston, 431 F. Supp. 941 (W.D. Tenn. 1977); United States *ex rel.* Reed v. Tinder, No. 75 0454 CH (S.D.W.Va. 1975); Shappy v. Knight, 251 Ark. 943, 475 S.W.2d 704 (1972); *In re* Rodriguez, 34 Cal. App.3d 510, 110 Cal.

Rptr. 56 (Ct. App. 1973); Chambers v. District Court of Dubuque County, 261 Iowa 31, 152 N.W.2d 818 (1967); Danforth v. Maine, 303 A.2d 794 (1973); Reist v. Bay County Circuit Judge, 396 Mich. 326, 241 N.W.2d 55 (1976); State v. Caha, 190 Neb. 347, 208 N.W.2d 259 (1973); Crist v. Division of Youth and Fam. Serv., 128 N.J.Super. 402, 320 A.2d 203 (1974); *In re* Ella B., 30 N.Y.2d 352, 285 N.E.2d 288 (1972); State v. Jamison, 251 Or. 114, 444 P.2d 15 (1968); *In re* R., 455 Pa. 29, 312 A.2d 601 (Pa. 1973); *In re* Myricks, 85 Wash.2d 252, 533 P.2d 841 (1975); State *ex rel.* Lemaster v. Oakley, 203 S.E.2d 140 (W. Va. 1974). *But see* Potvin v. Keller, 313 So.2d 703 (Fla. 1975).

60. *See* Child Abuse Prevention and Treatment Act of 1974, 42 U.S.C., §5103(b)(2)(G).

61. *See, e.g.*, N.Y. Civ. Prac. Law and Rules §4504; Cal. Evid. Code §§917, 992; Ill. Ann. Stat., ch. 51, §5.1

62. *See, e.g.*, *In re* Doe Children, 402 N.Y.S.2d 958 (Fam. Ct. 1978); N.Y. Fam. Ct. Act, §1046.

63. *See, e.g.*, American Medical Association, Principles of Ethics, §9.

64. Matter of S.W., 79 Cal. App.3d 719, 145 Cal. Rptr. 143 (Ct. of App. 1978)

65. *See, e.g.*, Wash. Rev. Code §5.60.060(1).

66. *See, e.g.*, State v. Waleczek, 585 P.2d 797 (Wash. 1978); Adams v. State, 563 S.W.2d 804 (Tenn. Civil App. 1978).

67. *See, e.g.*, Davis v. Page, 442 F. Supp. 258 (S.D. Fla. 1977).

VI

Termination of Parental Rights

What is the termination of parental rights?

The termination of parental rights is the permanent severance of the parent-child relationship. The effect of termination is that the parent is no longer legally related to the child and possesses neither rights to nor responsibilities for the child. The other effect of termination is that the child, no longer having any parents, is legally free to be adopted.[1] Not all children whose parents' rights have been terminated are adopted, but they may be adopted without their parent's permission since they have no legal "parents." Children whose parents' rights have been terminated but have not been adopted are wards of the state, and are legally related to no one.

How are parental rights terminated?

There are two ways of terminating parental rights: voluntary and involuntary.

The vast majority of terminations are effected voluntarily. This is accomplished by parents surrendering the child to a licensed child-care agency or placing the child with a relative or friend for a private adoption. (For a fuller discussion of adoption procedures, see Chapter X.)

Involuntary termination—the severance of the parent-child relationship without parental consent—is the primary focus of this chapter. All terminations made over the objection of parents occur by orders of courts, after hearings conducted pursuant to state laws. These laws vary somewhat from state to state, but there are common threads among them, which will be discussed in the following questions and answers.

99

For what reasons may a state seek to terminate parental rights?

In most states, the law that sets forth the conditions permitting termination of parental rights usually requires proof of a gross or long-standing neglect of parental obligations.

Every state law includes "abandonment" of children as a condition justifying termination, even though abandonment is defined differently by various state laws and courts. Most states also include repeated or unusually severe acts of neglect or abuse, and parental incapacity or inability to care for children. Many states include mental illness,[2] conviction of a crime affecting the fitness of a parent,[3] and financial nonsupport[4] as conditions justifying termination. A few states even include parental "debauchery," "depravity," adultery, and fornication.[5]

May a state terminate parental rights without *prior* proof of wrongdoing?

Usually not. In most states, involuntary termination may be ordered only if certain deleterious conditions have been in existence for a period of time (six months, a year, or more).

In New York, for example, the law of termination lists several conditions, all of which must be found, by a court, to be in existence for *one continuous year* before it will order the termination of parental rights. These conditions are: the child must be in the care of a licensed child-care agency; the agency must make diligent efforts to encourage the parent-child relationship; the parents must have failed to maintain contact with or plan for the future of the child; and the best interests of the child must require termination of parental rights.[6] There is no requirement that the original placement of a child in a child-care agency was involuntary or due to a court ruling of abuse or neglect, but unless all the conditions listed above exist for one year, parental rights may not be terminated.

Other states have similar requirements. In California, certain conditions must be proven to exist after parents have been involuntarily deprived of their child's custody for *one year,* or after their child has been in foster care for *two years.*[7] And in Connecticut, the conditions permitting a finding of termination must prevail for *one year* or more. These include abandonment, failure of parental rehabilitation, continuing physical or mental disability of the parent, or absence of an ongoing parent-child relationship.[8]

The wording of these statutes suggests that proceedings to terminate parental rights are usually instituted only after the child has already been under state care or supervision for some time or only after the parents have had some chance to correct their disabilities.

But not all termination proceedings are started after a period of time of "warning" to the parents; some are commenced upon the occurrence of a particularly grave or compelling circumstance such that parental behavior does not fall squarely into any of the enumerated statutory categories. Thus, in California, termination may result if parents are unable to care for their children because of the habitual use of alcohol or drugs, if they have been convicted of a felony or a crime which proves their unfitness, or if they are deemed developmentally disabled or mentally ill so severely that they are unable to raise children.[9] And in Connecticut, termination may be based on the statutory grounds mentioned above, or if the "totality of circumstances" dictates immediate termination.[10]

Moreover, in a few states, parental rights may be terminated without a special termination hearing, but may be terminated following an initial court ruling of neglect or abuse.[11]

What must the state prove if parents are charged with abandonment?

As mentioned earlier, *abandonment* is defined differently in various states.[12] Generally, the variations revolve around the length of time parents must be absent from their children before abandonment can be said to exist, and whether a parent's *intent* to abandon should be considered.

For many years, most states required the state to prove that parents not only abandoned their children but *intended* to abandon them as well. This meant that mere absence from the home or from one's children was insufficient to support an order of termination; the state had to prove that the parents meant to abandon their children "forever" or that their conduct indicated a "settled purpose" of relinquishing all interest in their children.[13] This requirement was very difficult for the state to meet, and, recently, states have been permitting termination upon proof that parents did not reside with their children for a certain length of time, whether they intended to return or not.[14]

But this change creates some problems of its own, such as how a court would interpret the facts in a situation where parents leave their child with a friend or relative so they can solve a specific problem without the demands of child-raising, but have every intention of returning to resume caring for their child after the passage of an uncertain amount of time.

This situation was faced a few years ago by a parent who was injured and placed her child with a friend while she recuperated. When she returned to pick up her child, she found that the friend had placed the child with the Massachusetts Department of Public Welfare. Upon seeking her child's return from the department, she was told that she could not resume custody because the child was declared "abandoned," even though she had given it to her friend less than two weeks before requesting its return, and the Department of Public Welfare had had custody for only two days! The Department claimed that they had reason to keep the child on authority of Massachusetts' definition of abandonment, which read:

> Any child under 14 who is left in any place and who is seemingly without a parent or legal guardian shall be reported to the Department which shall take temporary care and search for the parent. If the parent cannot be found or is unable or refuses to make *suitable provisions for the child,* the Department shall make provisions as seems in the best interest of the child [emphasis added].[15]

The mother took her case to court, claiming that the law was unconstitutional. The court did not agree that the Massachusetts definition of abandonment was unconstitutional, but it did rule that in this case it was applied in an unconstitutional manner because the mother was given no opportunity to contest the Department's decision that she was unable to make "suitable provisions for her child." [16]

In many states, this problem is resolved by permitting parents to disprove a charge of abandonment if they can show that they maintained continuous, periodic contact with their children, by visiting them, writing, speaking on the telephone, and the like. Rare and infrequent instances of contact, however, usually fail to overcome a ruling of abandonment.[17]

Is imprisonment grounds for termination of parental rights?

A few states mention imprisonment as grounds for termination of parental rights,[18] while others specifically *exclude* imprisonment as a condition permitting termination.[19]

In some cases, imprisonment may be considered grounds for termination because it falls into the definition of abandonment. But in most states, courts have ruled that imprisonment, by itself, cannot support a finding of abandonment since imprisonment does not establish a settled purpose to forego all parental duties.[20] In short, these states follow the rule that one's "intention" to abandon must be proven, and, using it as a guide, incarceration cannot constitute abandonment since being involuntarily sentenced to prison cannot be equated with a desire to forever abandon one's children.

As mentioned previously, in some states, conviction of a crime, if the crime is a serious one (murder, armed robbery, etc.), provides evidence of abuse or neglect and it may be grounds for termination of parental rights.[21]

May parental rights be terminated because of low intelligence or mental illness?

Perhaps, if the low intelligence or mental illness is so extreme that it makes parents incapable of caring for their children.

In light of the constitutional interests of natural parents in raising their children (see Chapter I), several federal courts have held that parents may not be involuntarily deprived of their children without a sufficient showing of harm to the child to justify termination.[22] A difficult problem arises, then, when a court must decide if parental rights should be terminated when evidence shows that certain parents are incapable of caring for their children due to their mental incapacity, *even though* there is no evidence of any past harm to the children or that the children have suffered under the care of their parents.

Some courts have found low or impaired intelligence alone—without any showing of harm to children—enough to justify termination.[23] And along similar lines, other courts have taken the position that if a parent has previously been judged mentally incompetent, that alone is sufficient to terminate the parent-child relationship.[24]

But a number of states do not permit termination merely because parents are thought to be incapable of caring for a child, without some proof that they are *in fact* incapable. For example, the Missouri statute authorizes termination when

the parent is so mentally deficient he is unable to form an interest or act knowingly *and* has substantially and continuously or repeatedly neglected the children or failed to give the child necessary care and protection [emphasis added].[25]

And an Oregon court ruled that simply because there was evidence of a mother's "antisocial personality," and that she was more likely than the average person to abuse her child "some day," it was insufficient reason to terminate her parental rights. The court required some showing of a present failure to perform her parental role or evidence of *substantial certainty* that she would not be able to perform with minimal adequacy.[26]

A middle ground is taken in Nebraska, where the law authorizes termination if "parents are unable to discharge parental responsibilities by cause of mental illness or a mental deficiency, *and* there are reasonable grounds to believe that such conditions will continue for a prolonged or indeterminate period." [27]

Does the state have a duty to provide supportive services to parents *before* parental rights may be terminated?

Usually. As mentioned previously, in most states, parental rights may be terminated only after a child has been involuntarily removed from the home or has been a ward of the state for a certain length of time. If the child was removed because of parental abuse, neglect, or some other wrongdoing, the state department of child welfare or other appropriate agency is usually charged with providing the parents supportive or rehabilitative services, such as counseling, homemaker assistance, parent training, employment training, individual or group therapy, and visits with the children. This duty to provide services is considered so essential in some states that parental rights may not be terminated subsequently if services were not provided, or, conversely, parental rights may be terminated only if services were provided but were either refused or ineffective. For example, the Indiana law reads:

> At the hearing on termination of parental rights, the person filing the petition shall show that reasonable services have, under the circumstances, been provided to the parents or were offered and refused by the parents, which services were designed to aid the parents in overcoming the problems which originally led to the deprivation of physical custody.[28]

And the Missouri law requires the Division of Family Services or other agency to use "reasonable, diligent, and continuing efforts to aid the parent to rectify the conditions." [29]

When the state is obligated to deliver these services and fails to do so, many courts will not permit a termination ruling to be made. Thus, to cite one of many examples, the Supreme Court of Utah overturned a finding of termination because the mother was never informed of her alleged inadequacies, how to remedy them, nor provided any training or rehabilitation.[30]

There are two exceptions to this rule. First, as noted earlier, in a few states, parental rights may be terminated upon the immediate conclusion of a neglect or abuse hearing; under such circumstances, obviously, there would be no duty to provide services since there is no time to do so. Second, even in states that require providing rehabilitative services before termination is permitted, the requirement is suspended if there is no possibility that the child's welfare will be improved as a result of such services. Thus, in New York, the law requires the agency to demonstrate that it put forth "diligent efforts to encourage and strengthen the parental relationship," but it adds, "when such efforts will not be detrimental to the best interests of the child." [31] Following this exception, some courts have ruled that when there is clearly no possibility of rehabilitation, parental rights may be terminated notwithstanding the lack of supportive services, because the welfare of the child could not be served.[32]

Do parents whose rights the state seeks to terminate have a right to be notified of the proceedings?

Yes. Fundamental aspects of the due process of law require that people be notified *prior* to proceedings in which their interests are at stake. Clearly, parents have a fundamental interest in the care and custody of their children (see Chapter I). Therefore, they have a right to receive prior, written notice of termination proceedings, including written notice of specific allegations against them, so that they know what they are accused of doing (or not doing) and to have a reasonable opportunity to prepare their defense.[33]

Do parents have a right to be heard at termination proceedings?

Yes. For the same reason that parents have a right to prior notice of termination proceedings, they have a right to be present and state their case at the hearing.[34] This also includes the right to present witnesses on their behalf and cross-examine witnesses against them.

If parents are not permitted to be present and to be heard at a termination hearing, it is probable that any decision made to terminate their rights could be attacked for constitutional irregularity.[35]

May parents be represented by an attorney in termination proceedings?

Yes. The crucial fact in termination proceedings is that parents are subject to state action which may result in loss of custody of their children. Because of the fundamental right of parents to the care, control, and custody of their children, the state may not prevent parents from having their own lawyer represent them.

Forty-eight years ago the Supreme Court established the right of accused criminals to be represented in court by an attorney. At that time the Court said:

> The right to be heard would be, in many cases, of little avail if it did not comprehend the right to be heard by counsel. . . . Without it, [the accused], though he

be not guilty, faces the danger of conviction because he does not know how to establish his innocence.[36]

There is little question that the Court's reasoning regarding criminal suspects is equally applicable to parents facing the loss of their children. (But it is important to note that because parents have the right to be represented by an attorney does not necessarily mean that they have the right to an attorney's services *free of charge*. This topic will be discussed next.)

In termination proceedings, do parents who cannot afford a lawyer have the right to have one free of charge?
Yes, but not in all states. The right of parents to court-appointed counsel (meaning a lawyer appointed by the court and paid by the public if the parents cannot afford to pay) is required by statute in at least fourteen states (Arizona, Colorado, Connecticut, Georgia, Idaho, Iowa, Kansas, Minnesota, North Dakota, Ohio, Oklahoma, Oregon, South Dakota, and Utah [37]). Moreover, court-appointed counsel for indigent parents have been required in at least seven other states (California, New Jersey, New York, Maine, Nebraska, Pennsylvania, and West Virginia [38]), by virtue of appellate-court rulings. Whether required by statute or case law, the end result is the same: in many states, parents who cannot afford an attorney to represent them in termination proceedings have the right to a court-appointed lawyer, free of charge.

There is no national rule concerning court-appointed lawyers for parents in termination proceedings though, because the Supreme Court has never addressed the issue. However, in 1963, the Supreme Court ruled that suspects facing serious *criminal* charges are entitled to a lawyer free of charge if they are unable to pay.[39] The Supreme Court based its decision in that case on the constitutional guarantee that every person must have "due process of law" when threatened with the loss of life, liberty or property, and it interpreted "due process" to mean that a person charged with a felony had a right to have an attorney represent him if he was unable to pay.

Since that landmark decision more than eighteen years ago, courts have extended the right to court-appointed lawyers to juveniles accused of committing delinquent acts,[40] persons facing involuntary confinement in mental hospitals,[41] persons charged with misdemeanor offenses,[42] and criminal defendants in the pretrial stage.[43]

In each of these cases, the person or group of people to whom the right of court-appointed counsel was extended was found to be in circumstances that placed their liberty in jeopardy; hence, all were guaranteed the right to "due process of law" (i.e., a court-appointed lawyer) *before* their liberty could be deprived.

Therefore, some courts and some legislatures have determined that parents subject to the loss of their children are entitled to the same due-process guarantee.

The reasoning employed by some of the state appellate courts in establishing the right to appointed counsel may be of interest to those who wish to pursue the right in states where it does not exist at present. The Oregon Supreme Court, for example, which mandated assigned counsel three years before the legislature required it, stated:

> The permanent termination of parental rights is one of the most drastic actions the state can take against its inhabitants. It would be unconscionable for the state forever to terminate the parental rights of the poor without allowing such parents to be assisted by counsel. . . . If the parents are too poor to employ counsel, the cost thereof must be born by the public.[44]

The New York Court of Appeals, which also paved the way for that state's legislature in requiring appointed counsel, concluded:

> A parent's interest in the liberty of the child, as well as in his care and control, is too fundamental an interest and right . . . to be relinquished to the state without the opportunity for a hearing with assigned counsel if the parent lacks the means to retain a lawyer. To deny legal assistance under such circumstances would . . . constitute a violation of his due process rights and . . . a denial of equal protection as well.[45]

And in California a federal court held that "due process requires the state to appoint counsel whenever an indigent parent, unable to present his or her case properly, faces a

substantial possibility of the loss of custody or of prolonged separation of a child." [46]

**In termination proceedings, is a lawyer provided to rep-
resent the child?**

Many states require courts to appoint a lawyer to represent the child in proceedings to terminate parental rights,
even if the child is an infant.[47] Even if state law does not
require that a lawyer be appointed, many courts will do so
on their own accord.[48] When a lawyer is appointed, it
means that he or she is paid by the court; neither the
child nor the parents are required to pay for this representation.

Children are frequently represented by lawyers in termination proceedings because of the importance of the
proceedings to the child—the possibility of being permanently separated from one's parents and made a ward of
the state. Lawyers are also provided children in recognition
of the fact that neither the state (which has charged the
parents with abandonment or wrongdoing) nor the parents
necessarily represent the interests of the children.

(Historically, it is interesting to note that the United
States Supreme Court has never ruled that a lawyer must
be appointed to represent the child in *termination* proceedings. In 1967, the Court required the appointment of
counsel in all juvenile delinquency hearings; it reasoned
that since children accused of wrongdoing faced the possible deprivation of their liberty by commitment to a reform
school or training school, they were entitled to the same
constitutional right of legal counsel as adults facing criminal charges.[49] Most states have taken this to mean that
they have a duty to appoint a lawyer to represent children
in other hearings involving children as well, or at least in
proceedings when the state seeks to intervene in a child's
family life and make a decision affecting his or her future
care and custody.)

However, there are still states that do *not* require separate counsel for the child. In one case in Pennsylvania,
the supreme court of that state affirmed an order terminating parental rights over the objection of the parents who
thought that the refusal of the lower court to appoint a
lawyer for the child made the decision constitutionally
defective.[50] (One judge dissented, saying that it is unjust

to deny the child personal representation. When parental rights are being terminated, he said, so too are the rights of the child. He reasoned that since children must be represented in delinquency cases, they should have the same right in termination proceedings. "Surely," he added, "a child's interest in and rights to his natural family should not be treated with any less concern.")

If a lawyer is appointed to represent the child in termination proceedings, must he or she reflect the wishes of the child's parents?

No. The point of having a lawyer appointed for children is to have someone available to represent their wishes and their interests alone. The theory is that the court needs the input and assistance of someone who represents neither the state (which seeks termination) nor the parents (who may resist it), but who is beholden only to the very subject of the proceeding, the child.

Moreover, children who are the subjects of termination proceedings are usually too young to speak for themselves, or if they are old enough to speak they may be unable to articulate or even identify their own interests. Their interests *may* be identical to their parents' position, they *may* be identical with the state's view, or they may be different from both. Therefore, a lawyer for the children is duty bound to take an independent role and advocate only the wishes and interests of his or her client, the child.

Do parents have a right to a trial by jury in a termination proceeding?

In most states the answer is no. The hearing is held by a judge only, who will make all final determinations of fact and law.[51]

How strongly must the state prove its case against parents?

At termination proceedings, the state has the burden of proving that parental rights should be terminated; parents do not have to prove their innocence, so to speak. If the state does not prove its case, parental rights will not be terminated.

The question then becomes, how *strongly* does the state have to prove its case; that is, what standard of proof is followed by the court in making its decision? In a criminal trial the state must prove the guilt of the defendant "beyond a reasonable doubt," which is a very high standard of evidence. In a civil trial, one party will win a case if they establish proof by a "preponderence" of the evidence, which is a less demanding standard. In civil cases, the party seeking to prove its point in court will succeed merely by showing more evidence on one side than the other.

Since termination proceedings are civil, about half of the states require only that proof need be established only by a preponderence of the evidence.[52] But since the *nature* of a termination case is so important, with the consequences being so severe—the possible loss of a child forever—a number of states have "raised" the standard from a "preponderence" of the evidence to "clear and convincing" evidence, which has the effect of making it more difficult for the state to prove its case; at least it makes the state prove its case in a "convincing" manner. If it cannot do this, parental rights will remain intact. States that have recently required "clear and convincing proof" are California, Iowa, Minnesota, New Mexico, Pennsylvania, and Washington.[53] At least one state, New Hampshire, has required proof "beyond a reasonable doubt." [54]

Do parents have a right to appeal a court decision to terminate their rights?

In most states, yes.[55] This would include a right to counsel to prepare the appeal, in those states where counsel is provided for the original hearing.[56]

May parental rights be terminated merely because termination is found in a court to be in the child's "best interests"?

Until recently, courts have refused to terminate parental rights without a clear showing of neglect, unfitness, harm, or abandonment.[57]

In the past several years, however, a few courts have utilized the child's "best interests" as the legal standard in authorizing termination of the rights of parents, even though they have not been shown to be unfit,[58] and some states have enacted laws to this effect.[59] A few laws go even so far as to allow an adoption without parental consent if it is in the child's best interests.[60] This means that the state does not have to prove any wrongdoing on the part of the parent or harm or injury to the child—it need only show that it would be in the child's best interests to be involuntarily taken from the custody of its parents. This new trend runs counter to the general rule that a parent's right to custody may not be defeated simply because a child might be better served by having different parents.[61] It is probable that these decisions are unconstitutional if they are reached without proof that the parents were unfit or that their child suffered some type of harm while under their care.

The U.S. Supreme Court has not handed down a clear opinion on this issue. Nevertheless, in 1977, after most of the state-court decisions alluded to above had been decided, the Supreme Court did provide some guidance in this area. The Court unanimously ruled that the right of natural parents to the care and custody of their children is a "constitutionally recognized liberty interest that derives from blood relationship, state law sanction, and basic human rights." [62] With this opinion, the Supreme Court reaffirmed the many cases decided in the past half century that gave constitutional protection to parental rights and legitimized the right of family integrity (see Chapter I). Then, in 1978, the Supreme Court unanimously declared that

> If a State were to attempt to force the breakup of a natural family, over the objections of the parents and their children, without some showing of unfitness and *for the sole reason that to do so was thought to be in the children's best interest,* we should have little doubt that the State would have intruded impermissibly on the "private realm of family life which the State cannot enter" [emphasis added].[63]

Subsequent to this U.S. Supreme Court decision, the Supreme Court of Montana interpreted its law (which provides for termination based on the best interests standard) [64] in such a manner that termination may be ordered only if a child is found to be abused, neglected, or dependent *first;* then, and only then, his or her future custody is based upon the best interest test. It stated:

The "best interests of the child" test is correctly used to determine custody rights between natural parents in divorce proceedings. . . . However, where third parties seek custody, it has long been the law in Montana that the right of the natural parent prevails until a showing of a forfeiture of this right. . . . This forfeiture can result only where the parent's conduct does not meet the minimum standards of the child abuse, neglect and dependency statutes.[65]

Similarly, the Massachusetts Supreme Judicial Court expressly overruled an earlier opinion authorizing the "best interests" standard for termination, declaring that the state may not break up a family without proof of parental unfitness.[66]

And in 1979, the highest court in New York cleared up a possible misunderstanding resulting from an earlier case which was being quoted by many to stand for the proposition that termination could be based on the best interests standard.[67] The court stated unequivocally:

A court may not terminate all parental rights by offering a child for adoption when there has been no parental consent, abandonment, neglect or proven unfitness, *even though some might find adoption to be in the child's best interests.*[68]

Are there any constitutional limits to the conditions for which parental rights may be terminated?

Yes. Because parents have a fundamental right to raise their children, states may not deprive them of the right except under *compelling* circumstances. Therefore, the grounds upon which a state may involuntarily terminate parental rights may not be minor ones, nor may they be defined in overly broad terms, such that the scope of potential termination could be interpreted in a way that sanctions termination for less-than-compelling reasons.

The best way to explain these principles is by example.

The first major test of overly vague and broad termination statutes was made in 1973 when a mother challenged an Iowa law that authorized termination for "refusal to give a child necessary parental care and protection." Another part of the same law permitted courts to order termination for parental conduct "likely to be detrimental to the physical or mental health or morals of a child." [69] Pursuant to this statute, the woman's parental rights to four of her five children had been terminated basically because her home was unkempt and her children were often dirty and unruly, even though there was no evidence or a judicial finding that they were harmed in any way. Nevertheless, a court terminated her rights because, in the language of the statute, she failed to provide "necessary parental care" and her conduct was "likely to be detrimental" to her children. She appealed this decision, claiming that the law was so vague that it was unconstitutional. A federal court agreed with her, saying that Iowa's law (1) did not give "fair warning of what parental conduct is proscribed, (2) permitted . . . arbitrary and discriminating termination, and (3) inhibited . . . the exercise of the fundamental right to family integrity." [70]

As a second example, an Arkansas law allowed termination if parents were found deficient in providing a child with "a proper home." [71] The Arkansas Supreme Court found this phrase unconstitutionally vague because it suggested a number of meanings. The court stated:

> Using any of these meanings does little to make the words, "a proper home," clearly understandable, so that it doesn't mean one thing to one judge, something else to another, and something yet different to still another. What is a proper home? A correct home? A suitable home? A fit home? Is propriety to be determined ethically, socially or economically? Or on the basis of morality? Or prosperity? Is the standard a maximum, a minimum, a mean or an average? [72]

Thus, state laws setting forth grounds for termination which use language as vague or broad as the laws of Iowa and Arkansas are vulnerable to constitutional attack.

On the other hand, a number of state laws have survived similar legal challenges in state courts, even though their grounds for termination could be said to be almost as vague as those discussed above. A Pennsylvania law that permitted termination if a child was "without essential parental care, control or subsistence necessary for his physical or mental well-being" was not found to violate constitutional principles. [73] A New York statute that permitted termination for parents' "failure to plan for the future of the child" was ruled not unconstitutionally vague.[74] Similarly, the Massachusetts standard of "best interest of the child" was found not to be vague,[75] nor was the Oklahoma standard that termination may result if a parent "fails to give the child the parental care or protection necessary for his physical or mental health." [76]

Perhaps the reason many courts are willing to find rather imprecise language constitutional, when they might rule otherwise in reviewing similarly worded laws not concerned with children, is because, in the words of the Oregon Supreme Court, "what might be unconstitutional if only the parents' rights were involved, is constitutional if the statute adopts legitimate and necessary means to protect the child's interests." [77]

NOTES

1. *See, e.g.,* ILL. ANN. STAT. ch. 4, §9.1–17; *In re* Workman, 38 Ill. App.3d 261, 344 N.E.2d 796 (1975).
2. ILL. ANN. STAT. ch. 4, §9.1–8(e); MO. ANN. STAT. §211.447(2)(2)(g).
3. CAL. CIV. CODE §232(a)(4); *In re* D.S.C., 155 Cal. Rptr. 406 (Ct. App. 1979).
4. MO. ANN. STAT. §211.477(2)(f).
5. *See, e.g.,* ILL. ANN. STAT. ch. 4, §§9.1–1D(h), 9.1–8; MO. ANN. STAT. §211.447(2)(2)(g); MINN. STAT. §260.221(b)(4).
6. N.Y. FAM. CT. ACT §614; N.Y. SOC. SERV. LAW §384-b(7).
7. CAL. CIV. CODE §232.1.
8. CONN. GEN. STAT. §17–43a.
9. CAL. CIV. CODE §§232.1(3), (4), (5), (6).
10. CONN. GEN. STAT. §17–43a.
11. *See, e.g.,* KAN. STAT. ANN. §38-824(c).
12. *See, e.g.* CAL. CIV. CODE §232(a)(1); N.Y. SOC. SERV. LAW §384-b. Thirty-five states cite abandonment as a ground for terminating parental rights. A comparative analysis of standards and state practices is given in U.S. DEPT. OF JUSTICE, ABUSE AND NEGLECT 1976.
13. *See, e.g., In re* Barazzi, 265 Cal. App.2d 282, 71 Cal. Rptr. 249 (1968); *In re* Adoption of Smith, 38 Ill. App.3d 217, 347 N.E.2d 292, *cert. denied* 431 U.S. 939, (1977).
14. *See, e.g., In re* B.J., 530 P.2d 747 (Alaska 1975); N.Y. SOC. SERV. LAW §384–b(5)(b).

15. Mass. Gen. Laws Ann. ch. 119, §23(e).
16. White v. Minter, 330 F. Supp. 1194 (D. Mass, 1971).
17. *See, e.g.,* Mo. Ann. Stat. §211.447(2)(2)(b).
18. *See, e.g.,* R.I. Gen. L. §15–7–7; Wise. Stats. Ann. §48.40.
19. *See, e.g.,* N.Y. Soc. Serv. Law, §384–b(7)(d)(iii).
20. *See, e.g.,* Murphy v. Vanderver, 349 N.E.2d 202 (Ind. App. 1976); *In re* Adoption of Mayhor, 248, S.E.2d 875 (N.C. App. 1978); *In re* Adoption of Jameson 20 Utah 2d 53, 432 P.2d 88 (1967).
21. Cal. Civ. Code §232(a)(4); *In re* D.S.C. 155 Cal. Rptr. 406 (Ct. App. 1979).
22. *See, e.g.,* Alsager v. District Court, 406 F. Supp. 10 (S.D. Iowa 1975); *aff'd.* 545 F.2d 1137 (8th Cir. 1976); Roe v. Conn, 417 F. Supp. 769 (M.D. Ala. 1976).
23. *See, e.g., In re* McDonald, 201 N.W.2d 447 (Iowa 1972); *In re* Paul, 170 So.2d 549 (La. Ct. App. 1965); *In re* William L., 427 Pa. 322, 383 A.2d 1228 (Pa. 1978), *cert. denied sub nom.* Lehman v. Lycoming County Children's Services, 439 U.S. 880 (1978); *In re* Telles, 151 Cal. Rptr. 263 (Ct. App. 1978).
24. *See, e.g., People ex rel* Nabsted v. Barger, 3 Ill.2d 511, 121 N.E.2d (1954); Strohsahl v. Strohsahl, 221 App. Div. 86, 222 N.Y.S. 319 (1st Dept. 1927).
25. Mo. Ann. Stat., §211.447(2)(2)(g).
26. *In re* Wyatt, 579 P.2d 889 (Or. App. 1978).
27. Neb. Rev. Stats. Supp. §43–209(5); State v. Metteer, Neb. Sup. Ct., *in* 5 Fam. L. Rptr. 2670 (June 26, 1979).
28. Ind. Code §31–3–1–7(e) (1971).
29. Mo. Ann. Stat. §211.447(2)(2)(b).
30. *In re* Walter B., 577 P.2d 119 (Utah 1978).
31. N.Y. Soc. Serv. Law §384–b(7)(a).
32. *See, e.g., In re* M.A. v. P.A., 529 P.2d 333 (Colo. Ct. App. 1974); *In re* Clear, 58 Misc.2d 699, 296 N.Y.S.2d 184 (Fam. Ct. 1969).
33. *See, e.g.,* Mass. Gen. Laws Ann. ch. 210, §4.
34. *See, e.g.,* Conn. Gen. Stat. §45–61f.
35. *See, e.g.,* Rodriguez v. Koschuy, 57 Ill. App.3d 355, 373 N.E.2d 47 (1978).
36. Powell v. Alabama, 187 U.S. 45, at 68–69 (1932).
37. Ariz. Rev. Stat. Ann. §8–225A; Colo. Rev. Stat. Ann. §22–1–6; Conn. Gen. Stat. §17–66b; Ohio Rev. Code §2151.35; Or. Rev. Stat. §419.498(2); S.D. Compiled Laws Ann. 26–8–22.2.
38. *In re* Ella B., 30 N.Y.2d 352, 285 N.E.2d 288 (1972); Danforth v. State Dept. of Health, Education and Welfare, 303 A.2d 794 (Maine 1973); State v. Caha, 190 Neb. 377, 208 N.W.2d 259 (1973); *In re* Adoption of R.I. 455

Pa. 29, 312 A.2d 601 (1973); *In re* Lemaster, 203 S.E.2d 140 (W. Va. 1974); Crist v. Division of Youth Services, 320 A.2d 203 (N.J. 1974); *In re* Norma M., 125 Cal. Rptr. 721, 53 Cal. App.3d 344 (1975); *In re* Rodriguez, 110 Cal. Rptr. 56, 34 Cal. App.3d 510 (1973).

39. Gideon v. Wainwright, 372 U.S. 335 (1963).

40. *In re* Gault, 387 U.S. 1 (1967).

41. Heryford v. Parker, 396 F.2d 383 (10th Cir. 1968).

42. Argersinger v. Hamlin, 407 U.S. 25 (1973).

43. Coleman v. Alabama, 399 U.S. 1 (1970).

44. State v. Jamison, 444 P.2d 15, at 17 (1968).

45. *In re* Ella B. *supra* note 38.

46. Cleaver v. Wilcox, 499 F.2d 940, 945 (9th Cir. 1975); *see also, In re* Rodriguez, 110 Cal. Rptr. 56 (1973).

47. *See, e.g.,* N.D. CODE §27–20–26 (1969); N.Y. FAM. CT. ACT §241 (1977).

48. *See, e.g.,* State *ex rel.* Juvenile Dept. of Multnomah County v. Wade, 527 P.2d 753 (Or. App. 1974). *In re* Orlando F., 40 N.Y.2d 103, 351 N.E.2d 711 (1976); *In re* Fish, 569 P.2d 924 (Mont. 1977); New Jersey Div. of Youth & Fam. Serv. v. Wandell, 382 A.2d 77 (Juv. & Dom. Rel. 1978); *In re* Richard E., 21 Cal.3d 349, 579 P.2d 495 (1978).

49. *In re* Gault, 387 U.S. 1 (1967).

50. *In re* D.E.T., Pa. Sup. Ct. in 5 FAM. L. RPTR. 2519 (April 5, 1979).

51. *See, e.g.,* J.V. v. State Department of Just. Soc. & Rehab Services, 572 P.2d 1283 (Okla. 1977).

52. *In re* N.J.W., 273 N.W.2d 134 (S. Dak. 1978); Woodard v. Texas Dept. of Human Resources, 573 S.W.2d 596 (Tex. Civ. App. 1978).

53. *In re* Hochmuth, 251 N.W.2d 484 (Iowa 1977); *In re* Welfare of Rosenbloom, 266 N.W.2d 888 (Minn. 1978); Huey v. Lente, 85 N.M. 597, 514 P.2d 1093 (1973); *In re* William L., 383 A.2d 1228 (Pa. 1978); *In re* Sego, 82 Wash.2d 736, 513 P.2d 831 (1973).

54. State v. Robert H., 393 A.2d 1387 (N.H. 1978).

55. *See, e.g.,* N.Y. FAM. CT. ACT, §1112; *In re* Workman, 14 Ill. Dec. 908, 373 N.E.2d 39 (1978).

56. *In re* Jacqueline H., 577 P.2d 683 (Cal. 1978). *In re* Brehm, 594 P.2d 269 (Kan. App. 1979), *See also, In re* Ward, 351 So.2d 571 (Ala. Civ. App. 1977) (right to a free transcript on appeal).

57. *See, e.g.,* People *ex rel.* Portney v. Strasser, 303 N.Y. 539, 104 N.E.2d 895 (1952); *In re* Appeal of Renker, 117 A.2d 780 (Pa. 1955); *In re* Clark's Adoption, 1 P.2d 112 (Ariz. 1931).

58. *See, e.g., In re* J.S.R., 374 A.2d 860 (D.C. App. 1977); *In re* New England Home for Little Wanderers, 328 N.E. 2d 854 (Mass. 1975); *In re* William L., *supra* note 23.

59. *See, e.g.,* COLO. REV. STAT. ANN. §19–3–110(2)(a); MONT. REV. CODES ANN. §§61–205(1)(c), 61–211; WASH, REV. CODE ANN. §§13.04.095, 26.32.040(2); W. VA. CODE ANN. §49–6-5(3).

60. *See, e.g.,* D.C. CODE §16–304(e); MASS. GEN. LAWS ANN. ch. 210, §3(a)(ii).

61. *See, e.g.,* Berrien v. Greene County Dept. of Pub. Welfare, 217 S.E.2d 854 (Va. 1975); Bennett v. Jeffries, 40 N.Y.2d 543, 356 N.E.2d 277 (1977).

62. Smith v. Organization of Foster Families, 431 U.S. 816, (1977).

63. Quilloin v. Walcott, 434 U.S. 246, 255 (1978).

64. See note 59, *supra.*

65. *In re* Fish, 569 P.2d 924 (Sup. Ct. Mont. 1977).

66. *In re* Custody of a Minor, 389 N.E.2d 68 (Mass. Sup. Jud. Ct. 1979), expressly overruling *In re* New England Home for Little Wanderers, *supra* note 58.

67. Bennett v. Jeffries, *supra* note 61.

68. *In re* Sanjivini K., 47 N.Y.2d 374 (1979); *see also, In re* Corey L. v. Martin L., 45 N.Y.2d 383, 380 N.E.2d 266 (1978).

69. IOWA CODE §§232–41(b),(d).

70. Alsager v. District Court, *supra* note 22.

71. ARK. STAT. ANN. §46.128(2)(h).

72. Davis v. Smith, 583 S.W.2d 37 (Ark. 1979).

73. *In re* William L., *supra* note 23 *construing* PA. ADOPTION ACT OF 1970 §311(2).

74. *In re* Carl & Annette N., 398 N.Y.S.2d 613 (Fam. Ct. 1977), *construing* N.Y. FAM. CT. ACT §614(1).

75. New England Home for Little Wanderers, *supra* note 58, *construing* MASS. GEN. LAWS ANN. ch. 210, §3.

76. Matter of Keyes, 574 P.2d 1026 (Okla. 1977), *appeal dismissed* 439 U.S. 804 (1978).

77. State v. McMaster, 259 Or. 291, 486 P.2d 567 (1971).

VII

Separated and Divorced Parents

CUSTODY AND VISITATION

How is custody of children determined between divorced or separated parents?

The mother and father may agree upon custody arrangements concerning their children.[1] If they cannot decide between themselves, a court may be asked by one or both parents to determine custody. The court will make its decision after a trial, at which both parents will have the right to be heard, to present witnesses on their own behalf, and to cross-examine witnesses against them.

If the dispute is to be settled by a court, the general rule is that neither parent has a greater right to custody than the other and that the judicial decision must be based upon the "best interests" of the child. Custody decisions are not meant to turn on which parent "deserves" custody; the focus is upon what is best for the child.[2]

What does the "best interests" of the child mean?

The "best interests" standard is extremely vague, and courts have wide discretion in determining which parent's environment and style of life best enhances the child's interests. Therefore, every case that is litigated must be decided upon its own special set of facts and circumstances.

Naturally, guidelines indicating the crucial factors to be considered in a custody case are difficult, if not impossible, to formulate. The "best interests" test is so elusive that if two judges tried the same case they might disagree as to the final outcome. Recently, the American Bar Association polled its members involved in custody litigation

119

and found that "there is total disagreement and variety as to what aspects of family life make up 'best interests and welfare.' " [3]

What if the parents agree about which parent should have custody?

If the parents agree between themselves who should be the primary caretaker of the child, this agreement normally binds both parties and will be honored by courts.[4]

Do mothers have an advantage in obtaining custody?

In most states, the technical response to this question is no, but in practice, the answer is often yes.

Through most of this century, courts honored what was known as the "tender years presumption" which favored mothers in custody disputes over young children. This meant that women were presumed by law to be better caretakers and better custodians than men, at least while their children were young. This legal presumption did not mean that women were guaranteed custody, but they had a decided advantage over fathers and were usually granted custody unless they were declared unfit.[5]

In recent years, all but a few states have abandoned this presumption because it discriminates against men on account of their gender and denies them equal protection of the laws.[6] Nonetheless, many courts still favor placing young children with their mothers, either because judges think that women make better caretakers or because, in many cases, women do in fact spend more time in the home with children, have more time to devote to their upbringing and, in the case of infants, may be breastfeeding them.

Has the "tender years presumption," which favors mothers, been abolished in all states?

No. There are a few states in which the presumption, prescribed by law, is still operative.

In West Virginia, for example, the state supreme court ruled that the law "still favors custody in the mother" of a very young child, when both parents are equally fit.[7] Previously, the same court ruled that the presumption was constitutional, especially when the child is being breastfed.[8]

In Virginia, the state supreme court held that the maternal presumption was legitimate, but could be used only when all other factors regarding the child's best interests were equal.[9]

The Utah Supreme Court also upheld the presumption, stating, "equal and just considerations [of the rights of parents to custody] does not mean that the law must pretend to be unaware of and blindly ignore obvious and essential biological differences." [10]

And in Oklahoma a law presuming the mother to be the better custodian of young children (and, surprisingly, presuming the father to be the better custodian of children "of an age to require education and preparation for labor or business") [11] was found not to violate the father's right to equal protection of the laws. The court claimed authority for its decision by referring with approval to the decision from Utah quoted above. The Oklahoma court did qualify its stand, however, by ruling that the maternal presumption applies only when the scales are relatively balanced between the attributes of both parents.[12]

What weight does a court give to the preference of the child in making custody determinations?

No court gives children a controlling voice in determining their custody, but virtually all states today allow courts to listen to the views of the children, at least those who are of an age of "discretion," such as children seven or eight years or older. (There are no guidelines regarding the exact age at which a child may be heard on the question of custody.) When a child is consulted for his or her preference, it usually takes place in the judge's chambers rather than in an open courtroom setting.

In any event, the views of the child, when ascertained, are only one factor a court takes into account in determining his or her "best interests" for the purpose of future custody.[13]

Can restrictions be placed on the custodial parent?

Yes. If parents agree to the terms of their custody arrangement, and set the terms down on paper, *including reasonable restrictions and obligations of the custodial or visiting parent,* their agreement becomes a contract and all terms are enforceable in a court of law. If parents cannot agree, and a court is called upon to determine the terms of custody, the court also may set conditions. (Once parents utilize contracts or courts to assist in working out custody matters, they lose their normal protection from state interference in matters of child rearing.)

May a court consider the religious preferences of parents in making an award of custody?

The general rule is that the First Amendment's guarantee of free exercise of religion and its prohibition of the establishment of religion forbids courts to consider the religious practices of parents in determining custody. The First Amendment, the Supreme Court has said, means that "No person can be punished for entertaining or professing religious beliefs or disbeliefs, for church attendance or non-attendance." [14]

A case that illustrates this point occurred in Missouri, where a court granted custody to a father solely because the mother was a Jehovah's Witness. The state supreme court reversed this decision, ruling that no court may determine custody based on its approval, disapproval, or interpretation of the beliefs or practices of a parent's religion. [15]

Some courts feel that they have a right to consider religion if a parent's particular practices impair the physical health or emotional development of the child. But courts that recognize this exception are still very cautious to interfere with a parent's religious preference. [16]

Another exception might occur if the child is mature enough to have developed an understanding of religion and considers it important in his or her own life. In that case, if one parent is able and willing to meet this need and the other is not, the court may take this into consideration. [17] In such cases, however, the court is really focusing more on the best interests of the child than the religious preferences of the parents.

May a court consider a parent's morals or "misconduct" in making an award of custody?

Yes. The "best interests of the child" standard virtually invites judges to base their decisions on a number of factors, including a parent's style of life. There is no way, therefore, that moral values can be excluded from consideration. But recently, courts have begun to frown upon decisions based *solely* on moral issues, especially when they have little or no impact on the interests or well-being of the child.

This trend is typified by a recent decision by the South Dakota Supreme Court in which custody was granted to the father.[18] Evidence at the trial indicated that the mother had engaged in two adulterous relationships during the marriage, went out drinking late three or four nights a week (often taking the child with her and driving while intoxicated), and frequently sleeping so late the following mornings that she neglected her child. The court ruled that misconduct which has not been proven to have a detrimental effect on children cannot deprive a parent of custody, but that in this case, the mother's behavior—especially driving with the child while intoxicated and neglecting the child in the morning—did have an adverse effect. Thus, the court concluded, awarding custody to the father was in the child's best interests.

Can the losing parent in a custody case regain custody years later?

Yes. Unlike most other legal decisions, which become final and irrevocable once all appeals are exhausted, custody decisions are never final. They are always subject to "modification" by courts after subsequent hearings. Modification means that the custody decision can be changed in some respect, including a reversal of the award of custody. (Of course, parents can always agree between themselves to modify previous custody agreements or orders, unless one parent has been previously declared unfit.)

Under what circumstances can a custody award be modified so that the noncustodial parent will regain custody?

First, the noncustodial parent must prove that there has been a "substantial change in circumstances" since the original award of custody. Second, the noncustodial parent must persuade a court that a change in custody is in the best interests of the child. Ordinarily, this is difficult to do, since most judges are reluctant to remove a child from the custody of the parent with whom he or she has lived for some time. The prevailing view is that establishing custody on a long-term basis maximizes the potential for a healthy parent-child relationship, since the parent will feel secure in his or her authority and the child will know that the relationship is permanent.[19] Therefore, to be successful, the noncustodial parent will probably have to prove that a "substantial change of circumstances" has occurred, that a transfer of custody is in the child's best interests, and that failure to change custody might result in harm to the child.[20]

Will a court rule that a "substantial change of circumstances" has occurred if the custodial parent begins to live with another person or acts immorally?

There is no way to predict a court's decision in this area. Certainly, if the custodial parent begins to live intimately with another person and he or she was not living with another at the time the original custody award was made, there has been a change of circumstance. But many courts require evidence that the change has in some way *harmed* the child before they will order the child transferred to the custody of the other parent.

For example, an Illinois court, noting the increasing number of unmarried couples living together, ruled that a divorced mother's cohabitation with a man did not justify transfer of custody to the father, since there was no showing of any detriment to the child resulting from the mother's living arrangement.[21] Other courts however, have ruled differently.[22]

With regard to other types of "immorality," the same theory holds. Thus, in a New York case, the transfer of children from the mother to the father was found not warranted merely because evidence showed that the mother associated with a married man, advertised in a "swingers" magazine, and read explicitly sexually oriented literature, when the children were at all times physically and psychologically well cared for.[23] And an appellate court in Oregon ruled that a mother's use of marijuana did not justify the transfer of children from her custody. While use of the illegal substance in front of her children indicated poor judgment, the court concluded, it was not as important as the overriding issue of whether the father's home was so much better that it outweighed the disadvantages of removing the children from their mother's stable home environment. The appellate court decided that the father was unable to meet this burden of proof.[24]

If a separated or divorced parent loses custody due to a court decision in one state, can he or she take the children to another state and try to win custody in a subsequent court proceeding there?

Probably not. A few years ago, the answer to this question might have been different, but in order to prevent this very occurrence, states have been passing laws that deny a losing parent in one state access to the courts of another state. The law is known as the Uniform Child Custody Jurisdiction Act, which will be discussed more fully in the following paragraphs.

What is the Uniform Child Custody Jurisdiction Act?

It is a law that has been enacted by most states which is intended to provide uniformity among the laws of all states so that "snatching" children and taking them to another state will be deterred. With uniform laws, it is anticipated that noncustodial parents will be discouraged from trying to interfere with a custody decision in one state and looking for a "second chance" in a different state. The Uniform Child Custody Jurisdiction Act accomplishes this end by requiring the court in the second state to defer to the order of the court in the first state which made the custody decision.

At the time of this writing, thirty-nine states have enacted the Uniform Act. They are: Alabama, Alaska, Arizona, Arkansas, California, Colorado, Connecticut, Delaware, Florida, Georgia, Hawaii, Idaho, Indiana, Iowa, Kansas, Louisiana, Maine, Maryland, Michigan, Minnesota, Missouri, Montana, Nebraska, Nevada, New Hampshire, New Jersey, New York, North Carolina, North Dakota, Ohio, Oregon, Pennsylvania, Rhode Island, South Dakota, Tennessee, Virginia, Washington, Wisconsin, and Wyoming. Two other states, Kentucky and Texas, have enacted laws similar to the Uniform Act.[25]

A copy of the Uniform Child Custody Jurisdiction Act, enforceable in all states mentioned above, is reprinted in this book in Appendix B.

Under the Uniform Child Custody Jurisdiction Act, are there any circumstances in which prior custody awards will not be honored?

Yes, if the original custody award was granted without prior notice to the noncustodial parent, if the prior decree was obtained fraudulently, or if factors concerning the child's best interest were not considered by the court making the first decision.[26]

Specifically, how does the Uniform Child Custody Jurisdiction Act work?

The best way to illustrate the Act's operation is with reference to a few representative court cases that have been decided in accordance with its terms.

For example, in one case a noncustodial parent had brought his child from Michigan to New York and asked a court in New York to award custody in his favor. The New York judge emphatically refused. He stated:

> The state of Michigan has adopted the UCCJA. We will in the future expect that courts of that state honor custody decrees of this state, just as they have a right to expect that we will honor their decrees. . . . [T]he mandate of the Act is clear. Absent the necessity for crisis intervention, the custody decrees of sister states entered pursuant to the UCCJA must be enforced. I do not find that there is a crisis situation before me. . . . Only one court should make a custody determination and that determination should not be challenged merely because the child is brought to another state. Any other view would negate completely the adoption of the UCCJA. We cannot allow this to happen; there is too much at stake.[27]

In another case, two parents received a divorce in South Dakota, where they had lived; the mother was granted custody of their daughter and the father was granted custody of the son. The mother and daughter moved to California. The father followed and removed the daughter from that state and returned with her to South Dakota. He then filed suit in a South Dakota court seeking custody of the girl. Even though the South Dakota court *could* have entertained the case, since South Dakota was the state in which custody was originally determined, it declined in order to uphold the purposes of the Uniform Child Custody Jurisdiction Act and to discourage abductions of children. The Supreme Court of South Dakota stated:

> We deem abductions and other unilateral removals of children without notice and approval . . . to be of no effect upon the residency of the child. . . . [T]he exercise of jurisdiction by South Dakota would tend to contravene the underlying purposes of the Act. We are primarily concerned with the deterrence of abductions and of the unilateral removals of children undertaken to obtain custody awards.[28]

In the cases mentioned above, all the states involved (Michigan, New York, California, and South Dakota) had adopted the Uniform Child Custody Jurisdiction Act. But even cases involving jurisdictional disputes between states which have not adopted the Act are apparently being decided in a similar fashion. For example, a couple was divorced in Illinois and the mother was awarded custody. The father then took the child with him to Iowa. When the mother came to Iowa to regain her child, the father objected on the ground that Iowa was not bound to honor Illinois's decision, since Illinois at that time had not enacted the UCCJA. The Iowa court disagreed and ordered the father to return the child to the mother, even though only one of the two states involved had adopted the Act.[29]

Aside from enforcing the Uniform Child Custody Jurisdiction Act, what recourse does a custodial parent have if the noncustodial parent absconds with the children?

With more and more separations and divorces taking place, naturally an increasing number of custody disputes arise. This has created a new phenomenon called child-snatching, or the act of one parent taking his or her children away from the other without the other's permission. Specialists estimate that more than 25,000 children are snatched from their custodial parents each year in this country.[30]

Child-snatching has been called the kidnapping of one's own children, but this is not quite accurate, since one cannot kidnap his own child. Kidnapping by definition is a case of a person being taken by a *non*parent. Thus, child-snatching by parents is not covered by the federal kidnapping law of 1934, and the FBI will not usually become involved in these cases. Moreover, if the child is taken by one parent *before* a court has determined custody, it is probable that no law has been broken, since both parents usually have an equal right to custody until custody is determined by a court.

However, if the child is taken by the noncustodial parent *after* a written custody agreement or judicial decision, it is likely that the noncustodial parent has committed a crime. Custodial interference is a misdemeanor in most states [31] and in a few it is a felony under certain circumstances. Thus, the custodial parent may rely on the criminal law in addition to the Uniform Child Custody Jurisdiction Act in order to seek the return of his or her children.

Regardless of what the law says, however, it may be difficult for a parent to interest the police or the district attorney in pursuing a child-snatching case. Law-enforcement officials are often predisposed to treat these cases lightly or merely as "family affairs."

Do parents have to accept an arrangement which makes one parent the custodian and the other a "visitor"?

No. It is possible that they can continue sharing custody more-or-less equally by agreeing to "joint custody." Joint custody is a relatively new legal concept, but it is gaining favor quite rapidly. Joint custody is not defined in most state family or domestic-relations codes, but it means that the children of divorced or separated parents remain in the custody of *both* parents, even though they are living apart. Thus, neither parent has any greater rights than the other in determining matters such as place of residence, education, religion, and medical care. Joint custody does not necessarily mean that each parent will reside with the child fifty percent of the time, but it is unlike normal custody arrangements in which the custodial parent enjoys greater rights than the noncustodial parent. Naturally, joint custody requires a great deal of cooperation between the parents and is probably unworkable if the parents have major differences between them or if they are bitter towards each other.

Joint custody is more often achieved by agreement than court order. This is due to the fact that parents who must resort to the courts to solve their custody arrangements are not often well disposed to working out the many problems that joint custody would require on a continuing basis. This led New York's highest court to observe:

> Joint custody is encouraged primarily as a voluntary alternative for relatively stable, amicable parents behaving in a mature civilized fashion. As a court-ordered arrangement imposed upon already embattled and embittered parents, accusing one another of serious vices and wrongs, it can only enhance familial chaos.[32]

But other courts are becoming more tolerant of joint custody orders under favorable circumstances.[33] As one New Hampshire Supreme Court judge recently stated in a dissenting opinion:

> The sole parent not only has to fulfill all family functions, but has little release from his or her burden. Thus one parent becomes overburdened and the other, in a sense, underburdened. . . . [T]he children who are free to develop full relationships with both parents fare best after divorce. Joint custody avoids subjecting the child completely to one parent's will, and instead affords the child in-depth exposure to both parents.[34]

And in California, a law was recently enacted which provides that when parents have agreed that they will be joint custodians, it will be presumed by courts that joint custody is in the best interest of the children if there is a subsequent court contest.[35]

Popular literature has also, of late, become increasingly supportive of the joint custody concept.[36]

What is visitation?

Visitation is the right granted to the noncustodial parent to spend a regular period of time each week, month or year with the child in the absence of the custodial parent. Visitation can include vacation periods and can be for several weeks or months at a time. The exact terms of visitation are normally contained in separation agreements between parents or in divorce or custody decrees determined by courts.

Does the noncustodial parent always have the right to visitation?

Almost always. It is almost automatic that the parent who does not have custody is granted the right of visitation.[37] This is because parents have a fundamental right to raise their children (see Chapter I), and because the status of separation or divorce does not abrogate this fundamental right.[38] Thus, visitation, being the "vestigial" right to custody, cannot be denied except under compelling circumstances, such as conditions that would seriously harm the child's welfare.[39]

If the noncustodial parent fails to make support payments, will a court deny visitation?

It depends on the state. Even *within* some states, courts are split over this issue. The predominant view is that a parent's visitation rights should not be made dependent upon his or her payment of child support, since visitation is supported by the independent premise that exposure to both parents is in the best interests of the child.[40] But some courts have ruled that since support payments are provided for the benefit of the child, nonpayment of support may be a ground for withdrawal of visitation privileges.[41]

What if the child doesn't want to visit with the non-custodial parent?

The child will probably be required to visit anyway. Courts will protect both the custodial and the noncustodial parent from attempts by the other to alienate the child's affections. Thus, courts will require the custodial parent to exert reasonable authority over the child to compel him or her to visit with the noncustodial parent.[42]

Can one parent be punished for interfering with the other parent's custodial or visitation rights?

Yes. To the greatest extent possible, courts try to assure that a child will grow up knowing both parents. Some courts have actually transferred custody from the custodial to the visiting parent because the custodial parent has encouraged the child to be hostile to the visiting parent or frequently interfered with the visitation of the noncustodial parent.[43] Similarly, courts have denied visitation to noncustodial parents who have attempted to alienate children from their custodial parents.[44]

Can a court place restrictions on the noncustodial parent's visitation rights?

Yes. Just as a court can restrict the terms of custody, so can it restrict aspects of visitation. Courts have restricted the places noncustodial parents may take their children as well as the people with whom they may associate during visitation hours.[45] Thus, by divorcing or separating, parents give power to the state to regulate certain aspects of their life that otherwise would be wholly beyond the power of the state to determine.

Can a court restrict the freedom of a custodial parent to move about?

Yes. This might come about in one of three situations: First, when parents have agreed to prohibit the custodial parent's move beyond a certain distance; second, when state law or the divorce decree contains a provision against a change of residence; and third, when the custodial parent tries to sneak the child out of the jurisdiction or attempts to move to a location so distant that visitation by the noncustodial parent becomes impossible.[46]

But restrictions on moving will not always be honored by courts, because they run counter to the constitutional right to travel. Thus, courts will decide these cases (usually brought by the noncustodial parent to prevent the custodian's move) on a case-by-case basis, with the "best interests of the child" as the governing standard.

One court in Minnesota avoided the conflict between the constitutional right to travel and a state law that required a custodial parent to seek court approval before moving out of the state by ruling that courts have the discretion to prohibit travel if it is in the best interests of the child.[47] A New York court prevented a move by a custodial mother and children to Florida because she had agreed not to in a prior separation agreement, because there was no evidence that the proposed move would benefit the children, and because the move would weaken the father's "natural rights of visitation and access to his children." [48] And a Wisconsin court succinctly stated:

A divorced man or woman is free to move about and pursue his or her life and living without restraint from his former spouse; [but] as divorced parents of minor children they may be required to curtail these liberties or forfeit some of their rights to custody or visitation, as the case may be, consistent with the best interests of the children and the rights of the other parent.[49]

DETAILS OF RAISING CHILDREN

Which parent has the primary responsibility for raising the child?

Generally, the custodial parent. Of course, divorced parents may agree between themselves which parent will make certain types of decisions about the children's upbringing, and these agreements are enforceable in court. If there is no such agreement, the custodial parent generally has the authority to determine the details of raising the child.

Medical Treatment

Who has the right to determine the medical treatment of the child?

The custodial parent is given the authority to make basic medical decisions.[50]

Is the custodial parent's right to determine the medical treatment of the child absolute?

No. As discussed in Chapter V, the state will order life-saving or crucial operations to be performed on the child over the parent's objections—even when religious beliefs prevent a parent from consenting to a particular medical plan.[51] As between parents, however, the opinion of the custodial parent will control unless the medical practice is not necessary (such as cosmetic surgery) and the objecting noncustodial parent is expected to pay for it. In such cases, the court will determine the reasonableness of the medical treatment from the point of view of the child's best interests.

Religion

Who has the authority to determine the religious up-bringing of the child?

Generally, the custodial parent. The right to determine the extent and kind of religious training for children is basic to the rights of *both* parents, but because of the constitutional principle of separation of church and state, courts are reluctant to resolve disputes *between* parents over religious matters. Normally, unless a child's physical health or emotional development is being significantly impaired, a court will not disturb the custodial parent's religious determination, even if the other parent objects.[52] In the few cases of this type in which courts have become involved, they have generally upheld the right of the custodial parent to control the child's religious training.[53]

What effect do premarital agreements concerning religious training have after divorce?

None. As a general rule, the parent with custody may select the religious training even if by doing so he or she is violating a premarital agreement to raise the child in a certain faith.[54] Basically, the reason for this is that enforcing such an agreement against the wishes of the custodial parent would create conflict that could be harmful to the child.[55] Another reason these agreements are not enforced is that if courts did enforce these agreements, they would violate the prohibition against the separation of church and state.

Name

Does a custodial parent have the right to change the name of his or her children without the consent of the other parent?

Generally, the answer would be no, but certain exceptions exist if it would be harmful to the children to retain their original name.

As discussed in Chapter I, parents have the right to name a child whatever they wish, including both first names and surnames. They may also change a child's name, but for this they must obtain court approval, and courts normally require consent of *both* parents. (Moreover, if the child is of a certain age, many courts require the consent of the child as well.) Therefore, one parent does not have the right to change the name of his or her child without the consent of the other. This rule holds true even when the parents are separated, divorced, or remarried.[56]

There are a few exceptions to this rule, however.

First, if the other parent cannot be found, or has abandoned the child, a court will not require his or her permission, so long as the court is satisfied that diligent attempts to find the absent parent were made but were unsuccessful.[57]

Second, even if the other parent withholds his or her consent to a change of name, a court may grant permission if it believes that the change would be in the child's best interests.

Even though the best interests exception exists, it should be noted that permission is rarely granted, simply because the right of natural parents to name their children is one that cannot be disturbed without compelling reasons. Mere inconvenience to the custodial parent or a child's embarrassment at having a different name than the custodial parent, stepparent, or siblings are not usually considered sufficient justifications.[58] As one court stated in response to a mother's desire to have a child's name changed to that of her new husband in opposition to the wishes of the natural father:

> The bond between a [visiting] father and his children . . . is tenuous at best and if the name is changed that bond may be weakened, if not destroyed. . . . When a father supports a child, and manifests a continuing interest in his welfare, and . . . objects to an attempted change of name, the court must decide the issue by determining what is for the child's best interest. A change of name may not be in the child's best interest if the effect of such change is to contribute to the further estrangement of the child from a father who exhibits a desire to preserve the parental relationship.[59]

What conditions might qualify as being in a child's best interests to justify a name change even if one parent objects?

In one case a New York court permitted a divorced mother to have her child's name changed to her maiden name when the father had seen his child only once in eight years and made no contribution towards the child's support.[60] A Georgia court granted a petition to have the name of two children changed to that of their stepfather when it was demonstrated that the children (ages eight and seven) wanted the change, and there was medical evidence indicating that one of the two children suffered from an emotional disturbance because his name was not the same as his mother's and stepfather's. In another case, a mother was granted permission to change the name of her children to her maiden name because her husband was serving a life sentence in prison for murder.[62]

If one parent seeks approval to change the name of a child, must the other parent be given prior notice of the proceedings?

Yes. The constitutional requirement of due process most likely requires notice to both parents of a pending court proceeding before an order granting a change of name may be made.[63] Prior notice means that both parents have a right to be informed that a court proceeding is about to take place and a right to appear at the proceeding and give their reasons for requesting or opposing such change. It is possible that an order granting one parent the right to change the name of a child without prior notice to the other parent may later be declared invalid.[64]

What if a child is adopted? Do the natural parents have a right to have the adopted child retain their surname?

No. When a child is adopted the natural parents no longer have any legal relationship to the child, which includes the loss of any right to determine the child's name. (See Chapter X for a discussion of adoption.)

Thus, if a mother and father are divorced and the child is adopted by the mother's new husband, the child will bear the name of the mother and adoptive father.[65]

May the custodial parent register a child in school under a different name without the consent of the noncustodial parent?

Probably not. Even though, in a situation such as this, the custodial parent is not seeking to have the child's name *officially* changed, he or she would be attempting to have a child known by a new name, which is tantamount to having it officially changed. Thus, the guidelines that limit one parent's changing the name of a child without the consent of the other, discussed above, would probably apply to nonofficial changes of name as well.

In the first known case dealing with this issue, a custodial mother had remarried and registered her children in school under the name of her new husband. The children's natural father protested. The court stated, "We recognize that here the [mother] may not have effected an actual change of the children's name but by registering them at school under the name [of her new husband] she has gone far in that direction." The court then had the matter sent to trial so that a judge could decide whether or not use of the new name was in the best welfare of the children.[66]

Education

Who has the right to determine the extent of the child's education?

Generally, the custodial parent.[67] Most courts subscribe to the view that upon losing the right to custody, one also loses "the corresponding privileges such as the right to decide the educational advantages such child shall receive." [68] The reason for this is that the custodial parent is deemed better situated to evaluate the child's needs.[69]

Can the custodial parent make the noncustodial parent pay for a child's private, secondary schooling?

Not usually. Courts have held that a custodial parent's demand to make the visiting parent pay for a child's education at a private school will not be honored unless there is proof of "special circumstances." Special circumstances might be the pre-separation plans of the parents, the financial abilities of the parents or the special needs or expectations of the child.[70]

Except for financial considerations, is the custodial parent's right to decide the education of the child absolute?
No. If the custodian's choice of a school will interfere with the noncustodial parent's visitation privileges, a court may not allow it.[71]

Of what effect are provisions in separation agreements concerning education?
These are generally enforceable. Unlike religious issues, courts are willing to enforce agreements between separated parents giving the noncustodial parent authority to decide educational matters.[72]

SUPPORT

Does a divorce free the noncustodial parent of parental obligations such as supporting the child?
No. Parents are legally obliged to support their children, commensurate with their ability and the needs of the offspring, whether or not they have custody of them.[73]

Upon what basis is an order of support made by a court?
The purpose of court-ordered support is to protect and advance the welfare of the child. Parents have a clear responsibility to support their child to the best of their ability, consistent with the life-style to which the child has been accustomed.[74]

What form does the obligation to support take?
Parents can agree, upon separating from each other, that *one or both* parents will support the child in a specific amount each month. If they do agree, this agreement may be (and often is) incorporated into the final order of divorce issued by the court. If parents cannot agree on an amount, the court can, after conducting a hearing on the matter, set the amount.

How long are parents obligated to support their children?
Child-support obligations normally extend until the child reaches the age of majority. This may mean eighteen or twenty-one, depending on the state and the intention of the parties at the time the support order was made.[75]

Can a noncustodial parent be required to pay for the college education of his or her children?

The most common rule is that when children reach the age of majority, they have no right to obtain support from their parents to secure an education.[76] But in some states, statutes explicitly provide that both parents may be required to continue support for school until the child reaches age twenty-one.[77] And in other states, "special circumstances" may be found to justify requiring parents to pay for their children's college education.[78] Finally, when parents have agreed (in separation agreements) that one parent will provide support payments for college education, courts will usually uphold the agreement and make that parent pay.[79]

Does a father's remarriage and responsibility to a new family eliminate his obligation to support the children of his first marrige?

Generally, no.[80] Although remarriage obviously constitutes a "substantial change in circumstances," courts rarely ignore the needs of the children of the first marriage.[81] Nonetheless, most people have a limited amount of money, and a reduction of the support obligation is sometimes ordered if it is impossible to meet the terms of the prior support order.

Can a woman married for the second time be ordered to support the children of her first marriage?

Yes.[82]

NOTES

1. Miner v. Miner, 10 Wis.2d 438, 103 N.W.2d 4 (1960); McMains v. McMains, 15 N.Y.2d 283, 206 N.E.2d 185 (1965); Elkind v. Byck, 68 Cal. App.2d 453, 439 P.2d 316 (1968); 60 KAN. STAT. 1610(d); Uniform Marriage and Divorce Act, §306.
2. Uniform Marriage and Divorce Act, §402; Fish v. Fish, 280 Minn. 316, 159 N.W.2d 271 (1968); Bell v. Eicholtz, 132 W. Va. 747, 53 S.E.2d 627 (1949).
3. Summary of Report in 2 FAM. L. RPTR. 2719 (Aug. 31, 1976).
4. Uniform Marriage and Divorce Act, §306; Miner v. Miner,

supra note 1; McMains v. McMains, *supra* note 1; Elkind v. Byck, *supra* note 1.

5. Meinhardt v. Meinhardt, 261 Minn. 272, 111 N.W.2d 782 (1961); Newman v. Newman, 179 Minn. 184, 228 N.W. 759 (1930); Jenkins v. Jenkins, 173 Wis. 592, 181 N.W. 826 (1921); Horst v. McLain, 466 S.W.2d 187 (Mo. 1971); Peavey v. Peavey, 85 Nev. 571, 460 P.2d 110 (1969).

6. McGowan v. McGowan, 374 A.2d 1306 (Pa. Super. 1977); McAndrew v. McAndrew, 39 Md. App. 1 382 A.2d 1081 (1978; Faro v. Faro, 579 P.2d 1377 (Alaska 1978); Bowen v. Bowen, 219 N.W.2d 683 (Iowa 1974); Watts v. Watts, 77 Misc.2d 178, 350 N.Y.S.2d 285 (Fam. Ct. 1973); Garrett v. Garrett 464 S.W.2d 740 (Mo. App. 1971).

7. Jeffries v. Jeffries (W. Va. Sup. Ct.), *in* 5 FAM. L. RPTR. 2543 (May 8, 1979).

8. J.B. v. A.B., 242 S.E.2d 248 (W. Va. 1978).

9. McCreery v. McCreery, 237 S.E.2d 167 (Va. 1977).

10. Cox v. Cox, 532 P.2d 994 (Utah 1975); *but see,* Jorgensen v. Jorgensen, in 5 FAM. L. RPTR. 2922 (Aug. 20, 1979).

11. 30 OKLA. STAT. ANN. §11(2).

12. Gordon v. Gordon, 577 P.2d 1271 (Okla. 1978).

13. Gillespie v. Gillespie, 40 Hawaii 315 (1953); Obey v. Degling, 37 N.Y.2d 768, 337 N.E. 601 (1975); Butler v. Perry, 210 Md. 332, 123 A.2d 453 (1956); Callen v. Gill, 7 N.J. 312, 81 A.2d 495 (1951); Goldstein v. Goldstein, 115 R.I. 152, 341 A.2d 51 (1975).

14. Everson v. Board of Education, 330 U.S. 1 (1946).

15. Waites v. Waites, 567 S.W.2d 326 (Mo. Sup. Ct. 1978); *see also* Mollish v. Mollish, 494 S.W.2d 145 (Tenn. 1972).

16. *See, e.g.,* Bonjour v. Bonjour, 592 P.2d 1233 (Alaska 1979); Wolfert v. Wolfert (Colo. Ct. App.), *in* 5 FAM. L. RPTR. 2658 (June 19, 1979).

17. Bonjour v. Bonjour, *supra* note 16.

18. Haskell v. Haskell (S.D. Sup. Ct.), *in* 5 FAM. L. RPTR. 2734 (July 24, 1979).

19. Perrault v. Cook, 114 N.H. 440, 322 A.2d 610 (1974); Obey v. Degling, *supra* note 13.

20. Uniform Marriage and Divorce Act, §409; Selivanoff v. Selivanoff, 12 Wash. App. 263, 529 P.2d 486 (1974); *but see, contra,* King. v. King., 114 R.I. 329, 333 A.2d 135 (1975); Blair v. Blair, 505 S.W.2d 444 (Mo. App. 1974).

21. Burris v. Burris, 383 N.E.2d 811 (Ill. App. 1979); *see also* Jarrett v. Jarrett, 382 N.E.2d 12 (Ill. App. 78).

22. *See, e.g.,* Jones v. Jones, 175 N.W.2d 389 (Iowa 1970).

23. Feldman v. Feldman, 45 A.D.2d 320, 358 N.Y.S.2d 507 (1974); *see also* Uniform Marriage and Divorce Act, §402.

24. *In re* Alderson 583 P.2d 31 (Or. App. Ct. 1978).

25. It is possible that, by the time this book is published, almost every state will subscribe to the Act.

26. *In re* Verbin, 595 P.2d 905 (Wash. 1979).

27. *In re* Irene R. (N.Y. Fam. Ct.,) *in* 5 FAM. L. RPTR. 2635 (June 12, 1979). *See also* Martin v. Martin, 45 N.Y.2d 739, 380 N.E.2d 333 (1978).

28. Winkelman v. Moses (S.D. Sup. Ct.), *in* 5 FAM. L. RPTR. 2709 (July 17, 1979).

29. Barcus v. Barcus, 278 N.W.2d 646 (Iowa 1979). *Accord, In re* Custody of Rector, 505 P.2d 950 (Colo. Ct. App. 1977); *In re* McDonald, 74 Mich. App. 119, 253 N.W.2d 678 (1977); Bergstrom v. Bergstrom, 271 N.W.3d 546 (N.D. 1978).

30. New York Times, May 18, 1979, p. C–14.

31. *See, e.g.,* PA. CRIMES CODE, §2904; Commonwealth v. Chubb, 395 A.2d 964, (Super. Ct. Pa. 1978).

32. Braiman v. Braiman, 44 N.Y.2d 584, 387 N.E.2d 1021 (1978); *See also In re* Marriage of Neal, 155 Cal. Rptr. 157 (Ct. App. 1979).

33. *See, e.g.,* Zinni v. Zinni, 103 R.I. 417 (1966); Winn v. Winn, 143 Cal. App.2d 84, 299 P.2d 721 (1956); Perotti v. Perotti, 78 Misc.2d 131, 355 N.Y.S.2d 68 (Sup. Ct. 1974).

34. Starkeson v. Starkeson, 397 A.2d 1043 (N.H. 1979).

35. S. B. 477 (Smith), July, 1979.

36. *See, e.g.,* Baum, *The Best of Both Parents,* N.Y. TIMES MAGAZINE, p. 45 (Oct. 31, 1976); M. GALBER, CO-PARENTING (1978); M. ROMAN & W. HADDAD, THE DISPOSABLE PARENT (1978).

37. Bartlett v. Bartlett, 175 Or. 215, 152 P.2d 402 (1944).

38. Cascio v. Cascio, 485 S.W.2d 857 (Mo. App. 1972).

39. Kellogg v. Kellogg, 187 Or. 617, 213 P.2d 172 (1949); Townsend v. Townsend, 205 Md.2d 591, 109 A.2d 765 (1954).

40. Griffin v. Griffin, 226 Ga. 781, 177 S.E.2d 696 (1970); Kane v. Kane, 391 P.2d 361, 363 (Colo. 1964).

41. Reardon v. Reardon, 3 Ariz. App. 475, 415 P.2d 571 (1966); *see also In re* Cardo (N.C. Court of Appeals), *in* 5 FAM. L. RPTR. 2712 (July 17, 1979).

42. Commonwealth v. Lotz, 188 Pa. Super. 241, 146 A.2d 362 (1958).

43. Ludlow v. Ludlow, 89 Cal. App.2d 210, 201 P.2d 579 (Dist. Ct. App. 1949); Emerson v. Quinn, 79 Idaho 358, 317 P.2d 344 (1957).

44. Kellogg v. Kellogg, 187 Or. 617, 213 P.2d 172 (1949); Nunnick v. Nunnick, 257 S.W. 832 (Mo. App. 1924).

45. Aud v. Etienne, 47 Ill.2d 110, 264 N.E.2d 196 (1976);

In re J.S. & C., 129 N.J. Super. 486, 324 A.2d 90 (1974), *aff'd.* 142 N.J. Super 499, 362 A.2d 54 (1976); *In re* Jane B., 85 Misc.2d 515, 380 N.Y.S.2d 848 (Sup. Ct. 1976).

46. *In re* Meier, 595 P.2d 474 (Or. 1979).
47. Ryan v. Ryan, 300 Minn. 244, 219 N.W.2d 912 (1974).
48. Strahl v. Strahl 414 N.Y.S.2d 184 (Sup. Ct. 1979).
49. Whitman v. Whitman, 28 Wis.2d 5058, 135 N.W.2d 835 (1965).
50. Lester v. Lester, 178 App. Div. 205, 165 N.Y.S. 187, *aff'd.* 222 N.Y. 546, 118 N.E. 1065 (1917).
51. State *ex rel.* Wallace v. Labrenz, 411 Ill. 618, 104 N.E.2d 69, *cert. denied* 344 U.S. 824 (1952); *In re* Sampson, 29 N.Y. 900, 278 N.E.2d 918 (1972).
52. Wolfert v. Wolfert *supra*, note 16.
53. *See, e.g.,* Miller v. Hedrick, 158 Cal. App.2d 281, 322 P.2d 231 (Ct. App. 1958).
54. Uniform Marriage and Divorce Act §402; Hackett v. Hackett, 146 N.E.2d 477 (Ohio C.P. 1957); Stanton v. Stanton, 213 Ga. 545, 100 S.E.2d 289 (1957).
55. Boerger v. Boerger, 26 N.J. Super. 90, 97 A.2d 419 (1953).
56. *See, e.g.,* Garnier v. Racivitch, 216 La. 241, 43 So.2d 595 (1949).
57. *In re* Larson, 81 Cal. App.2d 258, 183 P.2d 688 (1947); Application of DeJesus, 44 Misc.2d 833, 254 N.Y.S.2d 23 (Sup. Ct. 1954).
58. Hall v. Hall, 30 Md. App. 214, 351 A.2d 917 (1976).
59. Mark v. Kahn, 333 Mass. 517, 131 N.E.2d 758 (1956); *see also* Flowers v. Cain, 237 S.E.2d 111 (Sup. Ct. Va. 1977).
60. Application of Proman, 63 N.Y.S.2d 83 (City Ct. 1946); *see also In re* Williams, 86 Misc.2d 87, 381 N.Y.S.2d 944 (Civ. Ct. 1976).
61. Johnnson v. Coggins, 124 Ga. App. 603, 184 S.E.2d 696 (Ct. of App. 1971).
62. Application of Fein, 51 Misc.2d 1022, 274 N.Y.S.2d 547 (Civ. Ct. 1966). *See also* W. v. H., 103 N.J. Super. 24, 246 A.2d 501 (1968).
63. Roe v. Conn, 417 F. Supp. 769 (M.D. Ala. 1976).
64. Carroll v. Johnson, 565 S.W.2d 10 (Ark. 1978).
65. Stanfield v. Willoughby, 286 S.W.2d 908 (Ky. Ct. App., 1956); *In re* Adoption of Watson, 361 P.2d 1054 (Haw., 1961).
66. Mark v. Kahn, *supra* note 59. *See also* Sobel v. Sobel, 46 N.J. Super. 284, 134 A.2d 598 (1957).
67. Bateman v. Bateman, 234 Ga. 20, 159 S.E.2d 387 (1968).
68. *Id.,* 159 S.E.2d at 390.
69. Majnaric v. Majnaric, 46 Ohio Op.2d 250, 347 N.E.2d

552 (1975); Esteb v. Esteb, 138 Wash. 174, 244 P. 264 (1928).

70. Zirin v. Zirin, 409 N.Y.S.2d 13 (App. Div. 1978).

71. Lester v. Lester, *supra*, note 50.

72. *See, e.g.*, Taylor v. Taylor, 32 Ill. App.2d 45, 176 N.E.2d 640 (1961).

73. Anderson v. Anderson, 437 S.W.2d 704 (Kansas City Ct. of Appeals 1969).

74. Commonwealth *ex rel.* Kaplan v. Kaplan, 236 Pa. 526, 344 A.2d 578 (1975); Gitman v. Gitman, 428 Pa. 387, 237 A.2d 181 (1967); Hecht v. Hecht, 189 Pa. Super. 276, 150 A.2d 139 (1959).

75. *See* Stanton v. Stanton, 421 U.S. 7 (1975); Roe v. Doe, 29 N.Y.2d 188, 272 N.E.2d 567 (1971).

76. Philips v. Philips, 339 So.2d 1299 (La. App. 1976).

77. *See e.g.*, IOWA CODE §598.17.

78. *E.g.*, Kaplan v. Wallshein, 57 A.D.2d 828, 394 N.Y.S.2d 439 (2d Dept. 1977).

79. *E.g.*, Bethune v. Bethune, 46 N.Y.2d 913, 387 N.E.2d 1220 (1979); Carpenter v. Carpenter, 25 N.C. App. 235, 212 S.E.2d 911 (1975).

80. Anderson v. Anderson, *supra* note 73.

81. Anderson v. Anderson, *supra* note 73.

82. Alling v. Alling, 52 N.J. Eq. 92, 27 A. 655 (1893); Haugen v. Swanson, 23 N.W.2d 535 (Minn. 1946); McQuade v. McQuade, 145 Colo. 218, 358 P.2d 470 (1960); Conway v. Dana, 456 Pa. 536, 318 A.2d 324 (1974); Carter v. Carter, 58 A.D.2d 438, 397 N.Y.S.2d 88 (2d Dept. 1977).

VIII

Unwed Parents

Historically, children born to unmarried parents had no claim to support from their parents and no rights of inheritance. According to English common law, from which much of American law stems, an illegitimate child * was considered *filius nullius,* or a child of no one. As such, he or she enjoyed far fewer rights than legitimate children.

Legal discrimination against illegitimate children existed in America until the recent past. In the last few years, however, a number of laws that treated illegitimate children differently from legitimate children have been declared unconstitutional by the United States Supreme Court.

Even with recent changes in the law, illegitimate children are still treated differently than legitimate children in certain circumstances. Similarly, the rights and obligations of the *parents* of illegitimate and legitimate children differ in some respects as well, especially in the realms of child custody and the disposition of property and money when a parent dies.

DEFINITIONS

What makes a child illegitimate?

A child is considered illegitimate when he or she is born to a woman who is not married to the child's biological father at the time of birth. Conversely, a legitimate

* The authors find the word "illegitimate" distasteful, since it would seem to imply that a child bearing that label is something less than real. But since it is the word which presently denominates the legal status of children of unmarried parents, it is reluctantly used in this chapter.

child is one born to a woman who is married to the child's biological father.

Is the term "illegitimate" still in use today?

Yes. Statutes and courts today still use the terms "legitimate" and "illegitimate" to describe the legal status of children. In some state codes, children born of unmarried parents are still referred to as "bastards."

If the parents marry after the child is conceived but before it is born, is it considered illegitimate?

No. A child is considered illegitimate only when *born* to unwed parents. Therefore, parents who marry after conception (that is, during the mother's pregnancy), but before the child's birth, will not be considered the parents of an illegitimate child.

Is it possible for an illegitimate child to become legitimate?

Yes. In every state there is at least one way this could happen. Not all the state laws are the same, however.

The most common way that illegitimate children may be later *legitimized* is for the biological parents of the child to marry each other after the child's birth. This is the manner permitted in California, New York, Florida, Connecticut, and Michigan, among other states.[1]

In some states, such as Illinois and Massachusetts, not only must the parents marry each other but the father must acknowledge his paternity as well, either in writing or before a notary.[2] And in other states, acknowledgment alone, with or without marriage, is sufficient, as in Michigan, Alabama, and Wisconsin.[3]

CUSTODY AND ADOPTION

Do parents have the right to the custody of their illegitimate children?

Yes. *Against third parties* (meaning someone who is neither the father nor the mother), parents who have never married have the same right to the custody of their children as do married parents. This is because the Constitution and the policy of most states protect the right of *natural* parents to the care and custody of their children.[4] Thus, as a rule, unless parents have abandoned their children or been declared unfit, they have an absolute right to the custody of their children.[5] Marriage is simply irrelevant to parents' rights to raise their children.

Between themselves, however, unmarried mothers and fathers are subject to a more varied and complex scheme of rights than married parents in matters of custody.

Who may name a child born out of wedlock?

The mother. The father has no right to participate in the naming of his child when the parents are not married.

May a child born out of wedlock bear the name of the father?

Yes, if the mother desires, she has the right to give the child the surname of the child's father.

In a custody dispute between unmarried parents, who has the greater right—the mother or the father?

Generally, the mother. For a long time unmarried fathers were not allowed any legal interest in their children, including custody. Although the rights of unmarried fathers have been expanded in recent years, they still have greater difficulty than *married* fathers in obtaining custody of their children over the wishes of mothers.[6] In all custody disputes, whether between married or unmarried parents, the legal standard used to determine custody is the "best interests of the child." Thus, if the father has had a meaningful relationship with the child and the mother has not, a court may award custody to him if this would be in the child's best interests.[7] But as frequently happens in matters relating to children, bias and moral judgments frequently affect courts' views about the child's best interests. Practically speaking, it is far more difficult for unwed fathers to obtain custody than it is for wed fathers.[8]

May states grant unwed fathers fewer rights than wed fathers?

Yes. States may lawfully discriminate against certain kinds of unwed fathers, including those who have not had custody or lived with their children.[9] But the Constitution does not permit states to discriminate against *all* unwed fathers, simply because of their status. States may not invoke a broad, irrefutable presumption that unwed fathers do not have a sufficient interest in their children ever to be given custody.[10]

Can unmarried fathers obtain visitation privileges over the objection of the mother?

Yes. Since unmarried fathers have the right to seek and obtain custody, it is clear that they have the right to seek visitation as well. Of course, to secure visitation privileges, the father would probably have to prove his willingness to support the child and show more than a passing interest in the child's development and welfare. Thus, if an unmarried father has acknowledged his responsibility to the child and demonstrates a genuine interest in the welfare and support of the child, he will likely be entitled to visit unless his visits have an adverse impact on the child's well-being.[11]

Do unwed fathers have the same right to visit their children as separated or divorced fathers?

There is no definite answer to this question. Practically speaking, an unwed father will find it more difficult to obtain a court order for visitation than a married father who subsequently separated or divorced. This is partly due to the historical discrimination against all parties to an out-of-wedlock relationship.

But the situation is beginning to change. In recent years, the U.S. Supreme Court has struck down a number of laws that arbitrarily discriminate against children born to unwed parents.[12] Moreover, the Fourteenth Amendment to the Constitution requires that persons be granted equal protection of the laws. Many unwed fathers have successfully relied upon this guarantee to secure rights previously denied them. In the context of visitation, courts have long considered visitation to be both the child's *and* the parent's right. Thus, if a court were to deny visitation to an unwed father in a case where visitation would be granted to a wed father, the court's decision would probably unlawfully infringe on the rights of *both* the father and the child.

But the vital ingredient in this theory is this: if the

unwed father is to be granted visitation rights equal with those normally given formerly married fathers, he must stand in the same "position," except for his marital status; in short, the father must be more than a mere biological father. If he has lived with his child for a period of time and supported the child, and is then denied visitation by a court in a situation where a wed father would be granted visitation, there is a strong probability that the denial of visitation would be unconstitutional.[13]

If an unmarried mother surrenders her child for adoption, does the unmarried father have the right to prevent it?

It depends. If the father has lived with the mother and assisted in raising the child, he will have the right to oppose the adoption.[14] But if the father has never lived with the child, it is unclear if he would have this right. The degree to which an unmarried father has power to prevent the adoption would depend upon the degree of actual relationship he has had with the child, his concern for the child, and the child's age.[15] If the child is several years old and the father has rarely or never visited with him or her, he will not be allowed to interfere with the desire of the mother.[16] On the other hand, if the child is a newborn whom the mother wishes to surrender for adoption, in some states the father could prevent the adoption and would be allowed to obtain custody himself.[17]

If the mother of an illegitimate child marries someone other than the child's father, can the natural father prevent the adoption of his own child by the stepfather?

It depends on a number of factors. Generally, it is more difficult for an unmarried father to prevent the adoption of his child by the husband of the mother, than an adoption by strangers (as discussed in the previous question and answer). If the father once lived with the child and continues to show an interest in him or her through support payments and visitation, he may be able to prevent the adoption.[18] However, many courts want the stepfather to be able to adopt the child if that is the mother's wish. This is because many courts think that it is best for the child if it bears the same last name of the mother, stepfather and any half- or step-siblings. Accordingly, a father who rarely visits his illegitimate children and fails to maintain a substantial relationship with them may not be able to prevent their adoption by the stepfather.[19]

May a state allow the adoption of a child born out of wedlock over the objection of a nonabandoning, fit, custodial father?

Almost certainly not.[20] Distinctions between unwed mothers and fathers based on gender are valid, if at all, because of the greater likelihood that an unwed mother will exercise custody. But when an unwed father has custody, his substantive and procedural rights to the care and custody of his children are identical to that of an unwed mother. Thus, unwed custodial fathers have a right to a hearing on their fitness before the state may deprive them of the custody of their children. And in states where unwed custodial *mothers* must be proven unfit before they could be involuntarily deprived of their children, the state may not take away children from fathers "similarly situated" without proving *their* unfitness as well.

Can courts terminate the parental rights of the father of an infant born out of wedlock?

The answer to this is not clear. But it is likely that the general answer would be the same as the answers given to the three previous questions, since involuntary termination of parental rights and freeing a child for adoption over the objections of a parent involve essentially the same legal procedures. At least one court has held that it is unconstitutional to terminate a father's parental rights when he had acknowledged paternity and sought custody.[21]

Why are unwed fathers given fewer rights than wed fathers in matters of custody and adoption?

Several reasons have been given. One is that it promotes marriage and discourages extramarital relationships. Laws that discriminate against the unmarried generally reflect a legislature's displeasure with extramarital relationships. Another reason is that laws that make it easier for children of unwed fathers to be adopted facilitate adoptions and promote the best interests of the child. The U.S. Supreme Court has recognized the validity of this reasoning.[22] The Court said that the Constitution permits legal distinctions to be made between wed fathers and unwed fathers of infants because the likelihood is greater that unwed fathers will not have the same interest in their children as wed fathers.

But the Supreme Court has also said that *unwed fathers* who have a substantial relationship with their children cannot be treated differently than *unwed mothers*. Since no state authorizes adoption over the objection of nonabandoning, fit unwed mothers who have substantial relationships with their children, they may not do so for men.[23]

What is of particular concern to the courts and legislatures is that if they were to grant the same legal rights to unwed fathers that are enjoyed by wed fathers, an unwed father would be permitted to block the adoption of his child by another person, frequently a stepfather. This causes concern because it would give unwed fathers the power to prevent children from becoming "legitimate." And since illegitimate children are discriminated against in many ways, socially and legally, the state has an interest in seeing their number decreased.

This line of reasoning, it should be pointed out, is somewhat circular and aids potential adoptive fathers by keeping unwed fathers in their "place." First, the law classifies legitimate children differently from illegitimates and grants greater rights to the former. Then, in recognition of the discrimination against illegitimates, laws discriminating against unwed fathers are deemed valid.

A solution might be simply to say that a nonabandoning, fit, unwed father is possessed of all of the rights of a nonabandoning, fit, wed father. Unless a court rules that the unwed father did abandon his child, there could be no valid basis to disregard the wishes of the father. But this is not the route that courts have taken, since they have shown no hesitation to diminish the rights of parents who have not married.[24]

PATERNITY AND SUPPORT

What is a paternity action?

A paternity action is a lawsuit in which the object of the proceeding is to prove that a particular man is the natural father of a specific child. If a man denies being the father of a child, and if he was not married to the mother, he has a right to disclaim paternity and refuse support until proven to be the father in a court proceeding.

Can a man admit that he is the father of a child without a court proceeding?

Yes. However, if he wants to make his paternity legally binding in all respects, so that he enjoys all the rights of fatherhood (and his children have the right of inheritance), he should formally declare paternity in accordance with the laws in his state, which usually involve a judicial order.

Does a man have a right to a jury trial in a paternity action?

In most states, no.[25]

Do men charged with being fathers in paternity actions have a right to an attorney?

Frequently, yes. Many courts in recent years have recognized the serious consequences of being legally designated a father and have held as a matter of constitutional law that alleged fathers have a right to counsel in paternity proceedings.[26]

Not all states, however, give indigent men charged with paternity the right to court-assigned (free) counsel. But the trend is in the direction of granting court-assigned counsel as a legal right.[27]

If a blood test shows that a man charged with paternity cannot be the father of the child, can the results of that test be used in court to disprove paternity?

Yes.[28]

Is blood test evidence which fails to exclude the alleged father admissible in court to prove paternity?

No.[29] However, recent scientific advances in blood testing (especially in the development of the Human Leucocyte Antigen test, the results of which can determine paternity with an extremely high degree of accuracy) may result in the admissibility of affirmative blood test evidence in the future.

What are the consequences to a man who is legally declared to be the father of a child born out of wedlock?

The most important obligation imposed by a declaration of paternity, whether admitted voluntarily or ruled by a court, is the duty to support the child until the child reaches the age of majority.

Of course, the duty to support children applies to *all* parents, whether their children are legitimate or not. In 1973, the U.S. Supreme Court overturned a Texas law that said parents had no duty to support illegitimate children.[30] The Supreme Court ruled that there was no justification for denying children their right to support simply because their father and mother never married. The Court stated: "Once a state posts a judicially enforceable right on behalf of children to needed support from their natural father, there is no constitutionally sufficient justification for denying such an essential right to a child simply because its natural father has not married its mother."

Although unwed fathers have a legal obligation to support their children, this obligation commences only after there is a judicial ruling that a particular man is the father. But once that ruling is made, or if the father voluntarily acknowledges paternity, his support obligations are identical with those of all parents.

Is a husband of a woman who bears a child during marriage always considered the legal father of the child, with responsibilities for the support obligations of the child?

Yes, in most states. The general rule adopted from the English common law, known as the "Lord Mansfield Rule," is that offspring born during a marriage are presumed to be the legitimate children of both parents.

Although husbands are considered fathers of children born during their marriage, the presumption of paternity can be overcome by certain evidence.[31] In Maryland, for example, the presumption that a child is the legitimate child of the mother's husband can be rebutted by showing that at the time of conception the husband and wife were living separate and apart.[32] In other states, where blood-grouping tests conclusively show that the husband could not be the father of the child, courts have been unwilling to declare the husband as the father.[33]

Do unwed fathers have the right to seek declarations of paternity by commencing their own paternity proceedings?

Yes.[34] Although paternity proceedings normally are commenced by mothers on behalf of the children, courts have recently recognized the importance to fathers in having their relationship with children legally established.[35] In some states, men have the right to prove their paternity even if the mother of the child is or was married to someone else.[36]

PUBLIC ASSISTANCE

Do parents have the same right to have their illegitimate children supported by public assistance as do parents of legitimate children?

Yes, so long as they meet the financial qualifications for public assistance. In 1973, the U.S. Supreme Court struck down a New Jersey law that made families eligible for welfare payments only if their household contained two *married* adults and at least one legitimate or adopted child. [37] Spokesmen for New Jersey claimed that the law's purpose was to preserve and strengthen "traditional family life." But the Supreme Court disagreed and ruled that the statute denied illegitimate children equal protection of the laws, since the benefits of public assistance are indispensable to the health and well-being of *all* children, whether legitimate or not.

What is the Aid to Families with Dependent Children (AFDC) Program?

It is part of the federally sponsored Social Security program. Families are eligible for AFDC money if there are children under age eighteen in the home, or under age twenty-one and attending school, and the children are deprived of support because of the death, absence, or incapacity of one parent or both. Today such payments are made on behalf of one child in every eight under age eighteen in the United States.[38] As stated in the previous question and answer, AFDC funds are available to families whether children are legitimate or illegitimate.

Are all children born out of wedlock eligible for AFDC money?

No. They must meet certain qualifications. If a child (whether born out of wedlock or not) lives with both parents and both are able to support the child, the child does not come within the guidelines of the federal law. So long as the child's parents are available and able, they are obligated to support the child, and the family is ineligible for AFDC money.[39]

If the mother of an illegitimate child is receiving welfare payments for herself and the welfare department wants to learn the name of the child's father, will she be required to reveal it?

Yes. Federal law requires parents, as a condition of AFDC eligibility, to cooperate with state efforts to locate and obtain support from absent parents.[40] Unmarried mothers seeking to obtain welfare benefits for their child are required to cooperate with the state agency in locating the father and in attempting to establish paternity.[41] The purpose of this requirement is to get fathers to support their children, thereby eliminating or reducing the necessity for state support.

Specifically, an unwed mother is obliged to do the following three things as condition for receiving public benefits:

1. She must furnish the state agency with the Social Security numbers for herself, the father, the children, and other persons whose needs are considered in determining the family's AFDC grant.
2. She must assign to the state any rights to support that she or other members of the family unit may have.
3. She must cooperate with the state agency in locating the absent parent, establishing paternity, and securing support payments from him.

She may refuse to reveal the identity of the father or to assist in locating him only if there is good cause to do so.[42]

What constitutes "good cause" for refusing to reveal the identity of the father?

There is no precise answer to this. Each local agency

must make a case by case determination whether "good cause" has been shown. Generally, good cause for refusing to cooperate exists if cooperation might result in (1) physical or emotional harm to the child or (2) physical or emotional harm to the mother, including harm that "reduces the capacity to care for the child adequately." Additionally, if the child was conceived as a result of incest or rape, a mother would have good cause to refuse to identify the father.[43]

Does the mother's refusal to cooperate, without good cause, allow the state to cut off the child's AFDC benefits?

No. If the mother refuses to cooperate without good cause in the state's effort to locate the child's father, the state can retaliate by cutting off the *mother's* benefits, but not the child's support. If good cause cannot be shown and the mother is made ineligible, the child would still be eligible for aid, but in an amount determined without regard to the needs of the mother.[44]

Does the state have an obligation to try to find out the identity of the father as a condition of the state's receiving federal benefits?

Yes. Because the unwed father, if found, would be legally obligated to support his child, it is within the legal power of a state to try to ascertain the father's identity and location.[45] As a matter of fact, in 1975, Congress passed a law *requiring* states and the federal government to establish mechanisms for locating absent parents and for enforcing support obligations.[46] Thus, states are required to attempt to obtain the cooperation of the custodial parent in establishing paternity of an absent father.

Is it constitutional for a state to condition the continuation of AFDC payments on a recipient's willingness to admit into her home a social worker for periodic visits?

Yes. The U.S. Supreme Court has held that periodic visits to the home, even over the objection of the mother, are valid procedures in order to assure that public AFDC money is being properly spent.[47] The mother may refuse to allow the caseworker into her home, but in some states this would be at the peril of loss of eligibility.

INHERITANCE AND OTHER RIGHTS

Can an illegitimate child inherit money and property from his or her mother if the mother dies without a will?

Yes. In virtually every state, illegitimate children have the same inheritance rights as legitimate children to inherit from their mother if she dies "intestate"; that is, if she dies without a will. In most states, if a single mother dies without a will her estate would automatically be inherited by her children. This would be the case whether her children were legitimate or illegitimate.

Can an illegitimate child inherit money and property from his or her father if the father dies without a will?

It depends on the law in each state. A number of states make it more difficult for illegitimate children than legitimate children to inherit from their fathers if their fathers die without a will. This unequal treatment is usually justified on the ground that it is impossible to prove who the real father of an illegitimate child is. Even the U.S. Supreme Court has applied rather uneven standards in a number of cases, by ruling that some state laws that limit the right of inheritance of illegitimate children are constitutional while others are not.

For example, as recently as 1977 there was a law in Illinois that stated a child born to unmarried parents could not inherit from the intestate father if the father had not "acknowledged" the child and had not married the child's mother. A few years ago this law was challenged by an illegitimate child who was unable to inherit his deceased father's estate. Even though the father contributed to the child's support, he failed to fulfill the requirements of the law because he never formally "acknowledged" the child as his own nor did he ever marry the child's mother. The U.S. Supreme Court ruled that the Illinois law was unconstitutional because it discriminated against illegitimate children.[48] In its decision, the Supreme Court did not say that illegitimate children are to be given the same rights as legitimate children to the inheritance of estates from their fathers who die without a will, but it did say that the requirements established in Illinois imposed such a heavy burden on illegitimate children that the law was unconstitutional.[49] In short, the Supreme Court decided that state laws such as Illinois' (and at the time, there were about twenty other states that had similar laws) unfairly punished illegitimate children and denied them the "equal protection of the laws" as guaranteed all people by the Fourteenth Amendment to the Constitution.

On the other hand, within the last year the Supreme Court upheld another state law, which restricts the rights of illegitimate children in New York to inherit from their fathers.[50] The law requires the father to obtain a court order declaring his paternity before his child reaches the age of two; if he fails to do this, the child cannot inherit from the father if he dies without a will. The Supreme Court ruled that this law is rational, and therefore not unconstitutional, because the state has an interest in requiring proof, during a father's lifetime, that he really is the father of the illegitimate child. The Supreme Court said that New York's law was constitutional while Illinois' inheritance statute was not, because the latter, which required a father's acknowledgment *and* marriage, unduly burdened the rights of illegitimate children and bore little relation to the state's interest in having estates pass correctly.

This slender distinction illustrates the rather unsettled state of the law with regard to the right of illegitimate children to inherit from their fathers who die intestate. What the Supreme Court seems to have said, in sum, is that states are permitted to make rules that might restrict the succession of estates from fathers to their illegitimate children, even when no such rules apply to the succession of estates from fathers to their legitimate children. But these rules, whatever they may be, must bear some rational relation to the interest of the state in identifying actual fathers and in avoiding unnecessary disputes over the passing of property and money from one generation to the next.

Therefore, the right of inheritance of illegitimate children—and the equal right of fathers of illegitimate children to have their estates inherited by them—depend on the laws of each state.

Generally, what are the requirements in most states for fathers to have their estate inherited by their illegitimate children?

There is no consistency among various state laws.

Twenty states had laws similar to the Illinois law struck down by the Supreme Court, discussed in the previous answer. Most of those states, including Connecticut, the District of Columbia, Massachusetts, Ohio, Pennsylvania, and Texas, which required acknowledgment *and* marriage as a prerequisite for inheritance, are now in the process of rewriting their laws to conform with constitutionally acceptable guidelines.

Fifteen states, including Michigan, Minnesota, New York * and Wisconsin, permit inheritance if the father acknowledges the child in writing. Of these, eight also permit inheritance if paternity or filiation is declared by a court.

Eleven states, including Colorado, Delaware, Florida, and Indiana, permit inheritance if the father later marries the mother, is declared the father by a court, or if paternity is established after his death by convincing proof. To meet this latter test, the father must not have refused to support the child and he must have openly treated the child as his own.

In five states, including California, "open and notorious" recognition of an illegitimate child by the father during his lifetime is sufficient.

What if the father of an illegitimate child dies with a will and specifies that the child is to inherit all or part of his estate?

This presents no problem. So long as the child is mentioned by name in the will, the child will inherit accordingly. An adult has the right to will his property to anyone

---

* Interestingly, even though the Supreme Court ruled that New York's inheritance law was constitutionally permitted, as discussed in the previous answer, the legislature changed the law shortly afterward so that now fathers can pass their estate to their illegitimate children if they obtain an order of filiation within ten years of the child's birth (not two years, as the old law required) *or* if they sign an instrument acknowledging paternity, provided it is witnessed and filed according to law.[51]

—be it his child, friend, or chambermaid—or to any organization or charity he desires. Thus a father can designate an illegitimate child as the beneficiary of his estate just as he can designate anyone else. (In some states, however, the law requires that a certain percentage of a person's estate must be given to his surviving spouse or children even if the will directs otherwise.)

If the mother of an illegitimate child dies because of the fault or negligence of another person, does the illegitimate child have the right to sue the other person?

Yes. The U.S. Supreme Court answered this question in 1968 in the first of many cases that overturned long-standing laws discriminating against illegitimate children. In that case, entitled *Levy* v. *Louisiana*,[52] a woman was killed because of the negligence of another person. Generally, children of parents wrongfully killed by another are permitted to sue to recover the damages they have suffered because of the death. However, a law in Louisiana, where this woman lived, prohibited her child from suing the negligent person because her child was illegitimate. The Supreme Court found that law unconstitutional, because, it stated: "It is invidious to discriminate against [illegitimates] when no action, conduct or demeanor of theirs is possibly relevant to the harm that was done the mother."

While the *Levy* decision is viewed as a landmark case in establishing the rights of illegitimate children, it can be seen as furthering the rights of *parents* of illegitimate children as well. In fact, on the same day the Supreme Court ruled on the *Levy* case, it handed down another decision essentially upholding this very proposition. It is discussed next.

If an illegitimate child dies because of the negligence or fault of another, does the mother have the right to sue the person who caused her child's death?

Yes. For exactly the same reasons discussed in the *Levy* case, the U.S. Supreme Court has ruled that the right to recover damages extends not only to the illegitimate child (if his or her mother is wrongfully killed), but the child's *mother* as well, so that she has a right to sue the negligent person and seek monetary damages for the wrongful death of her illegitimate child, exactly like parents of a legitimate child.[53]

Does the father of an illegitimate child have the right to recover for the wrongful death of his child and does the child have the right to recover for the wrongful death of his or her father?

There is no blanket answer to this question, for the same reasons as those mentioned above in the discussion of the right of illegitimate children to *inherit* from their father. The problem revolves around establishing proof of paternity, and states have different requirements for this proof, such as acknowledgment or judicial orders of paternity. Of course, some states have no requirements at all. In any event, if the conditions of proof of fatherhood have been met, according to the particular state law, the right of an illegitimate child to bring suit to recover damages for the wrongful death of his or her father and the right of a father to sue for the wrongful death of his illegitimate child is secure.

The U.S. Supreme Court recently held, however, that if the father has *not* legitimized the child during the child's lifetime, it is not unconstitutional for a state to deny the father the right to sue for the wrongful death of the child.[54]

What about Social Security benefits? Can illegitimate children receive them from their parents?

Yes, but certain requirements must be met. Any child can inherit Social Security support through insured parents if the child is under eighteen (or under twenty-two for a full-time student). The child must also be dependent at the time of the parent's death. A child is considered "dependent," as defined in the Social Security Act, if the insured parent was living with the child or contributing to the child's support at the time of the parent's death.

Legitimate children do not have to prove their "dependency" in order to receive Social Security benefits, but illegitimate children must do so, *unless* (1) they were adopted by the deceased, (2) their parents married each other after the child was born, (3) the father acknowledged in writing that the child was his, (4) the father was declared the father by a court or was ordered by a court

to pay support for the child, or (5) the child was entitled
to inherit from the father under the state law governing
intestate inheritance.[55]

Even though the Social Security Act does not require
legitimate children to prove their "dependency," the Supreme Court ruled that this difference does not discriminate
against illegitimate children since the distinction is a "reasonable" one, related to the administration of the Social
Security Act.[56]

**If a parent of an illegitimate child is injured or killed
on the job, does his or her Workmen's Compensation
benefits go to the child?**

Yes. Laws restricting the right of illegitimate children
to claim Workmen's Compensation benefits have been declared illegal by the U.S. Supreme Court.[57] The purpose
of Workmen's Compensation, the Supreme Court ruled,
is to provide for the future of a person's dependents.
Therefore, laws that deny illegitimate children the right
to such support unnecessarily interfere with this purpose
and are unconstitutional.

Apparently, proof of paternity has not been as problem-
atic to the Supreme Court for Workmen's Compensation
cases as it has been in inheritance and wrongful-death
cases. The law that the Supreme Court ruled unconstitutional said that illegitimate children could not receive
Workmen's Compensation benefits from their father unless he acknowledged them as his children before he died
or was injured. It may therefore be presumed that an
illegitimate child can receive Workmen's Compensation
benefits from his or her mother and *father,* without first
having to satisfy complex acknowledgment or paternity
requirements.

**How does the government classify illegitimate children
of noncitizens for immigration purposes?**

Under the Immigration and Nationality Act of 1957, a
child or a parent of a United States citizen or a lawful
permanent resident is granted a "special preference" for
immigration and labor purposes.[58] However, the act grants
special preference only to parents of legitimate children
and to mothers—not fathers—of illegitimate children.
Therefore, the father of an illegitimate child who is a

United States citizen or a permanent resident alien is not entitled to special preference as a parent. This distinction was recently reviewed by the U.S. Supreme Court and found to be constitutional.[59]

May states punish a man for fathering a child out of wedlock and failing to provide support for the child?

Many states have so-called "bastardy statutes" in their criminal codes which permit such punishment. In recent years, however, attempts to enforce these statutes have been declared unconstitutional because they contravene the equal protection of the laws since *mothers* of illegitimate children are not subject to such punishment.[60]

NOTES

1. CAL. CIV. CODE §7004; CAL. PROB. CODE §255; N.Y. DOM. REL. LAW §24; FLA. STAT. ANN. §742.091; CONN. GEN. STAT. ANN. §45–274; MICH. CONSOL. LAWS ANN. §702.83.
2. ILL. REV. STAT. ch. 3, §12; MASS. GEN. LAWS ANN., ch. 190, §57.
3. ALA. CODE tit. 26, §11–2; WIS. STAT. ANN. §237.06; MICH. CONSOL. LAWS ANN. §702.83.
4. Meyer v. Nebraska, 262 U.S. 390 (1923).
5. Prince v. Massachusetts, 321 U.S. 158 (1944).
6. *See, e.g.,* People *ex rel.* Meredith v. Meredith, 272 App. Div. 79, 69 N.Y.S.2d 462 (2nd Dept, 1947), *aff'd.* 297 N.Y. 692, 77 N.E.2d (1947); Salk v. Salk, 89 Misc.2d 883, 393 N.Y.S.2d 84 (Sup. Ct.), *aff'd.* 53 A.D.2d 558, 385 N.Y.S.2d 1015 (1st Dept. 1976).
7. *E.g., In re* G.K. 248 N.W.2d 380 (S.D. 1977); Hyatte v. Lopez, 366 N.E.2d 676 (Ind. App. Ct. 1977); Boatwright v. Otero, 91 Misc.2d 653, 398 N.Y.S.2d 391 (Fam. Ct. 1977).
8. *See, e.g.,* Commonwealth *ex rel.* Gifford v. Miller, 213 Pa. Super. 269, 248 A.2d 63 (1968); *In re* H., 305 N.E.2d 815 (Ohio 1973). *But see, contra, In re* Mark T., 8 Mich. App. 122, 154 N.W.2d 27 (1967).
9. Caban v. Mohammed, 441 U.S. 380, 60 L. Ed.2d 297 (1979).
10. Stanley v. Illinois, 405 U.S. 645 (1972).
11. *See, e.g., In re* Guardianship of Smith, 42 Cal.2d 91, 265 P.2d 888 (1954); People *ex rel.* Francois v. Ivaneva, 14 A.D.2d 317, 221 N.Y.S.2d 75 (1st Dept. 1961); Slade v.

Dennis (Utah S. Ct.), in 5 Fam. L. Rptr. 2719 (April 19, 1979); Griffith v. Gibson, 73 Cal. App.3d 293, 142 Cal. Rptr. 176 (Ct. App. 1977).

12. Levy v. Louisiana, 391 U.S. 68 (1968).

13. See, e.g., Commonwealth v. Rozanski, 206 Pa. Super. 397, 213 A.2d 155 (1965); Mixon v. Mize, 198 So.2d 373 (Fla. Ct. App. 1967).

14. Stanley v. Illinois, supra note 10; Elmore v. Elmore, 5 Ill. Dec. 292, 361 N.E.2d 615 (1977); Irby v. Dubois, 354 N.E.2d 62 (Ill. App. 1977).

15. See, e.g., Caban v. Mohammed, supra note 9.

16. See, e.g., Quilloin v. Walcott, 434 U.S. 246 (1978).

17. Mich. Comp. Laws Ann. §710.33(3). Other states with similar statutes include: Colorado, Connecticut, Illinois, Indiana, Maine, Massachusetts, Minnesota, Nebraska, Nevada, New Mexico, New York, North Carolina, Oregon, South Dakota, Utah, Vermont, and West Virginia.

18. See, e.g., Caban v. Mohammed, supra note 9.

19. See, e.g., Quilloin v. Walcott, supra note 16.

20. Stanley v. Illinois, supra note 10; Caban v. Mohammed, supra note 9.

21. State ex rel. J.D.S. v. Edwards, 574 S.W.2d 405 (Mo. 1978).

22. Quilloin v. Walcott, supra note 16.

23. Caban v. Mohammed, supra note 9.

24. See, e.g., Parham v. Hughes, 441 U.S. 347, 60 L. Ed.2d 269 (1979).

25. See, e.g., Comish v. Smith, 540 P.2d 274 (Idaho 1975). Kansas, New York, and Pennsylvania are among the states which deny a right to trial by jury in paternity actions.

26. E.g., Salas v. Cortez, (Calif. Sup. Ct.), 5 Fam. L. Rptr. 2555; Reynolds v. Kimmons, 569 P.2d 799 (Alaska 1977); Artiber v. Cheboygan Circuit Judge, 397 Mich. 54, 243 N.W.2d 248 (1976). But see State v. Walker, 553 P.2d 1093 (Wash. 1976); Miller v. Gordon, 58 A.D.2d 1097, 397 N.Y.S.2d 500 (4th Dept. 1977).

27. E.g. Artibee v. Cheboygan Circuit Judge, supra note 26; Reynolds v. Kimmons, supra note 26.

28. See, e.g., N.Y. Fam. Ct. Act, §532.

29. See, e.g., Dodd v. Henkel, 148 Cal. Rptr. 780 (Ct. App. 1978).

30. Gomez v. Perez, 409 U.S. 535 (1973).

31. Taylor v. Richardson, 354 F. Supp. 13 (La. 1973).

32. Md. Ann. Code Art 16, §66 F (b); see also Taylor v. Richardson, 354 F. Supp. 13 (D. La. 1973).

33. Hanson v. Hanson, 249 N.W.2d 452 (Minn. 1977); see

also N.C. Gen. Stat. §8–50.1; Anonymous v. Anonymous, 1 A.D.2d 312, 150 N.Y.S.2d 344 (1st Dept. 1956).

34. *See, e.g.,* Johannesen v. Pfeiffer, 387 A.2d 1113 (Me. 1978).

35. *See, e.g.,* Donald J. v. Erma M.W., 147 Cal. Rptr. 15 (Ct. App. 1978).

36. *In re* R., 13 Cal.3d 636, 532 P.2d 123 (1975).

37. New Jersey Welfare Rights Org. v. Cahill, 411 U.S. 619 (1973).

38. L. Platky, Aid to Families with Dependent Children: An Overview 17 (Social Security Bulletin, Oct. 1977).

39. *See* King v. Smith, 392 U.S. 309 (1968).

40. 42 U.S.C. §654.

41. 42 U.S.C. §602(a)(26)(B); Doe v. Norton, 365 F. Supp. 65 (D. Conn. 1973), *vacated* 422 U.S. 391 (1975).

42. 43 Fed. Reg. 2170 (1978); 45 C.F.R. §232.13.

43. 45 C.F.R., §213.

44. 42 U.S.C. §602; Doe v. Norton, *supra* note 41.

45. Doe v. Norton, *supra* note 41.

46. 42 U.S.C. §§651–660.

47. Wyman v. James, 400 U.S. 309 (1971).

48. Trimble v. Gordon, 430 U.S. 762 (1977).

49. *See also* Labine v. Vincent, 401 U.S. 532 (1971).

50. Lalli v. Lalli, 439 U.S. 259 (1978).

51. N.Y. Est., Powers & Trusts Law, §4–1.2.

52. *Supra* note 12.

53. Glona v. American Guar. & Liab. Ins. Co. 391 U.S. 73 (1968).

54. Parham v. Hughes, *supra* note 24.

55. 42 U.S.C., §§402(d)(1), (d)(3); 416(h)(2), (h)(3) (1974).

56. Matthews v. Lucas, 427 U.S. 495 (1976). *But see* Davis v. Richardson, 342 F. Supp. 588 (D. Conn. 1972), *aff'd.* 409 U.S. 1069, *and* Griffin v. Richardson, 346 F. Supp. 1226 (D. Md. 1972), *aff'd.* 409 U.S. 1069 (1972).

57. Weber v. Aetna Cas. & Sur. Co., 400 U.S. 164 (1972).

58. 8 U.S.C., §§1101(b)(1)(D), (b)(2).

59. Fiallo v. Bell, 430 U.S. 787 (1977).

60. *See, e.g.,* Walker v. Stokes, 375 N.E.2d 1258 (Ohio App. 1978); Commonwealth v. MacKenzie, 334 N.E.2d 613 (Mass. 1975).

IX

Foster Parents

What is a foster parent?

There is no strict or universal definition. Generally, a foster parent can be any adult temporarily living with a child in place of the actual parent. It might be a relative or a stranger. The foster parent may have obtained temporary custody of the child by mutual agreement with the actual parent. Alternatively, the foster parent may have been given temporary custody by a state-licensed child-care agency or by virtue of a family- or juvenile-court decision.

A person who has extremely limited and short-lived custody, such as a baby-sitter or a relative taking care of a child whose parents are on a two-week vacation, is not considered a foster parent. Foster care is commonly used to mean family-type (noninstitutional) substitute parental care for a limited period when the child's actual parent is unable to provide care, but where adoption is not involved.[1]

What is a foster home?

There are many types of foster homes serving different functions. There are emergency or crisis homes, which receive children on very short notice for short-term care, perhaps only a few days, pending a court hearing. Children who are removed from their parents on an emergency basis typically are placed in this type of foster home.

Family-group homes, housing six to eight children living with a set of foster parents, are another type of foster home. This arrangement is most likely used for older children, including adolescents.

How do children come into foster care?

Children can come into foster care in a variety of ways. They may have been ordered in placement by a court because the parents are suspected or have been judicially found to have neglected or abused the children, or because the children have been found to be delinquent or in need of supervision. More commonly, children come into care because parents voluntarily place them there temporarily. This could happen for any number of reasons—parents' poor health, emotional illness, dire economic circumstances, drug or alcohol problems, or imprisonment. There are about 350,000 children in foster care on any given day in the United States.

Is foster care meant to be only temporary?

In most cases, yes. The foster parent-child relationship is designed to be a temporary relationship intended to provide the child with the benefits of a family setting (instead of institutional care) when placement out of the parental home is necessary. The ultimate goal is to reunite the child with his or her parents or, if necessary, to place the child in a permanent, adoptive relationship.

But this theoretical model frequently does not square with actual practice. Very often children are kept in foster care for many years longer than necessary.[2] As a result of remaining with the same foster family over a period of years, children and foster parents often develop very deep emotional attachments.

Do foster parents have any rights with respect to their foster children?

Yes. Although the social-services or child-care agency technically maintains the "care and custody" of the child, the responsibility for the day-to-day supervision of the child is upon the foster parents. As a result, foster parents have responsibility for and the right to make decisions on behalf of the child concerning such things as food, clothing, shelter, minor medical care, bedtime, etc. However, these rights are markedly less broad than those of natural parents. Thus the social-services agency may place restrictions on what the foster parents may do with the child—restrictions that could not be placed on natural parents. Examples of these restrictions include prohibiting corporal punishment, limiting the right of the family to move without agency approval, and restricting the right of the family to educate a foster child in a religious school if the natural parents object.[3]

What rights to the custody of foster children do foster parents have?

The answer to this question depends on the kind of foster parent involved. For example, foster parents who have been given children by actual parents and who have had custody of them for several years stand in a significantly different legal position than foster parents given a child by a child-care agency for two months while the mother recovers from an operation.

Foster parents who are given children for a temporary period by an officially recognized child-care agency usually are told before getting custody that the agency retains the right to return the child to the natural parents or even to place the child with another set of foster parents. In some states, at least ten days' notice must be given before the child will be removed (unless the foster parents are themselves suspected of abusing or harming the child, in which case removal may be immediate.)[4]

In most states, however, foster parents have virtually no rights to keep a child longer than the agency allows, or any due process rights, such as notice or a hearing, before the agency removes the child.

This is usually justified in three ways. First, foster care is designed to be temporary, with the ultimate purpose of reuniting the child with his or her parents. Second, it is the *agency*, and not the foster parents, that is legally responsible for the protection of the child.[5] Third, at the time that the foster parents are given custody by the agency, they often sign contracts expressly recognizing that the placement is temporary and that the agency making the placement retains the legal authority to remove the child upon notice at any time.

Can a child-care agency remove a child from foster parents on the ground that the foster parents and the child are developing too great an attachment for each other?

Yes. Since foster care is designed to provide a homelike setting for the *temporary* care of a child, with a view of ultimately reuniting the child with the natural parents, agencies will frequently remove children from one foster home into another when foster parents "become too emotionally involved with the child." [6]

Is an agreement between foster parents and a child-care agency that the foster parents will not adopt the foster child enforceable in court?

Usually, but courts may allow the adoption notwithstanding the existence of such an agreement. Since courts attempt to do what is in the best interests of the child in an adoption proceeding, foster parents, who initially had agreed not to adopt when they took the child into their home, have sometimes been allowed to adopt if the child has stayed in their home for a significant amount of time.[7]

Are foster parents given a preference to adopt once the children are adoptable?

Not necessarily. Because the agency usually has legal custody of the children and places them only temporarily with foster parents, the agency is allowed to choose the adoptive parents. Frequently, agencies give children to one set of foster parents for temporary foster care and then choose a different couple to adopt. A few states, however, give a statutory "preference" to foster parents to adopt the foster children who have remained in their home for at least eighteen months or two years.[8] California grants a preference for custody (and, ultimately, adoption) to the "person or persons in whose home the child has been living in a wholesome and stable environment," if it finds that return of custody to the natural parents will be detrimental to the child.[9]

Because foster care is temporary, agencies use different criteria in selecting prospective foster parents than for choosing prospective adoptive parents. Criteria for temporary foster parents concern such things as ability to provide a safe and healthy environment. For adoptive parents, however, other factors are included—the psychological characteristics of the parents, financial ability, the size of the family, as well as the race, age, and religion of the parents.

Can an agency refuse to allow an adoption by foster parents merely because, in the agency's view, the foster parents are too old?

Yes. The wide latitude to determine the child's best interests may permit blocking an adoption on the basis of the age of the foster parents.[10]

Do foster parents have the right to adopt their foster children after a period of time?

They have the right to *attempt* to adopt their foster children by legal means, but of course they have no guarantee of success. If the natural parents are still the legal parents, no adoption can take place until they give their permission or their parental rights are involuntarily terminated. Generally, the legal standard for terminating parental rights is severe due to the fundamental right of family integrity (see Chapters I and VI).

(As discussed earlier, however, there is a growing trend to allow an adoption, and to terminate parental rights, when it is found that doing so is in the child's best interests. This trend allows for what may be called no-fault termination of parental rights. The most common situation in which courts enter no-fault terminations is when children have lived with new parents for a significant period of time and consider the foster parents to be their "real" parents or their only parents. In these circumstances, some courts have permitted an adoption even where the natural parents are not unfit and have not abandoned the children. Thus, when the no-fault theory applies, the longer foster parents retain custody, the greater likelihood they will be permitted to adopt the children.)

Surprisingly, it is often the child-care agency that opposes adoption by the foster parents. For other than privately arranged foster care, the public child-welfare agency retains legal custody of children while in foster care, and they have the responsibility for making long-term decisions about the child's future. It is only recently that courts have been willing to overrule agency decisions. Nonetheless, an agency's view on the propriety of foster parents adopting still carries great weight in court proceedings.[11]

For example, one court held that an agency had the power to remove a child from one set of foster parents and place the child for adoption by a second set of parents. The foster parents from whose home the child was removed objected to the proposed adoption and sought to adopt the child themselves. The court had little difficulty siding with the agency on the strength of a state law that stated, "where a parent or parents place a child with an agency, only the prospective parents selected by the agency may adopt that child." [12]

Can foster parents who were given temporary custody of children directly by the natural parents continue to retain custody of the children over the objection of the parents?

Perhaps. After a period of time, usually at least several years, foster parents who may be regarded as the "psychological parents" [13] of the children may be awarded custody of the children by the court's finding this arrangement to be in the child's best interests.[14]

Do foster parents have a right to appear in every judicial proceeding concerning their foster children?

Some, but probably not all. In a very few states, once children have been in the custody of foster parents for a certain period, such as eighteen months, they have a right to intervene in any proceedings concerning the children.[15] One court recently denied the request of foster parents of ten years to appear as parties in a proceeding in which the natural mother sought return of her child. The court recognized that the foster parents "hold the same place in [the child's] emotional life . . . as a natural family." Nonetheless, because their legal relationship with their foster child was limited by the contract between the agency and the foster parents, they were not allowed to appear as parties to the action.[16]

Do foster parents have a right to a hearing before an agency removes a child from their custody, even when the child is being moved to a different foster family and not home to the natural parents?

No, not as a matter of constitutional right.[17] Some states, however, grant foster parents this right by statute, regulation, or court decision.[18]

Can foster parents challenge the decision of the agency to remove the child? If so, how?

Yes. Even if foster parents do not have the right to a hearing, they may sue in court by writ of *habeas corpus* to challenge the agency decision. This is not to suggest that the foster parent will succeed. It is important to recognize, however, that the agency decision can be challenged and reviewed by a court.

Are there risks if foster parents refuse to comply with an instruction by the agency to give it custody of the children?

Yes. In some states it is a crime, known as custodial interference, punishable by imprisonment, for foster parents to deliberately fail to surrender a child at the demand of the social-services agency.

Is periodic court review of foster-care arrangements constitutionally required?

The answer is uncertain. It is certain that there is no constitutional requirement to review foster-care arrangements more frequently than every eighteen months. In a case that challenged the New York scheme of reviewing the foster-care arrangement of each child every eighteen months, the U.S. Supreme Court upheld the practice.[19] But it is unclear if New York's schedule is required as a minimum.

Do foster parents have a right to appear in court in a review proceeding?

The few states that provide for review by statute also allow foster parents to appear. The U.S. Supreme Court has not decided the question of whether the right to appear is a constitutional one.

Do courts generally monitor the placement of children in foster care?

No. Because the social-services agency is legally charged with, and presumed to be acting in, the best interests of the child, courts and legislatures have rarely deemed it necessary to protect children from needless shifting from one foster home to another. Similarly, they have not required review of the length of time a child stays in foster status, before being returned to their natural parents or adopted by new parents.

Recent recognition that children have been harmed by needless prolongation of foster care has led a number of states to require periodic judicial review of the status of children in foster care.[20] In addition, Congress has passed laws that require states to continually supervise the care of children in foster care and periodically review the necessity of retaining each child in foster care and the appropriateness of the care being provided.[21]

Do local or state governments make any effort to monitor the placements of children in foster care other than by periodic court review?

Only a very few jurisdictions have established mechanisms for investigating complaints. In New York City, for example, the Department of Social Services created a Parents' Rights Unit to monitor placements and to help parents maintain relationships with children in foster care. Illinois and Texas also have special units to investigate complaints by parents or others concerning children in placement.

May children be placed in foster care out of state?

Yes. But the practice is coming under increasing attack, and states are beginning to curtail out-of-state placements.[22]

Do foster parents receive payments for taking care of children?

Yes. If foster parents obtain temporary custody of the child from a social-services agency, they will be paid for caring for the child.

What is AFDC–FC?

The Aid to Families with Dependent Children–Foster Care (AFDC–FC) program authorizes federal financial subsidies for the care and support of children who have been removed from their homes and made wards of the state, when a court has determined that their homes do not provide for their welfare.[23]

Are children who are living in foster homes of relatives entitled to AFDC–FC payments?

Yes. The U.S. Supreme Court has recently held that states may not exclude from AFDC–FC those children living with relatives. This is because such a law would conflict with Congress' preference that children who need foster care be cared for by relatives when feasible.[24]

Do natural parents retain any rights with respect to their children in foster care?

Yes. Parents who have not permanently given up custody of their children retain the power to make decisions for their children such as consent for nonemergency surgery [25] and their religious training.

Do natural parents have any responsibility for their children in foster care?

Yes. They have the obligation to visit their children and to plan for their future; failure to do this can result in a court order terminating parental rights.[26]

Do natural parents who have voluntarily placed their children in temporary foster care have the right to have their children returned to them on demand?

When parents have voluntarily placed their child in temporary foster care, a few states provide that they have a right to the return of the child on demand.[27] But when the department or agency does not want a child returned, it may file a petition in court alleging that the natural parents are unfit. (See Chapter VI.) Often when this is done, the natural parents are unsuccessful in obtaining speedy return of their children, and, at times, they are unsuccessful in securing their return at all.[28]

May a claim for custody by the natural parents be defeated if the foster parents show that returning the child to the natural parents will not be in the child's best interests?

In a few states, yes.[29] But in most states which give strong emphasis to the rights of natural parents, courts require a finding that, at the least, the child will be harmed if he or she is returned to the natural parents before they will allow foster parents to retain custody.[30]

NOTES

1. *See, e.g.,* Smith v. Organization of Foster Families for Equality and Reform, 431 U.S. 816 (1977).
2. Fanshel, *The Exit of Children from Foster Care: An Interim Research Report,* 50 CHILD WELFARE 65 (1971); Smith v. O.F.F.E.R., *supra* note 1.
3. KADUSHIN, CHILD WELFARE SERVICES 394–95 (1967).
4. *E.g.,* 18 N.Y.C.R.R. §450.10(a).
5. Smith v. O.F.F.E.R., *supra* note 1.
6. *In re* Jewish Child Care Ass'n, 5 N.Y.2d 222, 156 N.E.2d 700 (1959).
7. *See, e.g.,* Knight v. Dewers, 531 S.W.2d 252 (Ark. 1976); *In re* Adoption by Alexander, 206 So.2d 452 (App. Div. Fla. 1968).
8. N.Y. SOC. SERV. LAW §§374(1)(a), 383(3); MD. ANN. CODE art. 16 §75.
9. CAL. CIV. CODE §4600.
10. *See, e.g.,* Frantum v. Department of Pub. Welfare, 214 Md. 100, 133 A.2d 408 (1957), *cert. denied* 355 U.S. 882 (age of foster parents, 54 and 48); Bledsoe v. Dept. of Human Resources, 241 S.E.2d 304 (Ga. App. 1977).
11. *See, e.g.,* Drummond v. Fulton County Dept. of Family and Children's Serv., 563 F.2d 1200 (5th Cir. 1977) (*en banc*); Kyees v. County Dept. of Pub. Welfare, 600 F.2d 693 (7th Cir. 1979).
12. *In re* Adoption of Runyon, 268 Cal. App.2d 918, 74 Cal. Rptr. 514 (Ct. of App., 3d Dist. 1969).
13. *See* GOLDSTEIN, FREUD & SOLNIT, BEYOND THE BEST INTERESTS OF THE CHILD (1973).
14. *See, e.g.,* Bennett v. Jeffries, 40 N.Y.2d 543, 356 N.E.2d 277 (1976); Painter v. Bannister, 258 Iowa 1390, 140 N.W.2d 152; *cert. denied* 358 U.S. 949 (1966).
15. N.Y. SOC. SERV. LAW §383(3); CONN. GEN. STAT. ANN. §17–66c.
16. *In re* E.G., 268 N.W.2d 420 (Minn. 1978); *contra,* Doe v. State Dept. of Human Serv., 398 A.2d 562 (N.J. App. Div. 1979).
17. Smith v. O.F.F.E.R., *supra* note 1.
18. *E.g.,* C.V.C. v. Superior Court, 29 Cal. App.3d 909, 106 Cal. Rptr. 123 (1973); Doe v. State Dept. of Human Serv., 398 A.2d 562 (N.J. App. Div. 1979).
19. Smith v. O.F.F.E.R., *supra* note 1.

20. *See, e.g.,* N.Y. Soc. Serv. Law §392(2); 37 Ill. Ann. Stat. §701–20(2).
21. 42 U.S.C. §§608(a)(2), (f)(1); 45 C.F.R. §§220.19(b), (c), 233.110(a)(1)(ii)(1977).
22. *See, e.g.,* In Interest of V.M.C., 369 So.2d 660 (Fla. App. 1979); Sinhogar v. Parry, 412 N.Y.S.2d 966 (Sup. Ct. N.Y. Cty. 1979).
23. 42 U.S.C. §608(a)(1).
24. Miller v. Youakim, 440 U.S. 125 (1979).
25. Kadushin, *supra* note 3, at 355.
26. *See, e.g.,* N.Y. Soc. Serv. Law §§384–b(4), 384–b(7).
27. *E.g.,* Cal. Welf. & Inst. Code §16552.
28. *E.g., In re* Juvenile Appeal (Anonymous) v. Commissioner of Children and Youth Serv., 40 Conn. L.J. 50, —— A.2d —— (1979); *In re* New England Home for Little Wanderers, 367 Mass. 788, 328 N.E.2d 854 (1975).
29. *See, e.g., In re* Juvenile Appeal (Anonymous) v. Commissioner, *supra* note 28; Ross v. Hoffman, 33 Md. App. 333, 364 A.2d 596 (1976): *In re* New England Home for Little Wanderers, *supra* note 28; *In re* J.S.R., 374 A.2d 860 (D.C. App. 1977); *In re* J. & J.W., 134 Vt. 480, 365 A.2d 521 (1976).
30. *See, e.g., In re* B.G., 11 Cal.3d 679, 523 P.2d 244, 114 Cal. Rptr. 444 (1944); Bennett v. Jeffries, *supra* note 14; *In re* LaRue, 244 Pa. Super. 218, 366 A.2d 1271 (1976).

X

Adoptive Parents

What is an adoption?

An adoption is a procedure by which an adult and child become legally related to each other in the same respect as birth parents and children.

In order to effectuate this new legal relationship, the law goes so far as to "falsify" the original birth certificate of the child by creating a new one which lists the adoptive mother and father as the parents who gave birth to the child.

How can a child be adopted?

Any child to be adopted, whether born in or out of wedlock, must be "freed" for adoption by both natural parents. Generally there are two methods for freeing a minor child for adoption during the lives of his natural parents: by voluntary termination (parental consent) or by involuntary termination of parental rights.

What is involuntary termination of parental rights?

Involuntary termination of parental rights is discussed in detail in Chapter VI. In brief, parental rights may be terminated for persistent child neglect, parental unfitness, or abandonment of children. Termination of parental rights results in the permanent severance of all aspects of the parent-child relationship. Once their rights have been terminated, parents are no longer responsible for child support and lose all rights to child custody and visitation. They also lose the right to consent to their child's adoption; thus, their child may be adopted by others without their consent or approval.

What is voluntary termination of parental rights?

This is more commonly known as voluntarily surrendering a child for adoption. Once surrendered, a child may be adopted by others.

What happens to a child whose parents' parental rights have been terminated?

Until the child is adopted, such a child becomes a ward of the state. If the child is surrendered to the custody of a licensed child-care agency, the child becomes a ward of the agency. The child has no parents but does have a guardian. The legal status of the child is similar to that of an orphan, except that an orphan is likely to have living relatives. As a rule, once parental rights are terminated, whether by voluntary or involuntary means, no legal relationship exists between the parents and the child or between the relatives of the parents and the child.

May a child be adopted without the termination of rights of the natural parents?

No. If the natural parents do not consent to the adoption, thereby voluntarily terminating their parental rights, their child may not be adopted unless their relationship with their child is involuntarily severed by court order.

As discussed earlier, involuntary termination may be ordered only where the parent has abandoned the child or is unfit. However, four states (Arizona, Maryland, Massachusetts, and Virginia) and the District of Columbia permit adoptions to take place without the consent of the parents if a court rules that such consent is being withheld contrary to the best interests of the child.[1] As discussed in Chapter VI, the constitutionality of such laws is questionable.

How does one adopt a child?

There are two types of adoptions: agency and private. In some states only agency adoptions are permitted and all private adoptions are prohibited except by stepparents or blood relatives.[2]

What is an agency adoption?

Agency adoptions are handled through state-licensed adoptive agencies or state offices authorized to place children for adoption. In an agency adoption the child usually has been surrendered by the natural parents, but agencies may also receive children by court order after the involuntary termination of parental rights.

Parents who wish to adopt a child simply make an application to adoption agencies. They may or may not be foster parents at the time they apply. After receiving an application, the agency will interview and investigate the prospective adoptive parents in order to determine whether they are appropriate candidates. In the last several years the demand to adopt very young children has been much greater than the available supply. Accordingly, agencies have a large pool of people from which to choose a relatively small number of adoptive parents.

Having an overabundance of people from whom to choose, agencies are highly selective in making their decisions. Moreover, they may make many of their decisions in arbitrary ways. Some agencies give a preference to young couples (under forty years of age)[3] who have been married for several years and are of the same religion. Many agencies require that the couple have no children; some even require that they provide medical evidence that they cannot have their own children.

Adults who do not fit within such rigid schemes may, nevertheless, adopt children from agencies, but they may not be able to adopt healthy infants or very young children. There are many children eligible for adoption who are not adopted. These are usually older, nonwhite, or handicapped children.

What is a private adoption?

For those people who do not want to adopt a child through an agency, or for those who have not been successful with an agency, the alternative route to adoption is through private channels. Private adoptions are arranged by prospective adoptive parents either directly with natural parents or through nonlicensed intermediaries such as doctors, lawyers, relatives, or friends. Approximately one-quarter of all adoptions by nonrelatives in the United

States are arranged privately.[4] However, as previously stated, private adoptions have been made illegal in some states.

Private adoptions are usually arranged through lawyers and doctors. Gynecologists are considered by many to be excellent sources for adoptions because pregnant women who decide to give birth or who waited too long to obtain a legal abortion but who wish to give up their children for adoption frequently discuss the situation with their gynecologists. Occasionally, lawyers who are known in their community to arrange adoptions may be contacted by pregnant women or by doctors whose patients wish to surrender their children upon birth.

Why have private adoptions been outlawed in some states?

Private adoptions have been prohibited to reduce the possibility of extortion in unduly pressuring a mother to surrender her child. Additionally, opponents of private adoptions believe that requiring agency adoptions will provide greater assurance that the adoptive home will meet minimal state standards and thereby further the goal of having children raised adequately.

On the other hand, proponents of private adoptions point out that the private route often is better for the child since the adoption is completed much closer to the actual birth than is an agency adoption. Besides, proponents assert that private adoptions provide an important alternative for those persons deemed unacceptable by agency standards.

What are "gray-market adoptions"?

Because of the high demand for adoptable infants, many doctors and lawyers have found adoption to be a highly lucrative business. Couples have been known to spend twenty-five thousand dollars and more to adopt a child. The term "gray-market adoptions" refers to those adoptions in which the mother is being paid money to surrender her child for adoption. In a gray-market adoption, it is common for the mother, doctor, and lawyer to profit handsomely from what is the equivalent of baby-selling. Because it is not clear that the mother would have agreed to surrender her child (or even to have given birth in the first place) except for the payment of a substantial amount of money, such adoptions are considered repugnant to public policy.

Are gray-market adoptions illegal?

In most states, yes.[5] Generally, if the mother receives payment for more than her medical services, or if the intermediary who arranges the adoption receives payment greater than required for expenses and a nominal fee, it is a crime. But state officials are more likely to be interested in punishing the professionals involved than the adoptive parents.[6] Thus, when evidence is found that an unlawful payment was made for an adoption, the state usually will not remove the child from the adoptive parents.

In states that prohibit private adoptions except those made by the parents, is it illegal for a doctor or a lawyer to be an intermediary?

Not necessarily. In most states, it is illegal for doctors and lawyers to arrange for the adoption and *physically* hand over the child to the adoptive parents. It is the physical transfer that violates the law. In states that authorize only a parent, relative, or licensed agency to make an adoption placement, doctors or lawyers may still be permitted to play an important role in the adoption. But if the doctor or lawyer gets too involved and actually chooses the adoptive family and personally turns over the child, this would violate the law.[7]

Do natural parents have the right to choose who will adopt their child?

Not necessarily. If parental rights have been terminated involuntarily or if the parent has surrendered the child to the state or a licensed child-care agency, the parent's choice as to who should adopt the child will not be determinative. The agency or the court, in its role as surrogate parent, will decide which adoptive family will serve the child's best interests. The power of the state is so great that even if the child has lived with a particular foster family for several years, the agency or court may decide that adoption by that family is inappropriate.[8] Even when a *private* placement is made and the parents personally place the child with a new set of parents, the adoption must be approved by a court, with the standard for approval being the child's best interests.

If a child has been surrendered for adoption to a child-care agency, may the child be adopted by persons not of the agency's choosing?

It depends on the state. In some states, a refusal by an agency to give consent to adoptive parents it did not choose has been deemed an absolute bar to the adoption by those prospective parents.[9] In other states, courts have held that the agency's refusal does not prohibit a court from deciding the matter differently.[10]

May the parent who surrenders a child for adoption insist that the child be raised in a particular religion?

In many states, yes. In these states, parents who have surrendered their children for adoption with the promise or understanding that they will be raised according to a particular religious faith, have been allowed to *revoke* their consent to the adoption on the ground that the children were to be adopted by parents of a different religion.[11]

If children become eligible for adoption, do foster parents who have cared for them for a long period of time have a right to adopt them?

Not necessarily. It is common practice in many states for foster parents to sign an agreement upon first receiving a child from an agency that they will not try to adopt their foster child. Even when they have not signed such a form, and the child later becomes eligible for adoption, the agency or a court retains the power to determine whether permanent adoption by the foster couple should be allowed.

Practically, if foster care has been for a long period of time, and if the child considers his or her foster parents as "psychological parents," these will be factors favoring the adoption by the foster parents. But the adoption still may be disallowed, and the child may be removed from the home of the foster parents, if factors such as race, health, age, or any other condition such as problems in the family, lead a court to the conclusion that the adoption is not in the child's best interests.[12]

Why is it that foster parents, who have temporary custody of children, may not be granted the right to adopt them?

When the state or child-care agency has the responsibility to find an adoptive home for a child, a search for a permanent home will begin. This search usually takes time. Recognizing that children have continuing needs that are best met by loving adults in a setting comparable to a family, agencies usually try to place children *temporarily* in a foster home until it has decided which family should take the child on a permanent, adoptive basis.

Foster parents also are frequently relied upon when the state has temporary care of a child and it is expected that the child will ultimately be returned to the natural parents. In these circumstances, it is generally understood at the outset that the child may be removed from the foster parents at any time.

The criteria used for temporary foster care are different from those used for permanent care. Agencies are less selective in choosing foster parents than in choosing adoptive parents. Any family capable of giving love and comfort to a child on a temporary basis will be considered eligible foster parents. For an adoption, however, agencies seek a more "perfect" family. For example, the financial ability of adoptive parents to support a family is of greater concern to the agency, since foster parents usually receive financial subsidies to care for foster children, while adoptive parents often do not. Adoptive parents may also be selected on the basis of religious beliefs, and physical characteristics such as race or even complexion. Since these factors (and others) are not taken into account in selecting foster parents, it is not uncommon for agencies to reject foster parents when it comes to the adoption itself.

The problem with this system is that it frequently ignores reality. "Temporary" foster parents are very often the only parents children have known. Though these parents may not be ideal, removing children from their custody after a period of time can have the same detrimental effect upon the child as breaking up a stable, natural family. Severing this relationship often results in more trauma to the children (forcing them to endure the loss of the only parents they have known, having to readjust to strangers as new parents) than if they were left with the foster parents.

A better rule might be that unless it can be shown that permitting a child to be adopted by willing foster parents is *harmful* to the child, children should not be removed from foster parents over their objection in order to be adopted by a new set of parents. Although this is not the current law, a few courts have decided cases recently along these lines.[13]

Can a child be adopted by parents of a different religion?

Yes. However, some states require that the child be adopted by parents of the same religion as the natural parents "so far as consistent with the best interests of the child and where practicable." [14] Religious matching is required, where feasible, on the premise that natural parents have the right to determine the religious upbringing of their child, even if they are no longer the primary custodians. However, religious matching is never rigidly applied, even in states that recognize the principle, and children may be adopted by parents of a different religion in certain circumstances.

Are childless couples preferred as adoptive parents?

Yes, in many states. In fact, in some states agencies require couples who wish to adopt to submit medical evidence of their inability to have children of their own.[15] This requirement is based on the belief that parents with children of their own might treat an adopted child less than equally.

May atheists adopt?

Yes, but some parents have been barred from adopting because they do not believe in a "Supreme Being." [16] Although the First Amendment protects individuals from state interference with their beliefs (or non-beliefs), courts are granted extremely wide latitude in adoption cases to determine what is in a child's best interests. If it can be shown that the total absence of religious training would not be in a child's best interests, that may be sufficient ground to prohibit an adoption, even though the same facts would constitute an insufficient reason to remove a child from the custody of his or her natural parents.

May racially mixed couples adopt?

Yes, but racially mixed couples may find it extremely difficult. The law of supply and demand plays an important role in adoption decisions. Couples that present the least possible conflict or difficulty in raising children will be given the greatest selection of children from which to choose. Other couples, including racially mixed couples, couples of mixed religions, older couples, and couples in less than excellent health, are allowed to adopt but most likely will only be given children who are least likely to be adopted by more "conventional" couples.

May unmarried couples adopt?

Yes, but the same comments made about racially mixed couples applies to unmarried couples as well. Children that courts or agencies would be likely to allow unmarried people to adopt would be hard-to-place children.

May minors adopt?

No. In most states a person cannot adopt another unless he or she is at least eighteen years of age.[17]

May one spouse adopt wthout the consent of the other spouse?

No. If an adoptive parent is married, *both* spouses must either join in the proceeding or consent to the adoption.

May an adult be adopted?

In most states, yes.[18] Typically, when a person is over the age of fourteen years, his or her consent is required for the adoption to take place.[19]

Can parents who have surrendered their child change their minds and regain custody?

Perhaps. Many jurisdictions allow a parent an absolute right to regain custody (unless parental rights have been involuntarily terminated) prior to the final adoption decree.[20] Some states never allow a surrender to be rescinded unless there was evidence of fraud or duress in the original surrender. The majority of states, however, allow the parent to regain custody within a fixed period of time after the surrender (typically ranging from one to six months), but before the adoption becomes final.[21]

This recognition of natural parents' "second thoughts" is allowed in recognition of the trauma and uncertainty that frequently accompany a decision to surrender a child for adoption. At the same time, in order to protect adoptive parents, the surrender becomes irrevocable after a fixed period. From that point forward, natural parents no longer have any rights or relationship with the child, whether they change their minds or not.

May parents revoke the surrender of their child on the ground that it was given under duress?

Yes. However, definitions of duress will vary among the states. All states allow for revocation of a surrender if it was given under physical duress in which the parent was not making the surrender voluntarily.[22] However, if the duress was less direct and the parent claims, for example, that unemployment problems or sickness led to the surrender, courts may rule differently.[23]

Generally, a court will revoke a surrender if it can be proven that the parent did not fully understand the nature and consequences of the surrender. Accordingly, one court found duress and revoked the surrender because a minor parent was told by her own parents that she could not continue to live in her parents' home unless she surrendered her child for adoption.[24] Duress might also be present if a parent was paid a large amount of money as an inducement to surrender the child. Age itself may be a factor in finding that the surrender was not voluntary. When a mother is a minor, courts will be particularly sensitive to the possibility that the surrender was *not* a voluntary, knowing act.[25]

In one case, however, a mother's complaint that unsettling influences in her personal life including an unhappy marriage, divorce, quarreling with parents and relatives with whom she and her child were living, and financial and health problems all added up to duress was not sustained by a court.[26]

Is an agency adoption more secure than a private adoption against attack by the natural parent who changes her mind?

In some states, yes. In New Jersey, for example, a parent's consent to adopt will be set aside much more easily if the consent was made to a private party rather than an agency. To revoke a consent in a private adoption, courts will examine whether the parent really intended to abandon the child. But to revoke a consent given to an agency, the parent must show duress, fraud, or coercion.[27]

Are adoptions final once a court has entered its order?

No. When a child is not voluntarily surrendered, for example, if there were a failure to notify the parent of the adoption proceeding, it can be set aside.[28]

However, to protect the adoptive family, after a certain period of time, typically ranging from six months to three years, an adoption decree may not be disturbed by *any* challenge from a natural parent.

May *adoptive parents* change their minds after a final order of adoption and rescind the adoption?

Generally, no. Since adoption gives adoptive parents the same rights to the child as natural parents enjoy, the relationship is permanent.[29] However, a few states allow rescission or abrogation of the adoption if, within a specified number of years after the adoption, a significant change of circumstance occurs, such as divorce of the adoptive parents,[30] or undiagnosed mental illness or deficiency.[31]

May an adoptee learn the identity of his or her natural parents?

Generally, the identity of the natural parents will be revealed to the adoptee only if he or she goes to court and proves to a judge that there exists a strong justification for access to birth records.

In four states—Alabama, Arizona, Connecticut, and Kansas [32]—adoption records are not sealed. They are available to anyone, as are all court records, and may be seen on request. In two other states—South Dakota and Virginia—adoptees have the right to learn the identity of their biological parents when they become adults. In the vast majority of states, however, records are sealed and may be opened, if at all, only upon a court order, supported by a showing of "good cause." [33]

Why are limits placed on the adoptee's right to learn the identity of his or her natural parents?

There are a number of reasons offered for sealing adoption records. First, sealed records protect adopted children from the stigma of their adopted status. They also protect adopted children who were born to unmarried parents from the stigma of illegitimacy. Second, sealed records protect the adoptive family from possible intrusion into their lives by the natural parents. They also help insulate adoptive parents from fears that the child they have raised as their own might transfer his or her affections and loyalty to the natural parents at a later date. Third, sealed records protect the natural parents from future intrusion into their lives by the adopted child. Many children adopted years ago were children of unwed teen-age mothers who later married without telling their husbands of their secret past; since these women relied on the promises of sealed records, to be suddenly confronted with the appearance of an adopted child would be severely disruptive. Some courts have relied on this "contract of secrecy" as a basis for withholding the information. Fourth, it is often argued that a promise of secrecy is necessary to encourage parents to surrender their children to authorized agencies. For a variety of reasons, parents who have given up a child for adoption may never want anyone they know to find out. If the information could be brought out years later, this might discourage parents from surrendering unwanted children for adoption.

Proponents of making birth records available to adoptees disagree with all these reasons. They claim that many natural parents would not object to meeting their adult child if the child wished. If the adoptee is denied access to records because of the feelings of the natural parents, then natural parents could be contacted to determine their wishes before any request is denied. Also, they argue, respecting the wishes of natural parents has nothing to do with revealing certain *non-identifiable* information to the adoptee, such as relevant medical information; but even this is frequently withheld. Finally, many adoptees claim that preventing access to birth records is emotionally harmful to them. If providing adoptees access to records will be distressful to the natural or adoptive parents, they say, it is the parents who should suffer, rather than the adoptees.

Are laws that restrict an adoptee's access to his or her birth records constitutional?

Yes. Courts have consistently ruled that confidentiality statutes are constitutional, because legislatures may rationally conclude that sealed adoption records serve valid state interests in promoting adoptions.[34]

May natural parents find out information about their children who have been adopted?

In most states, no.

What are "subsidized adoptions"?

Subsidized adoptions are adoptions in which the state pays the adoptive family a fixed amount each month to care for the adopted child. Subsidized adoptions now exist in several states.[34] They have been created in recognition of the fact that many foster parents, although willing to adopt, cannot afford to lose the monthly payment they receive as foster parents. Subsidized adoptions are designed to give foster parents the incentive, and the means, to adopt.

Although all states subsidize foster care, only some pay adoptive parents. Partly as a result of this scheme, up to 300,000 children are in foster care in the United States who are eligible for adoption. Additionally, many of the large number of children in long-term foster care are "hard-to-place" children, being handicapped or emotionally disturbed. The absence of subsidized adoptions precludes many of these children from being adopted because of the inordinate expense involved in caring for them.

Some states, such as Vermont, allow subsidies only for the adoption of children who have been in foster care for at least two years and are adopted by their foster parents.[36]

What is an "open adoption"?

An *open adoption* is a modern alternative to traditional adoptions, because after a child is adopted, he or she still retains a relationship with the natural parents. This permits the child and the adoptive parents to benefit from the security of an adoption order and at the same time it permits the natural parents to retain visitation rights and to remain involved to a limited extent in the child's life. The "all-or-nothing" alternative of ordinary adoptions forces many natural parents to oppose the adoption of their child even in circumstances where they do not want actual custody. The classic case of this sort arises after a divorce and a proposed adoption by a stepparent. Open adoptions are rare, and they will be granted only on the consent of all parties. It is possible that these adoptions will become more popular in the next few years.

Does adoption cut off all ties of the child with former grandparents?

Not necessarily. Recent changes in adoption laws in some states have led to the possibility of grandparents retaining the right to visit in certain circumstances.[37] Thus, in California, when a parent has died and a stepparent adopts the child, grandparents (on the side of the deceased parent) have a statutory right to seek visitation.[38] But in most states, the rule is that adoption terminates the possible visitation rights of all relatives of the natural parents.[39] (For a fuller discussion of the rights of grandparents, see Chapter XI.)

Is it possible for a "common-law" adoption to occur?

In a few states, yes. A *common-law adoption* (meaning an adoption that is deemed to have taken place without formal legal procedures) may occur in situations where children who are not legally related to their "parents" have nevertheless lived in their homes for many years, have taken their last names, and have considered themselves publicly and privately as their legal children. In a few of these cases courts have considered the children to be legally related for purposes of recovering property from the parents' estate when no will was left.[40]

NOTES

1. Ariz. Rev. Stat. §8–106(c); D.C. Code §16–304(e); Md. Ann. Code art. 16, §74; Mass. Gen. Laws Ann. ch. 210, §3; Va. Code §63.1–225.
2. *See, e.g.,* Del. Code tit. 13, §904.

3. *See, e.g.,* Adoption of Michelle Lee T., 44 Cal. App.3d 699, 117 Cal. Rptr. 856 (Ct. of App. 1975).

4. U.S. DEPT. OF HEW, ADOPTION IN 1971 at 1 (Pub. No. 73–03259, 1973).

5. *See, e.g.,* D.C. CODE §§32–781–8; N.J. STAT. ANN. §2A: 96–7; DEL. CODE tit. 13, §904; MASS. GEN. ANN. LAWS ch. 210, §11A; OKLA. STAT. ANN. tit. 21, §866.

6. *See, e.g.,* People v. Schwartz, 64 Ill.2d 275, 356 N.E.2d 8 (1976).

7. *See* Note, *Black-Market Adoptions,* 22 CATH. LAWYER 48 (1976).

8. *E.g., In re* Adoption of Tachick, 60 Wisc.2d 540, 210 N.W.2d 865 (1973); Drummond v. Fulton County Dept. of Family & Children's Serv., 563 F.2d 1200 (5th Cir. 1977) (*en banc*).

9. *E.g.,* San Diego County Dept. of Public Welfare v. Superior Court of San Diego County, 7 Cal.3d 1, 496 P.2d 453 (1972); *In re* Spencer, 338 Mich. 50, 61 N.W.2d 75 (1953); *In re* Dougherty's Adoption, 358 Pa. 620, 58 A.2d 77 (1948).

10. *E.g.* Stines v. Vaughn, 23 Ill. App.3d 511, 319 N.E.2d 561 (1974); Ritchie v. Children's Home Soc., 299 Minn. 149, 216 N.W.2d 900 (1974); State *ex rel.* Portage County Welfare Dept. v. Summers, 38 Ohio St.2d 144, 311 N.E.2d 6 (1974).

11. *See, e.g.,* Ellis v. McCoy, 332 Mass. 254, 124 N.E.2d 266 (1954).

12. *See, e.g.,* Drummond v. Fulton County, *supra* note 8.

13. *See, e.g., In re* Adoption of Michelle Lee T., *supra* note 3.

14. *See* Dickens v. Ernesto, 30 N.Y.2d 61, 281 N.E.2d 153 (1972); app. dism'd, 407 U.S. 917 (1972); *see also* MASS. GEN. LAWS ANN., ch. 210 §5B; ILL. ANN. STAT. §9.1–15.

15. *E.g.,* New York, Kansas. *See* Comment, *A Reconsideration of the Religious Element in Adoption,* 56 CORNELL L. REV. 780, 782 n.13 (1971).

16. *See, e.g., In re* Adoption of "E," 59 N.J. 36, 279 A.2d 785 (1971).

17. *See* Wadlington, *Minimum Age Differences as a Requisite for Adoption,* 1966 DUKE L.J. 392.

18. *See, e.g.,* Wilson v. Johnson, 389 S.W.2d 634 (Ky. Ct. App. 1965).

19. ILL. ANN. STAT. §9.1–12.

20. *See, e.g.,* Martin v. Ford, 224 Ark, 993, 227 S.W.2d 842 (1955); *In re* Adoption of Lauless, 216 Or. 188, 338 P.2d 660 (1959); Wright v. Fitzgibbons, 198 Miss. 471, 21 So.2d 709 (1945). *Contra,* Bailey v. Mars, 138 Conn. 593, 87 A.2d 388 (1952); Duncan v. Harden, 234 Ga.

204, 214 S.E.2d 890 (1975); Barwin v. Reidy, 62 N.M. 183, 307 P.2d 175 (1957).

21. Scarpetta v. Spence-Chapin Adoption Serv., 28 N.Y.2d 185, 269 N.E.2d 787 (1971); *In re* Anderson, 589 P.2d 957 (Idaho 1978).

22. *See, eg.,* People *ex rel.* Drury v. Catholic Home Bureau, 34 Ill.2d 84, 213 N.E.2d 507 (1966).

23. For cases that allowed the revocation, *see, e.g., In re* D., 408 S.W.2d 361 (Mo. App. 1966); *In re* G., 389 S.W.2d 63 (Mo. App. 1965). For cases that disallowed the revocation, *see* Barwin v. Reidy, 62 N.M. 183, 307 P.2d 175 (1957); *In re* Surrender of Minor Children, 344 Mass. 230, 181 N.E.2d 836 (1962).

24. *See* Sims v. Sims, 30 Ill. App.3d 406, 332 N.E.2d 36 (1975). *Contra, In re* Adoption of Grimbrone, 262 So.2d 566 (La. App. 1972).

25. Janet G. v. New York Foundling Hospital, 94 Misc.2d 133, 403 N.Y.S.2d 646 (Fam. Ct. 1978).

26. Regenold v. Baby Fold, Inc., 369 N.E.2d 858 (Ill. 1977).

27. Sees v. Baber, 74 N.J. 201, 377 A.2d 628 (1977).

28. *See* Armstrong v. Manzo, 380 U.S. 545 (1965).

29. *See, e.g., In re* Adoption of G., 89 N.J. Super. 276, 214 A.2d 549 (Monmouth Cty. Ct., 1965).

30. ARK. STAT. ANN. §56–110.

31. CALIF. CIV. CODE §227b.

32. ALA. CODE tit. 27, §4; KAN. STAT. ANN. §59–2279; S.D. COMPILED LAWS ANN. §§34–25–16.4, 25–6–15; VA. CODE ANN. §§32–353.19, 63.1–236.

33. *E.g.,* N.Y. DOM. REL. LAW §114.

34. *See, e.g.,* Alma Society v. Mellon, 459 F.2d 912 (2nd Cir. 1979); Mills v. Atlantic City Dept. of Vital Statistics, 372 A.2d 646 (N.J. Super. 1977).

35. Among the states that provide for subsidized adoptions are Connecticut, District of Columbia, Illinois, Iowa, New Jersey, New York, and Vermont.

36. *Adoption and Foster Care, Hearings Before the Subcomm. on Children and Youth of the Senate Comm. on Labor and Public Welfare,* 94th Cong., 1st Sess. 726–38 (1976).

37. *See, e.g.,* M. y. Ford, 66 N.J. 426, 332 A.2d 199 (1975); People *ex rel.* Simmons v. Sherman, 414 N.Y.S.2d 83 (Sup. Ct. 1979).

38. CAL. CIV. CODE §197.5(c).

39. *See, e.g.,* Matter of Fox, 567 P.2d 985 (Okla. 1977).

40. *E.g.,* Kuchling v. California, 410 F.2d 222 (5th Cir. 1969).

XI

Grandparents

Grandparents have very few rights vis-à-vis their grandchildren. The law vests the primary right and power over children in the hands of their parents. As discussed earlier in this book, there are certain situations in which the state may intervene into the parent-child relationship and withdraw the parent's custodial rights to protect the interests of the child. Moreover, there are certain conditions that the state may impose upon a child, such as compulsory education or medical treatment, even if the child's parents are unwilling to provide them. But the fact that parents' rights are not absolute is not to say that *grandparents* have any rights in the upbringing of their grandchildren. In most situations, grandparents are regarded as strangers to their grandchildren in the eyes of the law.

There are two major exceptions to this general principle.

First, grandparents have the right to have their estate or any part of it inherited by their grandchildren, so long as they provide for such inheritance in their will. Money or property can be inherited directly by grandchildren if they have reached the age of majority when the grandparent dies, or through trust funds or guardians if they have not.

Second, grandparents in some states have a limited right to visit their grandchildren, even if the child's parents refuse. This right is discussed more fully in the questions and answers below.

Do grandparents have a right to visit their grandchildren, even if the children's parents object?

The answer is a qualified yes in some states.

Until recently, grandparents had no visitation rights at

all—their visits with their grandchildren were entirely at
the discretion of the children's parents. In the first known
case where this issue was discussed, a Louisiana court
ruled in 1894 that it is "desirable" that ties of affection
created by nature between grandparents and their de-
scendants be strengthened, but the father and mother
alone should be the judge. The court declined to order
visitation against the wishes of the parents, saying, "The
obligation to visit grandparents is moral and not legal." [1]

Lately, this view of grandparents' visitation has begun
to change.[2] Presently, about eighteen states authorize visitation if the matter is taken to court and the court finds
it is in the best interests of the grandchildren to have such
visitation.[3] In some states, laws permit court-ordered visitation only if the parents are separated, divorced, or at
least one parent is dead.[4] In a few of these states, a court
granting a divorce may simultaneously authorize visitation
to the children's grandparents.[5]

In other states, there are no laws dealing with grandparents' visitation at all. In these states, courts will usually refrain from granting grandparental visitation over
parental objections on the theory that they simply have no
jurisdiction or power to do so;[6] but even in the absence
of authorizing legislation, some courts have granted visitation under certain conditions.[7]

**What if one parent dies? Do grandparents on the side
of the deceased parent have a right to visit with their grandchildren even if the surviving parent objects?**

Only if a court agrees that such visitation would be in
the best interests of the grandchildren.[8]

In a number of states, including California, Georgia,
Louisiana, New Jersey, New York, Ohio, and Texas, there
are laws that specifically address this circumstance and
grant grandparents access to the courts to seek visitation.[9]
In these states, the law does not guarantee visitation, but
merely sets forth the procedure for requesting visitation
and permits a court to grant it if it is in the best interests
of the child.

**What circumstances would qualify for visitation under
the "best-interests-of-the-child" standard?**

The legal standard "best interests of the child" is purposely vague so that courts may inquire into the facts of family situations in each case and decide accordingly. It is therefore very difficult to point to certain facts and say that they will or will not qualify in all cases.

Generally, a court will look at the quality of the relationship that existed between the grandparent and grandchild before litigation commences. Courts will be favorably influenced if the child lived with the grandparents or spent a great deal of time with them. Thus, in a Pennsylvania case, where a child had resided with his maternal grandparents almost a full year following the death of his mother, the court granted visitation, saying, "We consider that it would be almost inhuman to completely isolate the child from his grandparents. . . . Unless there be some compelling reason, we do not believe that a grandchild should be denied visitation to his grandparents." [10]

And in a California case, a child lived with her mother and grandmother following the divorce of her parents. Three years later the mother disappeared and the father regained custody of the child. The grandmother was granted visitation privileges because, in the words of the court, "The grandmother undoubtedly occupied an important place in the life of the young child. . . . To have suddenly severed this close blood tie of love and affection and completely remove the child from its familiar surroundings might well have caused her considerable nervous and emotional disturbance." [11]

What circumstances might give a court reason to decide that visitation would *not* be in a child's best interests?

Factors that might discourage courts from granting visitation include circumstances that create adverse effects upon the child's health or serious differences between the child's parents and grandparents.

For example, a Pennsylvania court ruled that visitation should not be permitted when a child's natural mother and stepfather feuded with the child's grandparents. The court decided that "the health of the child was being seriously endangered by the emotional conflicts arising out of the manifest mutual animosities" between the parents and grandparents. Even though the grandparents had become deeply attached to the child, the court ruled that "sympathy from them cannot be permitted to interfere with the best interest and future welfare of the child." [12]

Similarly, another Pennsylvania court held that the best interests of a child could not be served by granting visitation to grandparents who participated in a serious feud for custody with the parents. In this case, the child had been living with its grandparents and the father successfully won custody from them. In justifying its decision to deny visitation, the court wrote, "There exists between the [grandparents] and the father of the child a deep and apparently irreconcilable animosity. . . . It engenders a contest for the child's affection, a contest which can lead only to the detriment of the child." [13]

What if a child's parents are divorced or one of them dies, and the child is subsequently adopted by another? Do the grandparents on the side of the deceased or displaced parent still have the right to seek visitation?

The general view is that once a child is adopted, the child's legal relationship with its former parent is terminated altogether. Therefore, logic would suggest that the child's legal relationship with its former grandparent would cease as well. Most courts accept this view and would not order a child's "new" parents to schedule visits with its "former" grandparents, if it was against the new parents' will.[14]

However, this general view of the law of adoption and its effect on former grandparents is not absolute; a few courts have ordered grandparental visitation even after adoption.[15]

A court in New Jersey, for example, ruled that visits with grandparents are such a "precious part of a child's experience" that the maternal grandmother of a child (whose mother had died and was later adopted by the father's second wife) would be granted this right.[16] In this case, the fact that the child had lived for a time with its grandmother before its adoption helped persuade the court. In another case, in Ohio, where two children whose father had died were later adopted by their mother's second husband, a court permitted grandparental visitation because the children had enjoyed frequent visitation in the past (the grandparents lived next door to the children); in light of their prior close relationship, the court decided that it would be in the children's best interests to have visitation continue.[17]

If grandparents seek court-ordered visitation, do the parents have to be notified of the court proceeding before it takes place so that they may contest visitation?

Yes. Fundamental principles of due process and fairness require prior notice to the natural parents if they are alive and if they can be located. There is some authority that suggests that a petition by grandparents for visitation will be denied if they cannot prove that notice of the petition has been served on the parents a reasonable period of time before the proceeding.[18] This is because parents have the right to have their objections to visitation heard by the court, and to argue why visitation might *not* be in the best interests of the grandchild.

NOTES

1. Succession of Reiss, 46 La. Ann. 347, 15 So. 151 (1894).
2. *See, generally,* Allen, *Visitation Rights of a Grandparent Over the Objections of the Parents,* 15 J. FAM. L. 51 (1976).
3. *See, e.g.,* N.J. STAT. ANN. §9:2–7.1; N.Y. DOM. REL. LAW §72; Lo Presti v. Lo Presti, 40 N.Y.2d 522, 387 N.Y.S.2d 412, 355 N.E.2d 372 (1976).
4. *See, e.g.,* CAL. CIV. CODE §197.5(a); *In re* Meier's Estate, 51 Cal. App.3d 120, 123 Cal. Rptr. 822 (1975).
5. *See, e.g.,* FLA. STAT. §61.13.
6. *See, e.g.,* Brotherton v. Boothe, 250 S.E.2d 36 (W. Va. 1978); Poe v. Case, 565 S.W.2d 612 (Ark., 1978).
7. Sparks v. Wigglesworth, (Ky. Ct. App.) in 5 FAM. L. RPTR. 3173 (July 17, 1979).
8. *See, e.g.,* Boyles v. Boyles, 14 Ill. App.3d 602, 302 N.E.2d 199 (1973); Mirto v. Bodine, 29 Conn. Supp. 510, 294 A.2d 336 (1972).
9. *See, e.g., In re* Meier's Estate, *supra* note 4; George v. Sizemore, 238 Ga. 525, 233 S.E.2d 779 (1977); Smith v. Trosclair, 321 So.2d 514 (1975); Mimkon v. Ford, 66 N.J. 426, 332 A.2d 199 (1975); People *ex rel.* Levine v. Rado, 54 Misc.2d 843, 283 N.Y.S.2d 483 (1967); *In re* Griffiths, 47 Ohio App.2d 238, 353 N.E.2d 884 (1975); Goolsbee v. Heft, 549 S.W.2d 34 (Tex. Civ. App. 1977).

10. Commonwealth *ex rel.* Goodman v. Dratch, 192 Pa. Super 1, 159 A.2d 70 (1960).

11. Benner v. Benner, 113 Cal. App.2d 531, 248 P.2d 425 (1952); *see also* Bookstein v. Bookstein, 7 Cal. App.3d 219, 86 Cal. Rptr. 495 (1970).

12. Commonwealth *ex rel.* Flannery v. Sharp, 151 Pa. Super. 612, 30 A.2d 810 (1943).

13. Commonwealth *ex rel.* McDonald v. Smith, 170 Pa. Super. 254, 85 A.2d 686 (1952).

14. *See, e.g.,* Lee v. Kepler, 197 So.2d 570 (Fla. App. 1967); Deweese v. Crawford, 520 S.W.2d 522 (Tex. Civ. App. 1975); Herman v. Lobovits, 66 Misc.2d 830, 322 N.Y.S.2d 123 (1971); CAL. CIV. CODE §197.5(c); Bikos v. Nobliski, 276 N.W.2d 541 (Mich. App. 1979); Commonwealth v. Cherry, 196 Pa. Super. 46, 173 A.2d 650 (1961).

15. *See, e.g.,* People *ex rel.* Simmons v. Sheridan, 414 N.Y.S. 2d 83 (Sup. Ct. 1979).

16. Mimkon v. Ford, *supra* note 9.

17. Graziano v. Davis, 50 Ohio App.2d 83, 361 N.E.2d 525 (1976).

18. *In re* Meier's Estate, *supra* note 4; N.Y. DOM. REL. LAW §72.

XII

Minor Parents

Do parents who are themselves minors have the right to the custody of their children?

Yes. A parent has the right to the custody of his or her child, whether or not the parent is an adult. In the first reported case to address this issue, the Oklahoma Supreme Court ruled in 1920 that simply because a parent was a minor did not mean that she could be denied the right to custody of her child.[1]

The law has not changed since then, and has in fact been made simpler for *married* minor parents, because presently marriage constitutes an automatic emancipation in every state.[2] Thus, by virtue of being married, minors are considered legal adults. (Of course, to be married in most states, minors need the permission of their parents.)

Parents who are *not* married are also entitled to the custody of their children even if they are minors.

As with adult parents, there may be a contest for custody of a child between the mother and father, and there may be state action to remove a child if it has been mistreated; but the right of parenthood itself—that is, the right to raise and bring up a child as one's own—is unaffected by the fact that a parent is not an adult.

Can minor parents consent to medical care for themselves and for their own children?

Usually. If young parents are *married,* they are automatically emancipated from their own parents, even if they are under age eighteen.[3] Emancipated minors gain legal power to consent to their own medical care as if they were adults, including power to provide consent for the care of their own children.

Similarly, in many states, minors who are parents, even if they are not married, may consent to medical care for themselves and their own children without their parents' permission.[4]

Can minor parents receive public assistance?

Yes. Minors who are parents are automatically considered emancipated from their parents for the purpose of seeking public assistance. In addition, minor mothers are entitled to AFDC payments if the father is not living in the home or contributing to the support of the child.[5]

An unmarried woman living with her parents who seeks to become eligible for welfare benefits for *herself* is obliged to furnish the state agency with the social security numbers of all other persons who are living in the home at that time. The income of her parents will be considered in determining her own eligibility for benefits. But an unmarried mother who seeks welfare benefits solely for her *child* need not furnish the authorities with information of the income of her own parents (even if she is living in the same home with them), since grandparents do not have the obligation to support their grandchildren.

Accordingly, if an adolescent mother is old enough to live with her child by herself and wants to do so, she may obtain public assistance to make it possible.

If a student is pregnant, can she still attend school?

Yes. Even though many schools have policies which prohibit pregnant girls from attending, these policies are illegal. Title IX of the Federal Educational Amendments of 1972 prohibits sex discrimination in all schools which receive federal funds.[6] Sex discrimination, in turn, has been interpreted by the Department of Health, Education, and Welfare (HEW) as including discrimination against pregnant females. Since virtually every school in the country receives federal funds, and since HEW is in charge of administering and enforcing this law, it may be concluded that discrimination against pregnant students, including denying them the right to attend classes, is illegal.

Does it matter if the pregnant student is married or single?

No. The law is the same, regardless of the marital status of the pregnant student. Title IX (mentioned above) makes no distinction between married and unmarried students.

Do students (male or female) who have their own children have the right to attend school?

Yes. This is supported by Title IX and by a number of judicial decisions that have addressed the issue.

As early as 1929, a court in Kansas ruled that a young parent had a right to attend high school. The court stated, "The public schools are for the benefit of children within school age, and . . . it is proper that no one within school age should be denied the privilege of attending school unless it is clear that the public interest demands the expulsion of such pupils.[7]

More recently, in 1969, a federal court in Mississippi ruled that the fact that an unmarried girl had given birth to a child "does not forever brand her as a scarlet woman undeserving of any chance for rehabilitation or the opportunity for future education."[8] From the court's language, it was clear that the judge considered motherhood of unmarried minors quite improper; nevertheless, the court ruled that pregnancy and motherhood was not a bar to an education unless school officials could show, at a hearing, that such students were "so lacking in moral character that their presence in the schools would taint the education of other students."

With less fanfare and moral judgment, a Texas court ordered the readmission of a young mother to high school simply because she was entitled to an education under state law.[9]

Do pregnant students and students with children have the right to participate in graduation and extracurricular activities?

Yes. Title IX, which prohibits sex discrimination in educational programs, includes extracurricular activities in its scope. Moreover, virtually every court case in which this question has been raised has been decided in favor of the pregnant student or student who is a parent.

Not too long ago, a Texas court ordered school officials to permit a divorced student, who had placed her child for adoption, to participate in extracurricular activities.[10] In reaching its decision, the court took cognizance of the fact that a student's record of participation in extracurricular activities often influences his or her chances for admission into college. A federal court in New Jersey also prohibited school officials from discriminating against students with respect to participation in extracurricular activities because of their parental status.[11]

The HEW regulations under Title IX do not mention graduation, but it is probable that a court would consider graduation to be an educational activity under Title IX. In New York, the State Commissioner of Education overrode the decision of a local board of education to prohibit a married pregnant student from attending her high-school graduation. He ruled that the legal decision was "clearly arbitrary, capricious and unreasonable," since the young woman had met all her academic requirements.[12]

The point to stress in any dispute with school officials involving pregnancy or parental status is that the burden is on the school to show a rational relationship between the prohibition and the functioning of the school. If no such relationship can be shown, as is usually the case, the exclusion may violate a student's right under the Fourteenth Amendment not to be arbitrarily and capriciously deprived of an education.[13]

Do pregnant students or students with children have the right *not* to attend school?

Yes. Most schools will allow pregnant students and students with children to drop out of school, even if the students are still within the compulsory school age. When schools have refused to grant such permission, courts have ruled that the refusal is illegal.[14] This means that while pregnant students and students with children have a right to continue with school, they do not have to if they do not desire.

NOTES

1. Coats v. Benton, 80 Okla, 93, 194 P. 198 (1920).
2. *See, e.g.,* Ditmar v. Ditmar, 48 Wash.2d 373, 293 P.2d 759 (1956).
3. *See, e.g.,* Commonwealth v. Graham, 157 Mass. 73, 31 N.E. 706 (1892); Gillikin v. Burbage, 263 N.C. 317, 139 S.E.2d 753 (1965).
4. *See, e.g.,* N.Y. PUB. HEALTH LAW §2504(1), (2); COLO. REV. STAT. §13–22–103; MINN. STAT. ANN. §144.342.
5. 42 U.S.C. §406(a).
6. 20 U.S.C. §1866.
7. Nutt v. Board of Educ., 128 Kan. 507, 278 P. 1065 (1929).
8. Perry v. Grenada Mun. Separate School Dist., 300 F. Supp. 748 (N.D. Miss. 1969). *See also* Shull v. Columbus Mun. Separate School Dist., 338 F. Supp. 1376 (N.D. Miss. 1972).
9. Alvin Indep. School Dist. v. Cooper, 404 S.W.2d 76 (Tex. Ct. Civ. App. 1966).
10. Romans v. Crenshaw, 354 F. Supp. 868 (S.D. Tex. 1972).
11. Johnson v. Board of Educ., Civ. No. 172–70 (D. N.J. 1970).
12. Matter of Murphy, 11 Ed. Dept. Rep. 180 (N.Y. Comm. Ed. 1972).
13. *See, e.g.,* Holt v. Shelton, 341 F. Supp. 821 (M.D. Tenn. 1972); Davis v. Meek, 344 F. Supp. 298 (N.D. Ohio 1972); Wellsand v. Valparaiso Community School Corp. Civ. No. 71 H 122(2) (N.D. Ind. 1971); Indiana High School Athletic Assn. v. Raike, 329 N.E.2d 66 (Ct. App. 1975); Moran v. School Dist. No. 7, 350 F. Supp. 1180 (D. Mont. 1972); Hollon v. Mathis Indep. School Dist., 358 F. Supp. 1269 (S.D. Tex. 1973).
14. *See, e.g.,* State v. Priest, 210 La. 389, 27 So.2d 173 (1946); *In re* Goodwin, 214 La. 1062, 39 So.2d 731 (1949); *In re* Rogers, 234 N.Y.S.2d 172 (1962).

XIII

Homosexual Parents

Homosexual parents have every right that heterosexual parents have, whether they are single, married, separated, or divorced. Therefore, the rights mentioned elsewhere in this book are applicable to all parents, regardless of their sexual orientation.

Nevertheless, homosexual parents may be discriminated against because of the prevailing social bias against them. And, of course, in all but ten states (California, Colorado, Connecticut, Delaware, Hawaii, Illinois, Massachusetts, New Jersey, Ohio, and Oregon), acts of homosexual contact between consenting adults are crimes. (*Being* a homosexual, however, is not illegal.)

Homosexuals, as parents, may expect to face discrimination at least in two areas: in seeking to adopt children and in seeking custody of their own children after a separation or divorce. In this chapter, we will deal primarily with the rights of homosexual parents in the realm of child custody and visitation. (For a fuller discussion of the rights of homosexuals, in family law and in all aspects of life, see *The Rights of Gay People,* by Boggan, Haft, Lister, and Rapp, one of the A.C.L.U. Handbooks in this series.)

In a child-custody dispute, if one of the parents is a homosexual, does he or she have any rights?

Yes, but since many judges believe that a child should not be brought up in a "homosexual environment," it would be fair to say that the homosexual parent suffers a disadvantage at the outset of a contest for child custody.

Recently, however, more and more admitted homosexuals have been successful in seeking court-ordered custody of their children.

Virtually every state employs the legal standard called the "best interests of the child" to resolve custody disputes. (See Chapter VII for a discussion of this standard.) This means that courts will attempt to take into consideration all aspects of the life of each parent in deciding which one could better promote the best interests of the child. In reaching its conclusion, a court will usually look at each parent's home, home-life, employment, past involvement with the child, time available to spend with the child, ability to provide for the child's future, fitness and ability to care for the child, and other child-related aspects of his or her life and social environment.

Sometimes, a court will examine each parent's morals, and if a court considers a person's behavior "immoral," it may base its decision on that finding. Naturally, prejudice against homosexuality weighs heavily against homosexual parents vying for custody against heterosexual spouses. Even if a court chooses to exclude moral considerations, it may decide that a homosexual parent, solely because of his or her sexual orientation, cannot provide a healthy environment for a child.

It is difficult to say to what degree a parent seeking custody is prejudiced by his or her sexual orientation. Since there is little law to guide custody determinations, other than the "best interests of the child" standard, individual judges have a wide range of discretion in making their decisions. Moreover, because there are relatively few reported decisions involving the rights of homosexual parents, there is too little law on the topic to permit the formulation of general statements or uniform answers.

What is the major legal problem faced by homosexual parents who seek court-ordered custody?

The major problem encountered by any homosexual parent is to convince the court that the parent's homosexuality, *per se,* is not harmful to a child. Until that hurdle is jumped, no homosexual parent will be in a position of parity with his or her adversary.

Judges will often assume that a homosexual environment, by itself, is harmful to a child, and hence that it is not in the child's best interest to live with a homosexual parent.[1] Judges in this frame of mind rarely find it necessary to require the nonhomosexual parent to prove a causal connection between homosexuality and harm. Therefore, the task of the homosexual parent is to urge the court to rule that unless harm to a child is *proven* by competent evidence, it may not be taken into consideration or even assumed in reaching a decision. The homosexual parent might then argue that any conclusion reached without proof of the connection between homosexuality and harm would be unreasonable and based on arbitrary grounds.

The assumption that parental homosexuality, *per se,* is harmful to children is deeply entrenched in the American judiciary. Many courts ignore all aspects of evidence regarding the best interests of children, including a parent's ability to care for them, and focus entirely on the homosexuality of a parent. For example, despite a lengthy trial and numerous issues raised on appeal, an Oregon appellate court awarded custody to a nonhomosexual parent, saying simply: "Because there is a potential for harm to persons involved, we conclude that no useful purpose would be served in publishing a detailed opinion." [2] In another case, an Ohio court deprived a mother of custody because she lived with another woman in a lesbian relationship which, according to the court, was "clearly to the neglect of supervision of the children." The court did not explain how the children were neglected or unsupervised, and it established "harm" to the children only because it believed that the homosexuality of the mother might result in the children being teased by their peers.[3]

Very few states require, as a matter of law, that connections between a parent's conduct and the welfare of the child must be proved. An exception is Colorado, where the law states that in determining the best interests of the child, a court "shall not consider the conduct of a proposed custodian that does not affect his relationship with the child." [4] And some courts refuse to consider personal morals unless they are shown to be harmful to the child. One California court declared: "A judge should not base his decision upon his disapproval of the morals or other personal characteristics of a parent that do not harm the child. It is not his function to punish a parent by taking away a child." [5]

A most interesting example of a case in which a veritable hodgepodge of standards was employed arose in California. A court decided that a mother's homosexuality, *per se,* made her unfit to have custody of her children. On appeal, the decision was reversed and a new trial was ordered because the trial judge failed to consider all the evidence as to what would be in the child's best interest.[6] But when the second trial was held, the judge ignored the instructions received from above, and commented from the bench: "We are dealing with a four-year-old child on the threshold of its development—just cannot take the chance that something untoward should happen to it. . . ." At the end of the second trial, custody was again awarded to the father.[7]

Have homosexual parents ever succeeded in gaining court-ordered custody?

Yes, and their success rate seems to be growing. As recently as 1975 there were only seven reported cases in which custody had been awarded to homosexual parents. Today there are literally hundreds of such cases.

In one of the first cases reported, in 1973, a Michigan court awarded custody of six children to two lesbian mothers who lived together. The court ruled that the private sexual relationship of the mothers did not detrimentally affect the children.[8] In the same year an Oregon appellate court granted custody to a homosexual father because there was no proof of any harm to the welfare of his children.[9] And in 1974, an Ohio court granted custody to a lesbian mother who was living with her lover.[10]

More recently, a Maine court granted custody to a lesbian mother after hearing testimony from a psychiatrist that the children, who had resided with the mother for some time, were well-adjusted and that the mother kept her life-style private.[11] And a Colorado court awarded custody to the lesbian companion of a deceased mother instead of the child's father because the mother's lover, in the words of the court, had become the child's "psychological parent," and her sexual preference "has not affected the child . . . and is not related to her ability to parent the child." [12]

In granting custody to homosexual parents, do courts ever impose certain conditions?

Yes. It appears that courts are so reluctant to grant custody to homosexuals that when they do, they often impose conditions that would not be imposed on heterosexual parents.

For example, in a joint decision involving the request of two lesbian mothers who lived together for custody of the children of their respective families, a court in Seattle granted each of them custody on condition that they separate and maintain separate homes for the children.[13] (Subsequently, the two women refused to live apart, causing one father to sue for a change of custody. The father not only lost the second case, but the judge removed his previous restraint on the mothers' living together.)[14] In a similar California case, a homosexual mother was granted custody of her children but only on condition that she not live with her lover and that she associate with her only when the children were out of the home.[15]

Restrictions on *visiting* privileges of homosexual parents have also been imposed. In a New York case a lesbian mother not only lost custody, but the court prohibited her from visiting with her child overnight, from having any homosexuals in her home when the child was present, from taking the child to any place where known homosexuals would be present, and from involving her child in any homosexual activities or publicity.[16] And in a New Jersey case, a noncustodial homosexual father was granted visitation during daylight hours only on alternate Sundays, and for three weeks during the summer at some place other than his home, during which time he was ordered not to sleep with anyone other than his lawful wife and not to see his male lover in the presence of his children.[17]

If a homosexual parent gains custody of his or her children by agreement with the other parent, is the agreement valid and enforceable?

Absolutely. As discussed in Capter VII, written agreements regarding custody and child support are contracts, enforceable in a court of law. Of course, as with all custody agreements, the noncustodial parent may ask a court to change custody based on a "change of circumstances" occurring since the date of the agreement.

So long as the custodial parent's homosexuality was known by both parties at the time of the agreement, it would be difficult for the noncustodial parent to argue that the custodian's homosexuality constituted a change of circumstances, since no "change" would have occurred. If, however, the custodial parent kept his or her homosexuality a secret at the time of the agreement, or if the custodial parent became engaged in homosexual relations *after* the agreement was made, this might qualify as a change of circumstances qualifying for court review.[18]

If the noncustodial parent learns that the custodial parent is or has become a homosexual and, for this reason, sues for a change of custody, will the nonhomosexual parent be victorious?

Not necessarily. As discussed above, if the noncustodial parent can prove that he or she was unaware at the time of the original custody agreement or decision that the other parent was a homosexual, or that since that time the custodial parent has become a homosexual, a court will entertain a petition on the grounds that a change of circumstances has occurred. But just because a court will hear the case does not mean that the noncustodial parent will be victorious.

As in all custody matters, the issues will revolve around the "best interests" of the child. And if at the time of the new custody contest the homosexual parent has previously exercised custody for a period of time, he or she will be in an advantageous position if it can be demonstrated that during this time the child has prospered and its interests have been well served. The noncustodial parent would have to show that the child's interests have not been met or that the child has suffered and that custody should be transferred.

The best example of a challenge to a homosexual parent's custody of a child is provided by a Washington case in which custody was originally granted to a lesbian mother with the understanding that she not live with her lover. Contrary to the court's direction, she lived with her lesbian friend, actively sought publicity, and "flaunted" her homosexual living arrangement. Based upon these facts, the father sued for custody upon the change-of-circumstances theory. The court not only denied the

father's request but removed its original restriction that
the mother live alone with her child. The court ruled that
the mother's living with another woman and the publicity,
while constituting a "change of circumstances," had not
harmed the child.[19]

In another case arising in Oregon, a mother sued to
have custody transferred to her, eleven years after custody had been awarded to the father, on the ground that
he was a homosexual and provided an unfit environment.
The mother's petition was denied and the mother appealed. The appellate court agreed that custody should remain with the father because the mother failed to prove
that the children "were being exposed to deviant sexual
acts or that the welfare of the [children] was being ad-
versely affected in any substantial way."[20] (In this case,
however, the father denied any homosexual activity even
though he had lived with another man for two years and
acknowledged "possible homosexual traits and tendencies." It is unknown what the outcome would have been
if he were as outwardly homosexual as the mother in the
previously mentioned Washington case.)

A different outcome was reached in a third case from
New York, when a father sued for change of custody because the mother lived in a homosexual relationship. The
court did not say that homosexuality itself was evidence
of unfitness, but ruled that the environment in a homosexual home is "not a proper atmosphere in which to bring
up a child or in the best interest of the child." [21] The court
did find that the ten-year-old child of the contesting parties was emotionally disturbed and it linked the child's
disturbance to the mother's lesbian environment, even
though there was no evidence upon which to base this
connection.

**May a parent be denied welfare or social-services bene-
fits because he or she is a homosexual?**

No. Any homosexual parent who has custody of a child
may receive assistance from the state in which he or she
resides through the Aid to Dependent Children law, so
long as all financial qualifications for assistance are met.[22]

NOTES

1. *See, e.g.*, Immerman v. Immerman, 176 Cal. App.2d 122, 1 Cal. Rptr. 298 (1959).
2. *See, e.g.*, Oharra v. Oharra, No. 73–384 E (Or. Cir. Ct., 13th Judic. Dist., June 18, 1974), *aff'd.* 530 P.2d 877 (Or. App. 1975).
3. Townend v. Townend, (Ohio Ct. Common Pleas, Portage County), *in* 1 FAM. L. RPTR. 2830 (March 14, 1975).
4. COLO. REV. STAT. §14–10–124(2).
5. Stack v. Stack, 189 Cal. App.2d 357, 11 Cal. Rptr. 177 (1961).
6. Nadler v. Superior Court, 255 Cal. App.2d 526, 63 Cal. Rptr. 352 (1967); *see also*, M.P. v. S.P., (N.J. Super. Ct.), *in* 5 FAM. L. RPTR. 2855 (July 3, 1979).
7. Transcript of hearing, p. 67, Nadler v. Nadler, No. 177331 (Cal. Super. Ct., Sacramento County, Nov. 15, 1967) *in* Hunter and Polikoff, *Custody Rights of Lesbian Mothers: Legal Theory and Litigation Strategy*, 25 BUFFALO L. REV. 691 (1976).
8. People v. Brown, 49 Mich. App. 358 (1973).
9. A. v. A., 15 Or. App. 353, 514 P.2d 358 (1973).
10. Hall v. Hall, No. 55900 (Ct. Common Pleas, Licking County, Ohio, Aug. 1974).
11. Whitehead v. Black (Maine Superior Ct.), *in* 2 FAM. L. RPTR. 2593 (July 7, 1976).
12. *In re* Hatzopoulos (Colo. Juv. Ct.), *in* 4 FAM. L. RPTR. 2075 (Dec. 6, 1977).
13. Schuster v. Schuster & Isaacson v. Isaacson, No. D-36867 (Wash. Super. Ct., Kings Co., Dec. 22, 1972).
14. 1 FAM. L. RPTR. 2004.
15. Mitchell v. Mitchell, No. 240665 (Cal. Super. Ct., Santa Clara County, June 8, 1972).
16. *In re* Jane B., 85 Misc.2d 515, 380 N.Y.S.2d 848 (Sup. Ct. 1976).
17. *In re* J.S. & C., 129 N.J. Super. 486, 324 A.2d 90 (1974).
18. Newsome v. Newsome, (N.C. Ct. App.) *in* 5 FAM. L. RPTR. 2907 (July 31, 1979).
19. Schuster v. Schuster, *supra* note 13.
20. A. v. A., *supra* note 9.
21. *In re* Jane B., *supra* note 16.
22. 42 U.S.C., §601–10.

XIV

Preventing Parenthood: Contraception, Sterilization, Abortion, and Restricting Marriage

CONTRACEPTION

May a state prohibit the use of contraceptives in a marital relationship?

No. Nor may a state enact a law restricting the *sale* of medically safe contraceptives, since such a law would interfere with the constitutional right of privacy.[1]

May a state prohibit the use of contraceptives by single persons?

No. The U.S. Supreme Court has made it clear that adults enjoy a constitutional right of privacy, which has been defined as "the right of the individual, *married or single,* to be free from unwarranted governmental intrusion into matters so fundamentally affecting a person as the decision whether to bear or beget a child."[2]

May a state bar the sale or distribution of contraceptive devices to minors?

No. The U.S. Supreme Court has ruled that state laws restricting the sale of contraceptives to minors are unconstitutional since they interfere with a *child's* right to privacy.[3] The Court noted that they are also unconstitutional because they unduly restrict the rights of parents to give or allow their children to use contraceptives.

STERILIZATION

May a person become voluntarily sterilized over the objection of his or her spouse?

Yes. Adults have the right to make basic decisions about their own bodies, including the decision to become sterilized, even over the objection of their spouse. This right is included in the constitutional right of individual and family privacy.[4]

Can a state prohibit an adult from becoming voluntarily sterilized?

No. Just as one *spouse* has no right to prevent the other from becoming sterilized, the *state* has no power to prevent an adult from making the same decision. The right to control one's body, including the right to make a decision whether or not to become a parent in the future, is protected by the Constitution.

Can a state prohibit a person from becoming a parent in the future by ordering involuntary sterilization?

In rare circumstances, yes. Although procreation is a fundamental right entitled to constitutional protection,[5] involuntary sterilizations have been ordered from time to time by various courts when they have been justified as being in the best interests of the person to be sterilized or being in the best interests of society.[6]

But the U.S. Supreme Court has not directly addressed this question since 1942, when it struck down a state law that authorized the involuntary sterilization of certain categories of criminals. In that case, the Court noted that the power of the state to order involuntary sterilization was extremely dangerous, and such power, "in evil or reckless hands . . . can cause races or types which are inimical to the dominant group to wither and disappear."[7] Thus, it is highly uncertain today if the Supreme Court would ever reaffirm a prior ruling made in 1927 that the sterilization of a "feeble minded" person was permissible for the purpose of eliminating negative genetic traits.[8]

ABORTION

Do pregnant women have the right to obtain an abortion?

Yes. If a woman finds a doctor willing to perform an abortion, the state may not restrict a woman's right to obtain one within the first two trimesters (the first six months) of her pregnancy.[9] Moreover, women have the constitutional right to obtain abortions even if they are minors [10] and even without permission of the father of the child.[11] (For a fuller discussion of the rights of pregnant minors to bear or not bear a child, see Chapter III.)

Is a woman's right to an abortion absolute?

No. During the first trimester of pregnancy, a woman may obtain an abortion without any state interference. In the second trimester, the state may require that the abortion be performed in a hospital or other similar facility. In the third trimester, the state may proscribe abortions except to preserve the life or health of the mother. And whenever an abortion is to be performed, the state may require that it be done by a licensed physician.[12]

Are indigent mothers allowed to have the cost of abortions paid by federal Medicaid funds?

It depends on the reason for the abortion. Under the so-called Hyde Amendment of 1978, the United States Congress voted that federal funds for medical care *excludes* coverage for abortions *unless* the abortion is required to protect the life of the mother, the pregnancy resulted from rape of incest, or "severe and long-standing physical health damage to the mother would result" if the abortion is not performed.[13] Thus, even though women have a right to have an abortion, and even though terminating one's pregnancy may be considered medically necessary, federal funds may not be used to pay for one if it does not come within the scope of any of the three categories mentioned above. At the time this answer is being written, however, the constitutionality of the Hyde Amendment is being received by the U.S. Supreme Court.

Do women receiving public assistance have a right to use *state* funds to pay for an abortion?

Again, it depends on the reason for the abortion. The Supreme Court has held that, although the state may not interfere with the freedom of a woman to terminate a pregnancy within the first two trimesters, the state is not obliged to allocate public funds to pay for medical services involving nontherapeutic abortions.[14] Nevertheless, about seventeen states still continue to permit the use of public funds for indigent women to obtain abortions.

Can a physician refuse to treat pregnant Medicaid patients who refuse to comply with his demand that they undergo sterilization after delivery of their third child?

Yes. Even though federal money is involved, courts have allowed physicians to do this.[15]

RESTRICTING MARRIAGE

Can a state prevent people from marrying on the basis of their race?

No. The Constitution prohibits states from attempting to prevent interracial marriage.[16]

May a state prohibit polygamous marriages?

Yes.[17] In fact, all states in the United States today prohibit polygamy.

Can parents prevent their minor children from marrying?

Yes. In most states, children under eighteen cannot marry without the written consent of their parents. Some states have different age thresholds, and some laws require court permission *in addition* to parental permission if the child is very young, but all states permit parents to veto the decision of minors under a certain age to marry.

May a state require an adult to obtain court permission to marry?

No. The U.S. Supreme Court recently reaffirmed the right to marry by striking down a Wisconsin law that required court permission for fathers to marry if they had minor children that were not in their custody and were not being supported. The Court said that even though the state has a legitimate interest in reducing the probability of children becoming public charges, the state cannot prevent a person's right to marry by requiring prior assurance that fathers already under an obligation to support their children are financially able to support additional ones.[18]

In some states, felons sentenced to life imprisonment are not allowed to marry. These laws have generally been upheld by federal courts, on the theory that a person under a "life" sentence has been lawfully deprived of his or her civil rights, including the right to marry.[19]

NOTES

1. Griswold v. Connecticut, 381 U.S. 479 (1965).
2. Eisenstadt v. Baird, 405 U.S. 438 (1972) (emphasis added).
3. Carey v. Population Serv. Int'l, 431 U.S. 678 (1977).
4. Ponter v. Ponter, 135 N.J. Super. 50, 342 A.2d 574 (1975); Doe v. Doe, 314 N.E.2d 128 (Mass. 1974).
5. Skinner v. Oklahoma, 316 U.S. 535 (1942).
6. North Carolina Ass'n for Retarded Children v. State of North Carolina, 420 F. Supp. 451 (M.D.N.C. 1976); Cook v. Oregon, 9 Or. App. 224, 495 P.2d 768 (1972). *In re* Cavett, 182 Neb. 712, 157 N.W.2d 171 (1968); Buck v. Bell, 274 U.S. 200 (1927).
7. Skinner v. Oklahoma, *supra* note 5.
8. Buck v. Bell, *supra* note 6.
9. Roe v. Wade, 410 U.S. 113 (1973).
10. Planned Parenthood v. Danforth, 428 U.S. 52 (1976); Bellotti v. Baird, 443 U.S. 622, 61 L. Ed.2d 797 (1979).
11. Planned Parenthood v. Danforth, *supra* note 10.
12. Roe v. Wade, *supra* note 9; Doe v. Bolton, 410 U.S. 179 1973).
13. Pub. L. 95–48, §210 (1978).
14. Beal v. Doe, 432 U.S. 438 (1977); Maher v. Doe, 432 U.S. 464 (1977).
15. Walker v. Pierce, 560 F.2d 609 (4th Cir. 1977).
16. Loving v. Virginia, 388 U.S. 1 (1967).
17. Reynolds v. United States, 98 U.S. 145 (1878).
18. Zablocki v. Redhail, 434 U.S. 374 (1978).
19. *See, e.g.*, N.Y. CIV. RTS. LAW §79–g; Johnson v. Rockefeller, 365 F. Supp. 377 (S.D.N.Y. 1973), *aff'd.* 415 U.S. 953 (1974).

Appendix A

Assistance Organizations for Parents

The following list includes a broad range of groups that deal with the rights of parents (and children).

Action for Children's
   Television
46 Austin Street
Newtonville, Ma. 02160

American Academy of
   Pediatrics
1801 Hinman Avenue
Evanston, Ill. 60204

ACLU Children's Rights
   Project
22 E. 40th St.
New York, N.Y. 10016

AFL-CIO
815 16th St., N.W.
Washington, D.C. 20006

American Friends Service
   Committee
1501 Cherry St.
Philadelphia, Pa. 19102

American Home
   Economics Association
2010 Massachusetts
   Ave., N.W.
Washington, D.C. 20036

American Humane
   Association
5351 S. Roslyn St.
Englewood, Colo. 80111

Association of Junior
   Leagues
National Child Advocacy
   Project
825 Third Avenue
New York, N.Y. 10022

Carnegie Council of Children
285 Prospect St.
New Haven, Conn. 06520

Child and Family Justice
Project
National Council of Churches
475 Riverside Dr., Rm. 560
New York, N.Y. 10027

Children's Defense Fund
1746 Cambridge St.
Cambridge, Mass. 02138

Children's Division, American Humane Ass'n
P.O. Box 1226
Denver, Colo, 80201

Children's Foundation
1028 Connecticut Ave., N.W.
Washington, D.C. 20036

Church Women United in
the U.S.A.
475 Riverside Dr., Rm. 812
New York, N.Y. 10027

Community Action Programs
Office of Community Action
1200 19th St., N.W.
Washington, D.C. 20006

Council for Exceptional
Children
1920 Association Dr.
Reston, Va. 22091

Day Care and Child Development Council of America
622 14th St., N.W.
Washington, D.C. 20005

Health Resources
Administration
Bureau of Health Planning
and Resources Development
3700 East-West Hwy.
Hyattsville, Md. 20782

League of Women Voters
1730 M St., N.W.
Washington, D.C. 20036

Legal Services Corporation
733 15th St., N.W.
Washington, D.C. 20036

Mental Health Association
1800 N. Kent St.
Arlington, Va. 22209

Mexican American Legal
Defense and Educational
Fund
145 Ninth Street
San Francisco, Calif. 94103

National Association for
the Advancement of
Colored People
1790 Broadway
New York, N.Y. 10019

NAACP Legal Defense and
Educational Fund
10 Columbus Circle
New York, N.Y. 10019

National Association for
the Education of Young
Children
1834 Connecticut Avenue,
N.W.
Washington, D.C. 20009

National Ass'n of Social
Workers
1425 H St., N.W.
Washington, D.C. 20005

National Black Child
  Development Institute
1463 Rhode Island Ave.,
  N.W.
Washington, D.C. 20005

National Center for Child
  Advocacy
Children's Bureau
Office of Child Development
P.O. Box 1182
Washington, D.C. 20013

National Coalition of ESEA
  Title I Parents
412 W. 6th St.
Wilmington, Del. 19801

National Committee for
  Citizens in Education
Wilde Lake Village, Suite 410
Columbia, Md. 21044

National Committee for
  Prevention of Child Abuse
111 E. Wacker Dr.,
  Suite 510
Chicago, Ill. 60601

National Congress of
  Parents and Teachers
700 N. Bush St.
Chicago, Ill. 60611

National Council of Jewish
  Women, Inc.
15 East 26th St., 8th fl.
New York, N.Y. 10010

National Council of Negro
  Women, Inc.
1346 Connecticut Ave., N.W.
Washington, D.C. 20036

National Head Start
  Association
c/o Community Teamwork,
  Inc.
10 Bridge St.
Lowell, Mass. 01852

National Health Law Program
2401 Main St.
Santa Monica, Calif. 90405

National Organization for
  Women
5 South Wabash, Suite 1615
Chicago, Ill. 60603

National Rural Center
1828 L St., N.W., Suite 1000
Washington, D.C. 20036

National Urban Coalition
1201 Connecticut Ave., N.W.
Washington, D.C. 20036

National Urban League
500 East 62nd St.
New York, N.Y. 10021

National Youth Alternatives
  Project
1820 Connecticut Ave., N.W.
Washington, D.C. 20009

Native American Rights Fund
1712 N St., N.W.
Washington, D.C. 20036

New York Coalition for
  Families
411 9th St.
Brooklyn, N.Y. 11215

North American Council on
    Adoptable Children
250 East Blaine
Riverside, Calif. 92507

Parents Anonymous
2009 Farrell Ave.
Redondo Beach, Calif. 90278

Puerto Rican Legal Defense
    and Educational Fund, Inc.
95 Madison Ave.
New York, N.Y. 10016

United Way of America
801 North Fairfax St.
Alexandria, Va. 22314

United Parents of Absconded
    Children
P.O. Box 127-A,
    Wolf Run Rd.
Cuba, N.Y. 14727

Youth Law Center
693 Mission St., 2nd fl.
San Francisco, Calif. 94105

Youth Liberation
2007 Washtenaw Ave.
Ann Arbor, Mich. 48104

Appendix B

Uniform State Laws

The following Uniform State Laws, promulgated by the National Conference of Commissioners on Uniform State Laws, have been passed as model laws for adoption by the states. Material which appear in brackets are optional or alternative provisions which are to be considered by a state in reviewing the laws. Each state decides for itself whether to follow all or any of these laws. Only some states have enacted some of these laws. A list of the states which have done so accompanies each law.

1. UNIFORM ADOPTION ACT
1969 REVISED ACT

§ 1. [Definitions]

As used in this Act, unless the context otherwise requires,

(1) "child" means a son or daughter, whether by birth or by adoption;

(2) "Court" means the [here insert name of the court or branch] court of this State, and when the context requires means the court of any other state empowered to grant petitions for adoption;

(3) "minor" means [a male] [an individual] under the age of [18] [21] years [and a female under the age of 18 years];

(4) "adult" means an individual who is not a minor;

(5) "agency" means any person certified, licensed, or otherwise specially empowered by law or rule to place minors for adoption;

(6) "person" means an individual, corporation, government

or governmental subdivision or agency, business trust, estate, trust, partnership or association, or any other legal entity.

§ 2. [Who May Be Adopted]
Any individual may be adopted.

§ 3. [Who May Adopt]
The following individuals may adopt:

(1) a husband and wife together although one or both are minors;

(2) an unmarried adult;

(3) the unmarried father or mother of the individual to be adopted;

(4) a married individual without the other spouse joining as a petitioner, if the individual to be adopted is not his spouse, and if

(i) the other spouse is a parent of the individual to be adopted and consents to the adoption;

(ii) the petitioner and the other spouse are legally separated; or

(iii) the failure of the other spouse to join in the petition or to consent to the adoption is excused by the Court by reason of prolonged unexplained absence, unavailability, incapacity, or circumstances constituuting an unreasonable withholding of consent.

§ 4. [Venue, Inconvenient Forum, Caption]
(a) Proceedings for adoption must be brought in the Court for the place in which, at the time of filing or granting the petition, the petitioner or the individual to be adopted resides or is in military service or in which the agency having the care, custody, or control of the minor is located.

(b) If the Court finds in the interest of substantial justice that the matter should be heard in another forum, the Court may [transfer,] stay or dismiss the proceeding in whole or in part on any conditions that are just.

(c) The caption of a petition for adoption shall be styled substantially "In the Matter of the Adoption of _____." The person to be adopted shall be designated in the caption under the name by which he is to be known if the petition is granted. If the child is placed for adoption by an agency, any name by which the child was previously known shall not be

disclosed in the petition, the notice of hearing, or in the decree
of adoption.

§ 5.   [Persons Required to Consent to Adoption]

(a) Unless consent is not required under section 6, a petition
to adopt a minor may be granted only if written consent to a
particular adoption has been executed by:

(1) the mother of the minor;

(2) the father of the minor if the father was married
to the mother at the time the minor was conceived or at
any time thereafter, the minor is his child by adoption, or
[he has otherwise legitimated the minor according to the
laws of the place in which the adoption proceeding is
brought] [his consent is required under the Uniform Legiti-
macy Act];

(3) any person lawfully entitled to custody of the
minor or empowered to consent;

(4) the court having jurisdiction to determine custody
of the minor, if the legal guardian or custodian of the
person of the minor is not empowered to consent to the
adoption;

(5) the minor, if more than [10] years of age, unless
the Court in the best interest of the minor dispenses with
the minor's consent; and

(6) the spouse of the minor to be adopted.

(b) A petition to adopt an adult may be granted only if
written consent to adoption has been executed by the adult and
the adult's spouse.

§ 6.   [Persons as to Whom Consent and Notice Not Re-
quired]

(a) Consent to adoption is not required of:

(1) a parent who has [deserted a child without afford-
ing means of identification, or who has] abandoned a
child;

(2) a parent of a child in the custody of another, if the
parent for a period of at least one year has failed significantly without justifiable cause (i) to communicate with
the child or (ii) to provide for the care and support of the
child as required by law or judicial decree;

(3) the father of a minor if the father's consent is not
required by section 5(a)(2);

(4) a parent who has relinquished his right to consent under section 19;

(5) a parent whose parental rights have been terminated by order of court under section 19;

(6) a parent judicially declared incompetent or mentally defective if the Court dispenses with the parent's consent;

(7) any parent of the individual to be adopted, if (i) the individual is a minor [18] or more years of age and the Court dispenses with the consent of the parent or (ii) the individual is an adult;

(8) any legal guardian or lawful custodian of the individual to be adopted, other than a parent, who has failed to respond in writing to a request for consent for a period of [60] days or who, after examination of his written reasons for withholding consent, is found by the Court to be withholding his consent unreasonably; or

(9) the spouse of the individual to be adopted, if the failure of the spouse to consent to the adoption is excused by the Court by reason of prolonged unexplained absence, unavailability, incapacity, or circumstances constituting an unreasonable withholding of consent.

(b) Except as provided in section 11, notice of a hearing on a petition for adoption need not be given to a person whose consent is not required or to a person whose consent or relinquishment has been filed with the petition.

§ 7. [How Consent is Executed]

(a) The required consent to adoption shall be executed at any time after the birth of the child and in the manner following:

(1) if by the individual to be adopted, in the presence of the court;

(2) if by an agency, by the executive head or other authorized representative, in the presence of a person authorized to take acknowledgments;

(3) if by any other person, in the presence of the Court [or in the presence of a person authorized to take acknowledgments];

(4) if by a court, by appropriate order or certificate.

(b) A consent which does not name or otherwise identify the adopting parent is valid if the consent [is executed in the presence of the Court and] contains a statement by the person whose consent it is that the person consenting voluntarily executed the consent irrespective of disclosure of the name or other identification of the adopting parent.

§ 8. [Withdrawal of Consent]

(a) A consent to adoption cannot be withdrawn after the entry of a decree of adoption.

(b) A consent to adoption may be withdrawn prior to the entry of a decree of adoption if the Court finds, after notice and opportunity to be heard is afforded to petitioner, the person seeking the withdrawal, and the agency placing a child for adoption, that the withdrawal is in the best interest of the individual to be adopted and the Court orders the withdrawal.

§ 9. [Petition for Adoption]

(a) A petition for adoption shall be signed and verified by the petitioner, filed with the clerk of the Court, and state:

   (1) the date and place of birth of the individual to be adopted, if known;

   (2) the name to be used for the individual to be adopted;

   (3) the date [petitioner acquired custody of the minor and] of placement of the minor and the name of the person placing the minor;

   (4) the full name, age, place and duration of residence of the petitioner;

   (5) the marital status of the petitioner, including the date and place of marriage, if married;

   (6) that the petitioner has facilities and resources, including those available under a subsidy agreement, suitable to provide for the nurture and care of the minor to be adopted, and that it is the desire of the petitioner to establish the relationship of parent and child with the individual to be adopted;

   (7) a description and estimate of value of any property of the individual to be adopted; and

   (8) the name of any person whose consent to the adoption is required, but who has not consented, and facts or circumstances which excuse the lack of his consent normally required to the adoption.

(b) A certified copy of the birth certificate or verification of birth record of the individual to be adopted, if available, and the required consents and relinquishments shall be filed with the clerk.

§ 10. [Report of Petitioner's Expenditures]

(a) Except as specified in subsection (b), the petitioner in any proceeding for the adoption of a minor shall file, before the petition is heard, a full accounting report in a manner acceptable to the Court of all disbursements of anything of value made or agreed to be made by or on behalf of the petitioner in connection with the adoption. The report shall show any expenses incurred in connection with:

(1) the birth of the minor;

(2) placement of the minor with petitioner;

(3) medical or hospital care received by the mother or by the minor during the mother's prenatal care and confinement; and

(4) services relating to the adoption or to the placement of the minor for adoption which were received by or on behalf of the petitioner, either natural parent of the minor, or any other person.

(b) This section does not apply to an adoption by a stepparent whose spouse is a natural or adoptive parent of the child.

(c) Any report made under this section must be signed and verified by the petitioner.

§ 11. [Notice of Petition, Investigation and Hearing]

(a) After the filing of a petition to adopt a minor, the Court shall fix a time and place for hearing the petition. At least 20 days before the date of hearing, notice of the filing of the petition and of the time and place of hearing shall be given by the petitioner to (1) [Public Welfare Department]; (2) any agency or person whose consent to the adoption is required by this Act but who has not consented; and (3) a person whose consent is dispensed with upon any ground mentioned in paragraphs (1), (2), (6), (8), and (9) of subsection (a) of section 6 but who has not consented. The notice to [Public Welfare Department] shall be accompanied by a copy of the petition.

(b) An investigation shall be made by the [Public Welfare Department] or any other qualified agency or person designated by the Court to inquire into the conditions and antecedents of a minor sought to be adopted and of the petitioner for the purpose of ascertaining whether the adoptive home is a suitable home for the minor and whether the proposed adoption is in the best interest of the minor.

(c) A written report of the investigation shall be filed with the Court by the investigator before the petition is heard.

(d) The report of the investigation shall contain an evaluation of the placement with a recommendation as to the granting of the petition for adoption and any other information the Court requires regarding the petitioner or the minor.

(e) Unless directed by the Court, an investigation and report is not required in cases in which an agency is a party or joins in the petition for adoption, a step-parent is the petitioner, or the person to be adopted is an adult. In other cases, the Court may waive the investigation only if it appears that waiver is in the best interest of the minor and that the adoptive home and the minor are suited to each other. The [Public Welfare Department] which is required to consent to the adoption may give consent without making the investigation.

(f) The [Public Welfare Department] or the agency or persons designated by the Court to make the required investigation may request other departments or agencies within or without this state to make investigations of designated portions of the inquiry as may be appropriate and to make a written report thereof as a supplemental report to the Court and shall make similar investigations and reports on behalf of other agencies or persons designated by the Courts of this state or another place.

(g) After the filing of a petition to adopt an adult the Court by order shall direct that a copy of the petition and a notice of the time and place of the hearing be given to any person whose consent to the adoption is required but who has not consented. The court may order an appropriate investigation to assist it in determining whether the adoption is in the best interest of the persons involved.

(h) Notice shall be given in the manner appropriate under rules of civil procedure for the service of process in a civil action in this state or in any manner the Court by order directs. Proof of the giving of the notice shall be filed with the Court before the petition is heard.

§ 12. [Required Residence of Minor]

A final decree of adoption shall not be issued and an interlocutory decree of adoption does not become final, until the minor to be adopted, other than a stepchild of the petitioner, has lived in the adoptive home for at least 6 months after placement by an agency, or for at least 6 months after the [Public Welfare Department] or the Court has been informed of the custody of the minor by the petitioner, and the department or Court has had an opportunity to observe or investigate the adoptive home.

§ 13. [Appearance; Continuance; Disposition of Petition]

(a) The petitioner and the individual to be adopted shall appear at the hearing on the petition, unless the presence of either is excused by the Court for good cause shown.

(b) The Court may continue the hearing from time to time to permit further observation, investigation, or consideration of any facts or circumstances affecting the granting of the petition.

(c) If at the conclusion of the hearing the Court determines that the required consents have been obtained or excused and that the adoption is in the best interest of the individual to be adopted, it may (1) issue a final decree of adoption; or (2) issue an interlocutory decree of adoption which by its own terms automatically becomes a final decree of adoption on a day therein specified, which day shall not be less than 6 months nor more than one year from the date of issuance of the decree, unless sooner vacated by the Court for good cause shown.

(d) If the requirements for a decree under subsection (c) have not been met, the court shall dismiss the petition and determine the person to have custody of the minor, including the petitioners if in the best interest of the minor. In an interlocutory decree of adoption the Court may provide for observation, investigation, and further report on the adoptive home during the interlocutory period.

§ 14. [Effect of Petition and Decree of Adoption]

(a) A final decree of adoption and an interlocutory decree of adoption which has become final, whether issued by a Court of this state or of any other place, have the following effect as to matters within the jurisdiction or before a court of this state:

    (1) except with respect to a spouse of the petitioner and relatives of the spouse, to relieve the natural parents of the adopted individual of all parental rights and responsibilities, and to terminate all legal relationships be-

tween the adopted individual and his relatives, including his natural parents, so that the adopted individual thereafter is a stranger to his former relatives for all purposes including inheritance and the interpretation or construction of documents, statutes, and instruments, whether executed before or after the adoption is decreed, which do not expressly include the individual by name or by some designation not based on a parent and child or blood relationship; and

(2) to create the relationship of parent and child between petitioner and the adopted individual, as if the adopted individual were a legitimate blood descendant of the petitioner, for all purposes including inheritance and applicability of statutes, documents, and instruments, whether executed before or after the adoption is decreed, which do not expressly exclude an adopted individual from their operation or effect.

(b) Notwithstanding the provisions of subsection (a), if a parent of a child dies without the relationship of parent and child having been previously terminated and a spouse of the living parent thereafter adopts the child, the child's right of interitance from or through the deceased parent is unaffected by the adopton.

(c) An interlocutory decree of adoption, while it is in force, has the same legal effect as a final decree of adoption. If an interlocutory decree of adoption is vacated, it shall be as though void from its issuance, and the rights, liabilities, and status of all affected persons which have not become vested shall be governed accordingly.

§ 15. [Appeal and Validation of Adoption Decree]

(a) An appeal from any final order or decree rendered under this Act may be taken in the manner and time provided for appeal from a [judgment in a civil action].

(b) Subject to the disposition of an appeal, upon the expiration of [one] year after an adoption decree is issued the decree cannot be questioned by any person including the petitioner, in any manner upon any ground, including fraud, misrepresentation, failure to give any required notice, or lack of jurisdiction of the parties or of the subject matter, unless, in the case of the adoption of a minor the petitioner has not taken custody of the minor, or, in the case of the adoption of an adult, the adult had no knowledge of the decree within the [one] year period.

§ 16. [Hearings and Records in Adoption Proceedings; Confidential Nature]

Notwithstanding any other law concerning public hearings and records,

(1) all hearings held in proceedings under this Act shall be held in closed Court without admittance of any person other than essential officers of the court, the parties, their witnesses, counsel, persons who have not previously consented to the adoption but are required to consent, and representatives of the agencies present to perform their official duties; and

(2) all papers and records pertaining to the adoption whether part of the permanent record of the court or of a file in the [Department of Welfare] or in an agency are subject to inspection only upon consent of the Court and all interested persons; or in exceptional cases, only upon an order of the Court for good cause shown; and

(3) except as authorized in writing by the adoptive parent, the adopted child, if [14] or more years of age, or upon order of the court for good cause shown in exceptional cases, no person is required to disclose the name or identity of either an adoptive parent or an adopted child.

§ 17. [Recognition of Foreign Decree Affecting Adoption]

A decree of court terminating the relationship of parent and child or establishing the relationship by adoption issued pursuant to due process of law by a court of any other jurisdiction within or without the United States shall be recognized in this state and the rights and obligations of the parties as to matters within the jurisdiction of this state shall be determined as though the decree were issued by a court of this state.

§ 18. [Application for New Birth Record]

Within 30 days after an adoption decree becomes final, the clerk of the court shall prepare an application for a birth record in the new name of the adopted individual and forward the application to the appropriate vital statistics office of the place, if known, where the adopted individual was born and forward a copy of the decree to the [Department of Welfare] of this state for statistical purposes.

§ 19. [Relinquishment and Termination of Parent and Child Relationship]

(a) The rights of a parent with reference to a child, including parental right to control the child or to withhold consent to an adoption, may be relinquished and the relationship of parent and child terminated in or prior to an adoption proceeding as provided in this section.

(b) All rights of a parent with reference to a child, including the right to receive notice of a hearing on a petition for adoption, may be relinquished and the relationship of parent and child terminated by a writing, signed by the parent, regardless of the age of the parent,

(1) in the presence of a representative of an agency taking custody of the child, whether the agency is within or without the state or in the presence and with the approval of a judge of a court of record within or without this state in which the minor was present or in which the parent resided at the time it was signed, which relinquishment may be withdrawn within 10 days after it is signed or the child is born, whichever is later; and the relinquishment is invalid unless it states that the parent has this right of withdrawal; or

(2) in any other situation if the petitioner has had custody of the minor for [2] years, but only if notice of the adoption proceeding has been given to the parent and the court finds, after considering the circumstances of the relinquishment and the long continued custody by the petitioner, that the best interest of the child requires the granting of the adoption.

(c) In addition to any other proceeding provided by law, the relationship of parent and child may be terminated by a court order issued in connection with an adoption proceeding under this Act on any ground provided by other law for termination of the relationship, and in any event on the ground (1) that the minor has been adandoned by the parent, (2) that by reason of the misconduct, faults, or habits of the parent or the repeated and continuous neglect or refusal of the parent, the minor is without proper parental care and control, or subsistence, education, or other care or control necessary for his physical, mental, or emotional health or morals, or, by reason of physical or mental incapacity the parent is unable to provide necessary parental care for the minor, and the court finds that the conditions and causes of the behavior, neglect, or incapacity are irremediable or will not be remedied by the parent, and that by reason thereof the minor is suffering or probably will suffer serious physical, mental, moral, or emotional harm, or (3) that in the case of a parent not having custody of a minor, his consent is being unreasonably withheld contrary to the best interest of the minor.

(d) For the purpose of proceeding under ths Act, a decree terminating all rights of a parent with reference to a child or the relationship of parent and child issued by a court of competent jurisdiction in this or any other state dispenses with the consent to adoption proceedings of a parent whose rights or parent and child relationship are terminated by the decree and with any required notice of an adoption proceeding other than as provided in this section.

(e) A petition for termination of the relationship of parent and child made in connection with an adoption proceeding may be made by:

> (1) either parent if termination of the relationship is sought with respect to the other parent;

> (2) the petitioner for adoption, the guardian of the person, the legal custodian of the child, or the individual standing in parental relationship to the child;

> (3) an agency; or

> (4) any other person having a legitimate interest in the matter.

(f) Before the petition is heard, notice of the hearing thereon and opportunity to be heard shall be given the parents of the child, the guardian of the person of the child, the person having legal custody of the child, and, in the discretion of the court, a person appointed to represent any party.

(g) Notwithstanding the provisions of subsection (b), a relinquishment of parental rights with respect to a child, executed under this section, may be withdrawn by the parent, and a decree of a court terminating the parent and child relationship under this section may be vacated by the Court upon motion of the parent, if the child is not on placement for adoption and the person having custody of the child consents in writing to the withdrawal or vacation of the decree.

§ 20. [Uniformity of Interpretation]

This Act shall be so interpreted and construed as to effectuate its general purpose to make uniform the law of those states which enact it.

231

The following states have adopted this Act as of August 1,
1979.
Arkansas
Iowa
Nebraska
New Mexico
North Dakota
Oklahoma

2. UNIFORM CHILD CUSTODY JURISDICTION ACT 1968 ACT

§ 1. [Purposes of Act; Construction of Provisions]

(a) The general purposes of this Act are to:

(1) avoid jursdictional competition and conflict with
courts of other states in matters of child custody which
have in the past resulted in the shifting of children from
state to state with harmful effects on their well-being;

(2) promote cooperation with the courts of other states
to the end that a custody decree is rendered in that state
which can best decide the case in the interest of the child;

(3) assure that litigation concerning the custody of a
child take place ordinarily in the state with which the child
and his family have the closest connection and where
significant evidence concerning his care, protection, training, and personal relationships is most readily available,
and that courts of this state decline the exercise of jurisdiction when the child and his family have a closer connection with another state;

(4) discourage continuing controversies over child custody in the interest of greater stability of home environment and of secure family relationships for the child;

(5) deter abductions and other unilateral removals of
children undertaken to obtain custody awards;

(6) avoid re-litigation of custody decisions of other
states in this state insofar as feasible;

(7) facilitate the enforcement of custody decrees of
other states;

(8) promote and expand the exchange of information
and other forms of mutual assistance between the courts

of this state and those of other states concerned with the same child; and

(9) make uniform the law of those states which enact it.

(b) This Act shall be construed to promote the general purposes stated in this section.

§ 2. [Definitions]

As used in this Act:

(1) "contestant" means a person, including a parent, who claims a right to custody or visitation rights with respect to a child;

(2) "custody determination" means a court decision and court orders and instructions providing for the custody of a child, including visitation rights; it does not include a decision relating to child support or any other monetary obligation of any person;

(3) "custody proceeding" includes proceedings in which a custody determination is one of several issues, such as an action for divorce or separation, and includes child neglect and dependency proceedings;

(4) "decree" or "custody decree" means a custody determination contained in a judicial decree or order made in a custody proceeding, and includes an initial decree and a modification decree;

(5) "home state" means the state in which the child immediately preceding the time involved lived with his parents, a parent, or a person acting as parent, for at least 6 consecutive months, and in the case of a child less than 6 months old the state in which the child lived from birth with any of the persons mentioned. Periods of temporary absence of any of the named persons are counted as part of the 6-month or other period;

(6) "initial decree" means the first custody decree concerning a particular child;

(7) "modification decree" means a custody decree which modifies or replaces a prior decree, whether made by the court which rendered the prior decree or by another court;

(8) "physical custody" means actual possession and control of a child;

(9) "person acting as parent" means a person, other than a parent, who has physical custody of a child and who has either been awarded custody by a court or claims a right to custody; and

(10) "state" means any state, territory, or possession of the United States, the Commonwealth of Puerto Rico, and the District of Columbia.

§ 3. [Jurisdiction]

(a) A court of this State which is competent to decide child custody matters has jurisdiction to make a child custody determination by initial or modification decree if:

    (1) this State (i) is the home state of the child at the time of commencement of the proceeding, or (ii) had been the child's home state within 6 months before commencement of the proceeding and the child is absent from this State because of his removal or retention by a person claiming his custody or for other reasons, and a parent or person acting as parent continues to live in this State; or

    (2) it is in the best interest of the child that a court of this State assume jurisdiction because (i) the child and his parents, or the child and at least one contestant, have a significant connection with this State, and (ii) there is available in this State substantial evidence concerning the child's present or future care, protection, training, and personal relationships; or

    (3) the child is physically present in this State and (i) the child has been abandoned or (ii) it is necessary in an emergency to protect the child because he has been subjected to or threatened with mistreatment or abuse or is otherwise neglected [or dependent]; or

    (4)(i) it appears that no other state would have jurisdiction under prerequisites substantially in accordance with paragraphs (1), (2), or (3), or another state has declined to exercise jurisdiction on the ground that this State is the more appropriate forum to determine the custody of the child, and (ii) it is in the best interest of the child that this court assume jurisdiction.

(b) Except under paragraphs (3) and (4) of subsection (a), physical presence in this State of the child, or of the child and one of the contestants, is not alone sufficient to confer jurisdiction on a court of this State to make a child custody determination.

(c) Physical presence of the child, while desirable, is not a prerequisite for jurisdiction to determine his custody.

§ 4. [Notice and Opportunity to be Heard]

Before making a decree under this Act, reasonable notice and opportunity to be heard shall be given to the contestants, any parent whose parental rights have not been previously terminated, and any person who has physical custody of the child. If any of these persons is outside this State, notice and opportunity to be heard shall be given pursuant to section 5.

§ 5. [Notice to Persons Outside this State; Submission to Jurisdiction]

(a) Notice required for the exercise of jurisdiction over a person outside this State shall be given in a manner reasonably calculated to give actual notice, and may be:

(1) by personal delivery outside this State in the manner prescribed for service of process within this State;

(2) in the manner prescribed by the law of the place in which the service is made for service of process in that place in an action in any of its courts of general jurisdiction;

(3) by any form of mail addressed to the person to be served and requesting a receipt; or

(4) as directed by the court [including publication, if other means of notification are ineffective].

(b) Notice under this section shall be served, mailed, or delivered, [or last published] at least [10, 20] days before any hearing in this State.

(c) Proof of service outside this State may be made by affidavit of the individual who made the service, or in the manner prescribed by the law of this State, the order pursuant to which the service is made, or the law of the place in which the service is made. If service is made by mail, proof may be a receipt signed by the addressee or other evidence of delivery to the addressee.

(d) Notice is not required if a person submits to the jurisdiction of the court.

§ 6. [Simultaneous Proceedings in Other States]

(a) A court of this State shall not exercise its jurisdiction under this Act if at the time of filing the petition a proceeding concerning the custody of the child was pending in a court of another state exercising jurisdiction substantially in conformity with this Act, unless the proceeding is stayed by the court of the other state because this State is a more appropriate forum or for other reasons.

(b)   Before hearing the petition in a custody proceeding the court shall examine the pleadings and other information supplied by the parties under section 9 and shall consult the child custody registry established under section 16 concerning the pendency of proceedings with respect to the child in other states. If the court has reason to believe that proceedings may be pending in another state it shall direct an inquiry to the state court administrator or other appropriate official of the other state.

(c) If the court is informed during the course of the proceeding that a proceeding concerning the custody of the child was pending in another state before the court assumed jurisdiction it shall stay the proceeding and communicate with the court in which the other proceeding is pending to the end that the issue may be litigated in the more appropriate forum and that information be exchanged in accordance with sections 19 through 22. If a court of this state has made a custody decree before being informed of a pending proceeding in a court of another state it shall immediately inform that court of the fact. If the court is informed that a proceeding was commenced in another state after it assumed jurisdiction it shall likewise inform the other court to the end that the issues may be litigated in the more appropriate forum.

§ 7.   [Inconvenient Forum]

(a) A court which has jurisdiction under this Act to make an initial or modification decree may decline to exercise its jurisdiction any time before making a decree if it finds that it is an inconvenient forum to make a custody determination under the circumstances of the case and that a court of another state is a more appropriate forum.

(b) A finding of inconvenient forum may be made upon the court's own motion or upon motion of a party or a guardian ad litem or other representative of the child.

(c) In determining if it is an inconvenient forum, the court shall consider if it is in the interest of the child that another state assume jurisdiction. For this purpose it may take into account the following factors, among others:

    (1) if another state is or recently was the child's home state;

    (2) if another state has a closer connection with the

child and his family or with the child and one or more of the contestants;

(3) if substantial evidence concerning the child's present or future care, protection, training, and personal relationships is more readily available in another state;

(4) if the parties have agreed on another forum which is no less appropriate; and

(5) if the exercise of jurisdiction by a court of this state would contravene any of the purposes stated in section 1.

(d) Before determining whether to decline or retain jurisdiction the court may communicate with a court of another state and exchange information pertinent to the assumption of jurisdicion by either court with a view to assuring that jurisdiction will be exercised by the more appropriate court and that a forum will be available to the parties.

(e) If the court finds that it is an inconvenient forum and that a court of another state is a more appropriate forum, it may dismiss the proceedings, or it may stay the proceedings upon condition that a custody proceeding be promptly commenced in another named state or upon any other conditions which may be just and proper, including the condition that a moving party stipulate his consent and submission to the jurisdiction of the other forum.

(f) The court may decline to exercise its jurisdiction under this Act if a custody determination is incidental to an action for divorce or another proceeding while retaining jurisdiction over the divorce or other proceeding.

(g) If it appears to the court that it is clearly an inappropriate forum it may require the party who commenced the proceedings to pay, in addition to the costs of the proceedings in this State, necessary travel and other expenses, including attorneys' fees, incurred by other parties or their witnesses. Payment is to be made to the clerk of the court for remittance to the proper party.

(h) Upon dismissal or stay of proceedings under this section the court shall inform the court found to be the more appropriate forum of this fact or, if the court which would have jurisdiction in the other state is not certainly known, shall transmit the information to the court administrator or other appropriate official for forwarding to the appropriate court.

(i) Any communication received from another state informing this State of a finding of inconvenient forum because a court of this State is the more appropriate forum shall be filed in the custody registry of the appropriate court. Upon assuming jurisdiction the court of this State shall inform the original court of this fact.

§ 8. [Jurisdiction Declined by Reason of Conduct]

(a) If the petitioner for an initial decree has wrongfully taken the child from another state or has engaged in similar reprehensible conduct the court may decline to exercise jurisdiction if this is just and proper under the circumstances.

(b) Unless required in the interest of the child, the court shall not exercise its jurisdiction to modify a custody decree of another state if the petitioner, without consent of the person entitled to custody, has improperly removed the child from the physical custody of the person entitled to custody or has improperly retained the child after a visit or other temporary relinquishment of physical custody. If the petitioner has violated any other provision of a custody decree of another state the court may decline to exercise its jurisdiction if this is just and proper under the circumstances.

(c) In appropriate cases a court dismissing a petition under this section may charge the petitioner with necessary travel and other expenses, including attorneys' fees, incurred by other parties or their witnesses.

§ 9. [Information under Oath to be Submitted to the Court]

(a) Every party in a custody proceeding in his first pleading or in an affidavit attached to that pleading shall give information under oath as to the child's present address, the places where the child has lived within the last 5 years, and the names and present addresses of the persons with whom the child has lived during that period. In this pleading or affidavit every party shall further declare under oath whether:

(1) he has participated (as a party, witness, or in any other capacity) in any other litigation concerning the custody of the same child in this or any other state;

(2) he has information of any custody proceeding concerning the child pending in a court of this or any other state; and

(3) he knows of any person not a party to the proceedings who has physical custody of the child or claims to have custody or visitation rights with respect to the child.

(b) If the declaration as to any of the above items is in the affirmative the declarant shall give additional information under oath as required by the court. The court may examine the parties under oath as to details of the information furnished and as to other matters pertinent to the court's jurisdiction and the disposition of the case.

(c) Each party has a continuing duty to inform the court of any custody proceeding concerning the child in this or any other state of which he obtained information during this proceeding.

§ 10.   [Additional Parties]

If the court learns from information furnished by the parties pursuant to section 9 or from other sources that a person not a party to the custody proceeding has physical custody of the child or claims to have custody or visitation rights with respect to the child, it shall order that person to be joined as a party and to be duly notified of the pendency of the proceeding and of his joinder as a party. If the person joined as a party is outside this State he shall be served with process or otherwise notified in accordance with section 5.

§ 11.   [Appearance of Parties and the Child]

[(a)   The court may order any party to the proceeding who is in this State to appear personally before the court. If that party has physical custody of the child the court may order that he appear personally with the child.]

(b) If a party to the proceeding whose presence is desired by the court is outside this State with or without the child the court may order that the notice given under section 5 include a statement directing that party to appear personally with or without the child and declaring that failure to appear may result in a decision adverse to that party.

(c) If a party to the proceeding who is outside this State is directed to appear under subsection (b) or desires to appear personally before the court with or without the child, the court may require another party to pay to the clerk of the court travel and other necessary expenses of the party so appearing and of the child if this is just and proper under the circumstances.

§ 12.   [Binding Force and Res Judicata Effect of Custody Decree]

A custody decree rendered by a court of this State which had jurisdiction under section 3 binds all parties who have

been served in this State or notified in accordance with section
5 or who have submitted to the jurisdiction of the court, and
who have been given an opportunity to be heard. As to these
parties the custody decree is conclusive as to all issues of law
and fact decided and as to the custody determination made
unless and until that determination is modified pursuant to law,
including the provisions of this Act.

§ 13.　[Recognition of Out-of-State Custody Decrees]

The courts of this State shall recognize and enforce an initial
or modification decree of a court of another state which had
assumed jurisdiction under statutory provisions substantially in
accordance with this Act or which was made under factual circumstances meeting the jurisdictional standards of the Act, so
long as this decree has not been modified in accordance with
jurisdictional standards substantially similar to those of this
Act.

§ 14.　[Modification of Custody Decree of Another State]

(a) If a court of another state has made a custody decree,
a court of this State shall not modify that decree unless (1) it
appears to the court of this State that the court which rendered
the decree does not now have jurisdiction under jurisdictional
prerequisites substantially in accordance with this Act or has
declined to assume jurisdiction to modify the decree and (2)
the court of this State has jurisdiction.

(b) If a court of this State is authorized under subsection
(a) and section 8 to modify a custody decree of another state
it shall give due consideration to the transcript of the record
and other documents of all previous proceedings submitted to
it in accordance with section 22.

§ 15.　[Filing and Enforcement of Custody Decree of An-
other State]

(a) A certified copy of a custody decree of another state
may be filed in the office of the clerk of any [District Court,
Family Court] of this State. The clerk shall treat the decree in
the same manner as a custody decree of the [District Court,
Family Court] of this State. A custody decree so filed has the
same effect and shall be enforced in like manner as a custody
decree rendered by a court of this State.

(b) A person violating a custody decree of another state
which makes it necessary to enforce the decree in this State

may be required to pay necessary travel and other expenses, including attorneys' fees, incurred by the party entitled to the custody or his witnesses.

§ 16. [Registry of Out-of-State Custody Decrees and Proceedings]

The clerk of each [District Court, Family Court] shall maintain a registry in which he shall enter the following:

(1) certified copies of custody decrees of other states received for filing;

(2) communications as to the pendency of custody proceedings in other states;

(3) communications concerning a finding of inconvenient forum by a court of another state; and

(4) other communications or documents concerning custody proceedings in another state which may affect the jurisdiction of a court of this State or the disposition to be made by it in a custody proceeding.

§ 17. [Certified Copies of Custody Decree]

The Clerk of the [District Court, Family Court] of this State, at the request of the court of another state or at the request of any person who is affected by or has a legitimate interest in a custody decree, shall certify and forward a copy of the decree to that court or person.

§ 18. [Taking Testimony in Another State]

In addition to other procedural devices available to a party, any party to the proceeding or a guardian ad litem or other representative of the child may adduce testimony of witnesses, including parties and the child, by deposition or otherwise, in another state. The court on its own motion may direct that the testimony of a person be taken in another state and may prescribe the manner in which and the terms upon which the testimony shall be taken.

§ 19. [Hearings and Studies in Another State; Orders to Appear]

(a) A court of this State may request the appropriate court of another state to hold a hearing to adduce evidence, to order a party to produce or give evidence under other procedures of that state, or to have social studies made with respect to the custody of a child involved in proceedings pending in the court of this State; and to forward to the court of this State certified copies of the transcript of the record of the hearing, the evidence otherwise adduced, or any social studies prepared in compliance with the request. The cost of the services may be assessed against the parties or, if necessary, ordered paid by the [County, State].

(b) A court of this State may request the appropriate court of another state to order a party to custody proceedings pending in the court of this State to appear in the proceedings, and if that party has physical custody of the child, to appear with the child. The request may state that travel and other necessary expenses of the party and of the child whose appearance is desired will be assessed against another party or will otherwise be paid.

§ 20.   [Assistance to Courts of Other States]

(a) Upon request of the court of another state the courts of this State which are competent to hear custody matters may order a person in this State to appear at a hearing to adduce evidence or to produce or give evidence under other procedures available in this State [or may order social studies to be made for use in a custody proceeding in another state]. A certified copy of the transcript of the record of the hearing or the evidence otherwise adduced [and any social studies prepared] shall be forwarded by the clerk of the court to the requesting court.

(b) A person within this State may voluntarily give his testimony or statement in this State for use in a custody proceeding outside this State.

(c) Upon request of the court of another state a competent court of this State may order a person in this State to appear alone or with the child in a custody proceeding in another state. The court may condition compliance with the request upon assurance by the other state that state travel and other necessary expenses will be advanced or reimbursed.

§ 21.   [Preservation of Documents for Use in Other States]

In any custody proceeding in this State the court shall preserve the pleadings, orders and decrees, any record that has been made of its hearings, social studies, and other pertinent documents until the child reaches [18, 21] years of age. Upon appropriate request of the court of another state the court shall forward to the other court certified copies of any or all of such documents.

§ 22. [Request for Court Records of Another State]

If a custody decree has been rendered in another state concerning a child involved in a custody proceeding pending in a court of this State, the court of this State upon taking jurisdiction of the case shall request of the court of the other state a certified copy of the transcript of any court record and other documents mentioned in section 21.

§ 23. [International Application]

The general policies of this Act extend to the international area. The provisions of this Act relating to the recognition and enforcement of custody decrees of other states apply to custody decrees and decrees involving legal institutions similar in nature to custody institutions rendered by appropriate authorities of other nations if reasonable notice and opportunity to be heard were given to all affected persons.

§ 24. [Priority]

Upon the request of a party to a custody proceeding which raises a question of existence or exercise of jurisdiction under this Act the case shall be given calendar priority and handled expeditiously.]

The following states have adopted this Act as of August 1, 1979.

Alabama	Louisiana
Alaska	Maine
Arizona	Maryland
Arkansas	Michigan
California	Minnesota
Colorado	Missouri
Connecticut	Montana
Delaware	Nebraska
Florida	Nevada
Georgia	New Hampshire
Hawaii	New Jersey
Idaho	New York
Indiana	North Carolina
Iowa	North Dakota
Kansas	Ohio

Oregon   Tennessee
Pennsylvania   Virginia
Rhode Island   Washington
South Dakota   Wisconsin
                    Wyoming

3. UNIFORM ENFORCEMENT OF SUPPORT ACT 1968 ACT

§ 1. [Purposes]

The purposes of this Act are to improve and extend by reciprocal legislation the enforcement of duties of support.

§ 2. [Definitions]

(a) "Court" means the [here insert name] court of this State and when the context requires means the court of any other state as defined in a substantially similar reciprocal law.

(b) "Duty of support" means a duty of support whether imposed or imposable by law or by order, decree, or judgment of any court, whether interlocutory or final or whether incidental to an action for divorce, separation, separate maintenance, or otherwise and includes the duty to pay arrearages of support past due and unpaid.

(c) "Governor" includes any person performing the functions of Governor or the executive authority of any state covered by this Act.

(d) "Initiating state" means a state in which a proceeding pursuant to this or a substantially similar reciprocal law is commenced. "Initiating court" means the court in which a proceeding is commenced.

(e) "Law" includes both common and statutory law.

(f) "Obligee" means a person including a state or political subdivision to whom a duty of support is owed or a person including a state or political subdivision that has commenced a proceeding for enforcement of an alleged duty of support or for registration of a support order. It is immaterial if the person to whom a duty of support is owed is a recipient of public assistance.

(g) "Obligor" means any person owing a duty of support

or against whom a proceeding for the enforcement of a duty of support or registration of a support order is commenced.

(h) "Prosecuting attorney" means the public official in the appropriate place who has the duty to enforce criminal laws relating to the failure to provide for the support of any person.

(i) "Register" means to [record] [file] in the Registry of Foreign Support Orders.

(j) "Registering court" means any court of this State in which a support order of a rendering state is registered.

(k) "Rendering state" means a state in which the court has issued a support order for which registration is sought or granted in the court of another state.

(l) "Responding state" means a state in which any responsive proceeding pursuant to the proceeding in the initiating state is commenced. "Responding court" means the court in which the responsive proceeding is commenced.

(m) "State" includes a state, territory, or possession of the United States, the District of Columbia, the Commonwealth of Puerto Rico, and any foreign jurisdiction in which this or a substantially similar reciprocal law is in effect.

(n) "Support order" means any judgment, decree, or order of support in favor of an obligee whether temporary or final, or subject to modification, revocation, or remission, regardless of the kind of action or proceeding in which it is entered.

§ 3. [Remedies Additional to Those Now Existing]

The remedies herein provided are in addition to and not in substitution for any other remedies.

§ 4. [Extent of Duties of Support]

Duties of support arising under the law of this State, when applicable under section 7, bind the obligor present in this State regardless of the presence or residence of the obligee.

§ 5. [Interstate Rendition]

The Governor of this State may

(1) demand of the Governor of another state the surrender of a person found in that state who is charged criminally in this State with failing to provide for the support of any person; or

(2) surrender on demand by the Governor of another state a person found in this State who is charged criminally in that

state with failing to provide for the support of any person. Provisions for extradition of criminals not inconsistent with this Act apply to the demand even if the person whose surrender is demanded was not in the demanding state at the time of the commission of the crime and has not fled therefrom. The demand, the oath, and any proceedings for extradition pursuant to this section need not state or show that the person whose surrender is demanded has fled from justice or at the time of the commission of the crime was in the demanding state.

§ 6. [Conditions of Interstate Rendition]

(a) Before making the demand upon the Governor of another state for the surrender of a person charged criminally in this State with failing to provide for the support of a person, the Governor of this State may requre any prosecuting attorney of this State to satisfy him that at least [60] days prior thereto the obligee initiated proceedings for support under this Act or that any proceeding would be of no avail.

(b) If, under a substantially similar Act, the Governor of another state makes a demand upon the Governor of this State for the surrender of a person charged criminally in that state with failure to provide for the support of a person, the Governor may require any prosecuting attorney to investigate the demand and to report to him whether proceedings for support have been initiated or would be effective. If it appears to the Governor that a proceeding would be effective but has not been initiated he may delay honoring the demand for a reasonable time to permit the initiation of a proceeding.

(c) If proceedings have been initiated and the person demanded has prevailed therein the Governor may decline to honor the demand. If the obligee prevailed and the person demanded is subject to a support order, the Governor may decline to honor the demand if the person demanded is complying with the support order.

§ 7. [Choice of Law]

Duties of support applicable under this Act are those imposed under the laws of any state where the obligor was present for the period during which support is sought. The obligor is presumed to have been present in the responding state during the period for which support is sought until otherwise shown.

§ 8. [Remedies of State or Political Subdivision Furnishing Support]

If a state or a political subdivision furnishes support to an individual obligee it has the same right to initiate a proceeding under this Act as the individual obligee for the purpose of securing reimbursement for support furnished and of obtaining continuing support.

§ 9. [How Duties of Support Enforced]

All duties of support, including the duty to pay arrearages, are enforceable by a proceeding under this Act including a proceeding for civil contempt. The defense that the parties are immune to suit because of their relationship as husband and wife or parent and child is not available to the obligor.

§ 10. [Jurisdiction]

Jurisdiction of any proceeding under this Act is vested in the [here insert title of court desired.]

§ 11. [Contents and Filing of [Petition] for Support; Venue]

(a) The [petition] shall be verified and shall state the name and, so far as known to the obligee, the address and circumstances of the obligor and the persons for whom support is sought, and all other pertinent information. The obligee may include in or attach to the [petition] any information which may help in locating or identifying the obligor including a photograph of the obligor, a description of any distinguishing marks on his person, other names and aliases by which he has been or is known, the name of his employer, his fingerprints, and his Social Security number.

(b) The [petition] may be filed in the appropriate court of any state in which the obligee resides. The court shall not decline or refuse to accept and forward the [petition] on the ground that it should be filed with some other court of this or any other state where there is pending another action for divorce, separation, annulment, dissolution, habeas corpus, adoption, or custody between the same parties or where another court has already issued a support order in some other proceeding and has retained jurisdiction for its enforcement.

§ 12. [Officials to Represent Obligee]

If this State is acting as an initiating state the prosecuting attorney upon the request of the court [a state department of welfare, a county commissioner, an overseer of the poor, or other local welfare officer] shall represent the obligee in any proceeding under this Act. [If the prosecuting attorney neglects or refuses to represent the obligee the [Attorney General] may order him to comply with the request of the court or may undertake the representation.] [If the prosecuting attorney neglects or refuses to represent the obligee, the [Attorney General] [State Director of Public Welfare] may undertake the representation.]

§ 13. [Petition for a Minor]

A [petition] on behalf of a minor obligee may be executed and filed by a person having legal custody of the minor without appointment as guardian ad litem.

§ 14. [Duty of Initiating Court]

If the initiating court finds that the [petition] sets forth facts from which it may be determined that the obligor owes a duty of support and that a court of the responding state may obtain jurisdiction of the obligor or his property it shall so certify and cause 3 copies of the [petition] and its certificate and one copy of this Act to be sent to the responding court. Certification shall be in accordance with the requirements of the initiating state. If the name and address of the responding court is unknown and the responding state has an information agency comparable to that established in the initiating state it shall cause the copies to be sent to the state information agency or other proper official of the responding state, with a request that the agency or official forward them to the proper court and that the court of the responding state acknowledge their receipt to the initiating court.

§ 15. [Costs and Fees]

An initiating court shall not require payment of either a filing fee or other costs from the obligee but may request the responding court to collect fees and costs from the obligor. A responding court shall not require payment of a filing fee or other costs from the obligee but it may direct that all fees and costs requested by the initiating court and incurred in this State when acting as a responding state, including fees for filing of pleadings, service of process, seizure of property, stenographic or duplication service, or other service supplied to the obligor, be paid in whole or in part by the obligor or by the [state or political subdivision thereof.] These costs or fees do not have priority over amounts due to the obligee.

§ 16. [Jurisdiction by Arrest]

If the court of this State believes that the obligor may flee it may

> (1) as an initiating court, request in its certificate that the responding court obtain the body of the obligor by appropriate process; or
>
> (2) as a responding court, obtain the body of the obligor by appropriate process. Thereupon it may release him upon his own recognizance or upon his giving a bond in an amount set by the court to assure his appearance at the hearing.

§ 17. [State Information Agency]

(a) The [Attorney General's Office, State Attorney's Office, Welfare Department or other Information Agency] is designated as the state information agency under this Act, it shall

> (1) compile a list of the courts and their addresses in this State having jurisdiction under this Act and transmit it to the state information agency of every other state which has adopted this or a substantially similar Act. Upon the adjournment of each session of the [legislature] the agency shall distribute copies of any amendments to the Act and a statement of their effective date to all other state information agencies;
>
> (2) maintain a register of lists of courts received from other states and transmit copies thereof promptly to every court in this state having jurisdiction under this Act; and
>
> (3) forward to the court in this State which has jurisdiction over the obligor or his property petitions, certificates and copies of the Act it receives from courts or information agencies of other states.

(b) If the state information agency does not know the location of the obligor or his property in the state and no state location service is available it shall use all means at its disposal to obtain this information, including the examination of official records in the state and other sources such as telephone directories, real property records, vital statistics records, police records, requests for the name and address from employers who are able or willing to cooperate, records of motor vehicle license offices, requests made to the tax offices both state and federal where such offices are able to cooperate, and requests made to the Social Security Administration as permitted by the Social Security Act as amended.

(c) After the deposit of 3 copies of the [petition] and certificate and one copy of the Act of the initiating state with the clerk of the appropriate court, if the state information agency knows or believes that the prosecuting attorney is not prosecuting the case diligently it shall inform the [Attorney General] [State Director of Public Welfare,] who may undertake the representation.

§ 18. [Duty of the Court and Officials of This State as Responding State]

(a) After the responding court receives copies of the [petition], certificate and Act from the initiating court the clerk of the court shall docket the case and notify the prosecuting attorney of his action.

(b) The prosecuting attorney shall prosecute the case diligently. He shall take all action necessary in accordance with the laws of this State to enable the court to obtain jurisdiction over the obligor or his property and shall request the court [clerk of the court] to set a time and place for a hearing and give notice thereof to the obligor in accordance with law.

(c) [If the prosecuting attorney neglects or refuses to represent the obligee the [Attorney General] may order him to comply with the request of the court or may undertake the representation.] [If the prosecuting attorney neglects or refuses to represent the obligee, the [Attorney General] [State Director of Public Welfare] may undertake the representation.]

§ 19. [Further Duties of Court and Officials in the Responding State]

(a) The prosecuting attorney on his own initiative shall use all means at his disposal to locate the obligor or his property, and if because of inaccuracies in the [petition] or otherwise the court cannot obtain jurisdiction the prosecuting attorney shall inform the court of what he has done and request the court to continue the case pending receipt of more accurate information or an amended [petition] from the initiating court.

(b) If the obligor or his property is not found in the [county], and the prosecuting attorney discovers that the obligor or his property may be found in another [county] of this State or in another state he shall so inform the court. Thereupon the

clerk of the court shall forward the documents received from
the court in the initiating state to a court in the other [county]
or to a court in the other state or to the information agency or
other proper official of the other state with a request that the
documents be forwarded to the proper court. All powers and
duties provided by this Act apply to the recipient of the documents so forwarded. If the clerk of a court of this State for-
wards documents to another court he shall forthwith notify the
initiating court.

(c) If the prosecuting attorney has no information as to the
location of the obligor or his property he shall so inform the
initiating court.

§ 20. [Hearing and Continuance]

If the obligee is not present at the hearing and the obligor
denies owing the duty of support alleged in the petition or offers
evidence constituting a defense the court, upon request of either
party, continue the hearing to permit evidence relative to the
duty to be adduced by either party by deposition or by appearing in person before the court. The court may designate the
judge of the initiating court as a person before whom a deposition may be taken.

§ 21. [Immunity from Criminal Prosecution]

If at the hearing the obligor is called for examination as an
adverse party and he declines to answer upon the ground that
his testimony may tend to incriminate him, the court may require him to answer, in which event he is immune from criminal prosecution with respect to matters revealed by his
testimony, except for perjury committed in this testimony.

§ 22. [Evidence of Husband and Wife]

Laws attaching a privilege against the disclosure of communications between husband and wife are inapplicable to
proceedings under this Act. Husband and wife are competent
witnesses [and may be compelled] to testify to any relevant
matter, including marriage and parentage.

§ 23. [Rules of Evidence]

In any hearing for the civil enforcement of this Act the court
is governed by the rules of evidence applicable in a civil court
action in the _____ Court. If the action is based on a support order issued by another court a certified copy of the order

shall be received as evidence of the duty of support, subject only to any defenses available to an obligor with respect to paternity (Section 27) or to a defendant in an action or a proceeding to enforce a foreign money judgment. The determination or enforcement of a duty of support owed to one obligee is unaffected by any interference by another obligee with rights of custody or visitation granted by a court.

§ 24 [Order of Support]

If the responding court finds a duty of support it may order the obligor to furnish support or reimbursement therefor and subject the property of the obligor to the order. Support orders made pursuant to this Act shall require that payments be made to the [clerk] [bureau] [probation department] of the court of the responding state. [The court and prosecuting attorney of any [county] in which the obligor is present or has property have the same powers and duties to enforce the order as have those of the [county] in which it was first issued. If enforcement is impossible or cannot be completed in the [county] in which the order was issued, the prosecuting attorney shall send a certified copy of the order to the prosecuting attorney of any [county] in which it appears that proceedings to enforce the order would be effective. The prosecuting attorney to whom the certified copy of the order is forwarded shall proceed with enforcement and report the results of the proceedings to the court first issuing the order.]

§ 25. [Responding Court to Transmit Copies to Initiating Court]

The responding court shall cause a copy of all support orders to be sent to the initiating court.

§ 26. [Additional Powers of Responding Court]

In addition to the foregoing powers a responding court may subject the obligor to any terms and conditions proper to assure compliance with its orders and in particular to:

(1) require the obligor to furnish a cash deposit or a bond of a character and amount to assure payment of any amount due;

(2) require the obligor to report personally and to make payments at specified intervals to the [clerk] [bureau] [probation department] of the court; and

(3) punish under the power of contempt the obligor who violates any order of the court.

§ 27. [Paternity]

If the obligor asserts as a defense that he is not the father of the child for whom support is sought and it appears to the court that the defense is not frivolous, and if both of the parties are present at the hearing or the proof required in the case indicates that the presence of either or both of the parties is not necessary, the court may adjudicate the paternity issue. Otherwise the court may adjourn the hearing until the paternity issue has been adjudicated.

§ 28. [Additional Duties of Responding Court]

A responding court has the following duties which may be carried out through the [clerk] [bureau] [probation department] of the court:

(1) to transmit to the initiating court any payment made by the obligor pursuant to any order of the court or otherwise; and

(2) to furnish to the initiating court upon request a certified statement of all payments made by the obligor.

§ 29. [Additional Duty of Initiating Court]

An initiating court shall receive and disburse forthwith all payments made by the obligor or sent by the responding court. This duty may be carried out through the [clerk] [bureau] [probation department] of the court.

§ 30. [Proceedings Not to be Stayed]

A responding court shall not stay the proceeding or refuse a hearing under this Act because of any pending or prior action or proceeding for divorce, separation, annulment, dissolution, habeas corpus, adoption, or custody in this or any other state. The court shall hold a hearing and may issue a support order pendente lite. In aid thereof it may require the obligor to give a bond for the prompt prosecution of the pending proceeding. If the other action or proceeding is concluded before the hearing in the instant proceeding and the judgment therein provides for the support demanded in the [petition] being heard the court must conform its support order to the amount allowed in the other action or proceeding. Thereafter the court shall not stay enforcement of its support order because of the retention of jurisdiction for enforcement purposes by the court in the other action or proceeding.

§ 31. [Application of Payments]

A support order made by a court of this State pursuant to this Act does not nullify and is not nullified by a support order made by a court of this State pursuant to any other law or by a support order made by a court of any other state pursuant to a substantially similar act or any other law, regardless of priority of issuance, unless otherwise specifically provided by the court. Amounts paid for a particular period pursuant to any support order made by the court of another state shall be credited against the amounts accruing or accrued for the same period under any support order made by the court of this State.

[§ 32. [Effect of Participation in Proceeding]

Participation in any proceeding under this Act does not confer jurisdiction upon any court over any of the parties thereto in any other proceeding.]

[§ 33. [Intrastate Application]

This Act applies if both the obligee and the obligor are in this State but in different [counties.] If the court of the [county] in which the [petition] is filed finds that the [petition] sets forth facts from which it may be determined that the obligor owes a duty of support and finds that a court of another [county] in this State may obtain jurisdiction over the obligor or his property, the clerk of the court shall send the [petition] and a certification of the findings to the court of the [county] in which the obligor or his property is found. The clerk of the court of the [county] receiving these documents shall notify the prosecuting attorney of their receipt. The prosecuting attorney and the court in the [county] to which the copies are forwarded then shall have duties corresponding to those imposed upon them when acting for this State as a responding state.]

§ 34. [Appeals]

If the [Attorney General] [State Director of Public Welfare] is of the opinion that a support order is erroneous and presents a question of law warranting an appeal in the public interest, he may

(a) perfect an appeal to the proper appellate court if the support order was issued by a court of this State, or

(b) if the support order was issued in another state, cause the appeal to be taken in the other state. In either case expenses of appeal may be paid on his order from funds appropriated for his office.

§ 35. [Additional Remedies]

If the duty of support is based on a foreign support order, the obligee has the additional remedies provided in the following sections.

§ 36. [Registration]

The obligee may register the foreign support order in a court of this State in the manner, with the effect, and for the purposes herein provided.

§ 37. [Registry of Foreign Support Orders]

The clerk of the court shall maintain a Registry of Foreign Support Orders in which he shall [file] foreign support orders.

§ 38. [Official to Represent Obligee]

If this State is acting either as a rendering or a registering state the prosecuting attorney upon the request of the court [a state department of welfare, a county commissioner, and overseer of the poor, or other local welfare official] shall represent the obligee in proceedings under this Part.

[If the prosecuting attorney neglects or refuses to represent the obligee, the [Attorney General] may order him to comply with the request of the court or may undertake the representation.] [If the prosecuting attorney neglects or refuses to represent the obligee, the [Attorney General] [State Director of Public Welfare] may undertake the representation.]

§ 39. [Registration Procedure; Notice]

(a) An obligee seeking to register a foreign support order in a court of this State shall transmit to the clerk of the court (1) three certified copies of the order with all modifications thereof, (2) one copy of the reciprocal enforcement of support act of the state in which the order was made, and (3) a statement verified and signed by the obligee, showing the post office address of the obligee, the last known place of residence and post office address of the obligor, the amount of support remaining unpaid, a description and the location of any property of the obligor available upon execution, and a list of the states in which the order is registered. Upon receipt of these documents the clerk of the court, without payment of a filing fee or other cost to the obligee, shall file them in the Registry of Foreign Support Orders. The filing constitutes registration under this Act.

(b) Promptly upon registration the clerk of the court shall send by certified or registered mail to the obligor at the address given a notice of the registration with a copy of the registered support order and the post office address of the obligee. He shall also docket the case and notify the prosecuting attorney of his action. The prosecuting attorney shall proceed diligently to enforce the order.

§ 40.   [Effect of Registration; Enforcement Procedure]

(a) Upon registration the registered foreign support order shall be treated in the same manner as a support order issued by a court of this State. It has the same effect and is subject to the same procedures, defenses, and proceedings for reopening, vacating, or staying as a support order of this State and may be enforced and satisfied in like manner.

(b) The obligor has [20] days after the mailing of notice of the registration in which to petition the court to vacate the registration or for other relief. If he does not so petition the registered support order is confirmed.

(c) At the hearing to enforce the registered support order the obligor may present only matters that would be available to him as defenses in an action to enforce a foreign money judgment. If he shows to the court that an appeal from the order is pending or will be taken or that a stay of execution has been granted the court shall stay enforcement of the order until the appeal is concluded, the time for appeal has expired, or the order is vacated, upon satisfactory proof that the obligor has furnished security for payment of the support ordered as required by the rendering state. If he shows to the court any ground upon which enforcement of a support order of this State may be stayed the court shall stay enforcement of the order for an appropriate period if the obligor furnishes the same security for payment of the support ordered that is required for a support order of this State.

§ 41. [Uniformity of Interpretation]

This Act shall be so construed as to effectuate its general purpose to make uniform the law of those states which enact it.

Every state plus the District of Columbia, Puerto Rico and the Virgin Islands have adopted this Act.

4. UNIFORM MARRIAGE AND DIVORCE ACT
Custody Provisions

§ 401. [Jurisdiction; Commencement of Proceeding]

(a) A court of this State competent to decide child custody matters has jurisdiction to make a child custody determination by initial or modification decree if:

(1) this State (i) is the home state of the child at the time of commencement of the proceeding, or (ii) had been the child's home state within 6 months before commencement of the proceeding and the child is absent from this State because of his removal or retention by a person claiming his custody or for other reason, and a parent or person acting as parent continues to live in this State; or

(2) it is in the best interest of the child that a court of this State assume jurisdiction because (i) the child and his parents, or the child and at least one contestant, have a significant connection with this State, and (ii) there is available in this State substantial evidence concerning the child's present or future care, protection, training, and personal relationships; or

(3) the child is physically present in this State and (i) has been abandoned or (ii) it is necessary in an emergency to protect him because he has been subjected to or threatened with mistreatment or abuse or is neglected or dependent; or

(4) (i) no other state has jurisdiction under prerequisites substantially in accordance with paragraphs (1), (2) or (3), or another state has declined to exercise jurisdiction on the ground that this State is the more appropriate forum to determine custody of the child, and (ii) it is in his best interest that the court assume jurisdiction.

(b) Except under paragraphs (3) and (4) of subsection (a), physical presence in this State of the child, or of the child and one of the contestants, is not alone sufficient to confer jurisdiction on a court of this State to make a child custody determination.

(c) Physical presence of the child, while desirable, is not a prerequisite for jurisdiction to determine his custody.

(d) A child custody proceeding is commenced in the [_____] court:

    (1) by a parent, by filing a petition

        (i) for dissolution or legal separation; or

        (ii) for custody of the child in the [county, judicial district] in which he is permanently resident or found; or

    (2) by a person other than a parent, by filing a petition for custody of the child in the [county, judicial district] in which he is permanently resident or found, but only if he is not in the physical custody of one of his parents.

(e) Notice of a child custody proceeding shall be given to the child's parent, guardian, and custodian, who may appear, be heard, and file a responsive pleading. The court, upon a showing of good cause, may permit intervention of other interested parties.

§ 402. [Best Interest of Child]

The court shall determine custody in accordance with the best interest of the child. The court shall consider all relevant factors including:

    (1) the wishes of the child's parent or parents as to his custody;

    (2) the wishes of the child as to his custodian;

    (3) the interaction and interrelationship of the child with his parent or parents, his siblings, and any other person who may significantly affect the child's best interest;

    (4) the child's adjustment to his home, school, and community; and

    (5) the mental and physical health of all individuals involved.

The court shall not consider conduct of a proposed custodian that does not affect his relationship to the child.

§ 403. [Temporary Orders]

(a) A party to a custody proceeding may move for a temporary custody order. The motion must be supported by an affidavit as provided in Section 410. The court may award temporary custody under the standards of Section 402 after a hearing, or, if there is no objection, solely on the basis of the affidavits.

(b) If a proceeding for dissolution of marriage or legal separation is dismissed, any temporary custody order is vacated unless a parent or the child's custodian moves that the proceeding continue as a custody proceeding and the court finds, after a hearing, that the circumstances of the parents and the best interest of the child requires that a custody decree be issued.

(c) If a custody proceeding commenced in the absence of a petition for dissolution of marriage or legal separation under subsection (1)(ii) or (2) of Section 401 is dismissed, any temporary custody order is vacated.

§ 404. [Interviews]

(a) The court may interview the child in chambers to ascertain the child's wishes as to his custodian and as to visitation. The court may permit counsel to be present at the interview. The court shall cause a record of the interview to be made and to be part of the record in the case.

(b) The court may seek the advice of professional personnel, whether or not employed by the court on a regular basis. The advice given shall be in writing and made available by the court to counsel upon request. Counsel may examine as a witness any professional personnel consulted by the court.

§ 405. [Investigations and Reports]

(a) In contested custody proceedings, and in other custody proceedings if a parent or the child's custodian so requests, the court may order an investigation and report concerning custodial arrangements for the child. The investigation and report may be made by [the court social service agency, the staff of the juvenile court, the local probation or welfare department, or a private agency employed by the court for the purpose].

(b) In preparing his report concerning a child, the investigator may consult any person who may have information about the child and his potential custodial arrangements. Upon order of the court, the investigator may refer the child to professional personnel for diagnosis. The investigator may consult with and obtain information from medical, psychiatric, or other expert persons who have served the child in the past without obtaining the consent of the parent or the child's custodian; but the child's consent must be obtained if he has reached the age of 16, unless the court finds that he lacks mental capactiy to consent. If the requirements of subsection (c) are fulfilled, the investigator's report may be received in evidence at the hearing.

(c) The court shall mail the investigator's report to counsel and to any party not represented by counsel at least 10 days prior to the hearing. The investigator shall make available to counsel and to any party not represented by counsel the investigator's file of underlying data, and reports, complete texts of diagnostic reports made to the investigator pursuant to the provisions of subsection (b), and the names and addresses of all persons whom the investigator has consulted. Any party to the proceeding may call the investigator and any person whom he has consulted for cross-examination. A party may not waive his right of cross-examination prior to the hearing.

§ 406. [Hearings]

(a) Custody proceedings shall receive priority in being set for hearing.

(b) The court may tax as costs the payment of necessary travel and other expenses incurred by any person whose presence at the hearing the court deems necessary to determine the best interest of the child.

(c) The court without a jury shall determine questions of law and fact. If it finds that a public hearing may be detrimental to the child's best interest, the court may exclude the public from a custody hearing, but may admit any person who has a direct and legitimate interest in the particular case or a legitimate educational or research interest in the work of the court.

(d) If the court finds it necessary to protect the child's welfare that the record of any interview, report, investigation, or testimony in a custody proceeding be kept secret, the court may make an appropriate order sealing the record.

§ 407. [Visitation]

(a) A parent not granted custody of the child is entitled to reasonable visitation rights unless the court finds, after a hearing, that visitation would endanger seriously the child's physical, mental, moral, or emotional health.

(b) The court may modify an order granting or denying

visitation rights whenever modification would serve the best interest of the child; but the court shall not restrict a parent's visitation rights unless it finds that the visitation would endanger seriously the child's physical, mental, moral, or emotional health.

§ 408. [Judicial Supervision]

(a) Except as otherwise agreed by the parties in writing at the time of the custody decree, the custodian may determine the child's upbringing, including his education, health care, and religious training, unless the court after hearing, finds, upon motion by the noncustodial parent, that in the absence of a specific limitation of the custodian's authority, the child's physical health would be endangered or his emotional development significantly impaired.

(b) If both parents or all contestants agree to the order, or if the court finds that in the absence of the order the child's physical health would be endangered or his emotional development significantly impaired, the court may order the [local probation or welfare department, court social service agency] to exercise continuing supervision over the case to assure that the custodial or visitation terms of the decree are carried out.

§ 409. [Modification]

(a) No motion to modify a custody decree may be made earlier than 2 years after its date, unless the court permits it to be made on the basis of affidavits that there is reason to believe the child's present environment may endanger seriously his physical, mental, moral, or emotional health.

(b) If a court of this State has jurisdiction pursuant to the Uniform Child Custody Jurisdiction Act, the court shall not modify a prior custody decree unless it finds, upon the basis of facts that have arisen since the prior decree or that were unknown to the court at the time of entry of the prior decree, that a change has occurred in the circumstances of the child or his custodian, and that the modification is necessary to serve the best interest of the child. In applying these standards the court shall retain the custodian appointed pursuant to the prior decree unless:

(1) the custodian agrees to the modification;

(2) the child has been integrated into the family of the petitioner with consent of the custodian; or

(3) the child's present environment endangers seriously his physical, mental, moral, or emotional health, and the harm likely to be caused by a change of environment is outweighed by its advantages to him.

(c) Attorney fees and costs shall be assessed against a party seeking modification if the court finds that the modification action is vexatious and constitutes harassment.

§ 410. [Affidavit Practice]

A party seeking a termporary custody order or modification of a custody decree shall submit together with his moving papers an affidavit setting forth facts supporting the requested order or modification and shall give notice, together with a copy of his affidavit, to other parties to the proceeding, who may file opposing affidavits. The court shall deny the motion unless it finds that adequate cause for hearing the motion is established by the affidavits, in which case it shall set a date for hearing on an order to show cause why the requested order or modification should not be granted.

The following states have enacted this Act as of August 1, 1979.

Arkansas
Colorado
Georgia (substantially similar)
Kentucky
Minnesota (substantially similar)
Montana
Washington (substantially similar)

5. UNIFORM PARENTAGE ACT

§ 1. [Parent and Child Relationship Defined]

As used in this Act, "parent and child relationship" means the legal relationship existing between a child and his natural or adoptive parents incident to which the law confers or imposes rights, privileges, duties, and obligations. It includes the mother and child relationship and the father and child relationship.

§ 2. [Relationship Not Dependent on Marriage]

The parent and child relationship extends equally to every

child and to every parent, regardless of the marital status of the parents.

§ 3.   [How Parent and Child Relationship Established]

The parent and child relationship between a child and

(1) the natural mother may be established by proof of her having given birth to the child, or under this Act;

(2) the natural father may be established under this Act;

(3) an adoptive parent may be established by proof of adoption or under the [Revised Uniform Adoption Act].

§ 4.   [Presumption of Paternity]

(a) A man is presumed to be the natural father of a child if:

(1) he and the child's natural mother are or have been married to each other and the child is born during the marriage, or within 300 days after the marriage is terminated by death, annulment, declaration of invalidity, or divorce, or after a decree of separation is entered by a court;

(2) before the child's birth, he and the child's natural mother have attempted to marry each other by a marriage solemnized in apparent compliance with law, although the attempted marriage is or could be declared invalid, and,

(i) if the attempted marriage could be declared invalid only by a court, the child is born during the attempted marriage, or within 300 days after its termination by death, annulment, declaration of invalidity, or divorce; or

(ii) if the attempted marriage is invalid without a court order, the child is born within 300 days after the termination of cohabitation;

(3) after the child's birth, he and the child's natural mother have married, or attempted to marry, each other by a marriage solemnized in apparent compliance with law, although the attempted marriage is or could be declared invalid, and

(i) he has acknowledged his paternity of the child in writing filed with the [appropriate court or Vital Statistics Bureau].

(ii) with his consent, he is named as the child's father on the child's birth certificate, or

(iii) he is obligated to support the child under a written voluntary promise or by court order;

(4) while the child is under the age of majority, he receives the child into his home and openly holds out the child as his natural child; or

(5) he acknowledges his paternity of the child in a writing filed with the [appropriate court or Vital Statistics Bureau], which shall promptly inform the mother of the filing of the acknowledgment, and she does not dispute the acknowledgment within a reasonable time after being informed thereof, in a writing filed with the [appropriate court or Vital Statistics Bureau]. If another man is presumed under this section to be the child's father, acknowledgment may be effected only with the written consent of the presumed father or after the presumption has been rebutted.

(b) A presumption under this section may be rebutted in an appropriate action only by clear and convincing evidence. If two or more presumptions arise which conflict with each other, the presumption which on the facts is founded on the weightier considerations of policy and logic controls. The presumption is rebutted by a court decree establishing paternity of the child by another man.

§ 5. [Artificial Insemination]

(a) If, under the supervision of a licensed physician and with the consent of her husband, a wife is inseminated artificially with semen donated by a man not her husband, the husband is treated in law as if he were the natural father of a child thereby conceived. The husband's consent must be in writing and signed by him and his wife. The physician shall certify their signatures and the date of the insemination, and file the husband's consent with the [State Deparement of Health], where it shall be kept confidential and in a sealed file. However, the physician's failure to do so does not affect the father and child relationship. All papers and records pertaining to the insemination, whether part of the permanent record of a court or of a file held by the supervising physician or elsewhere, are subject to inspection only upon an order of the court for good cause shown.

(b) The donor of semen provided to a licensed physician for use in artificial insemination of a married woman other than the donor's wife is treated in law as if he were not the natural father of a child thereby conceived.

§ 6.   [Determination of Father and Child Relationship; Who May Bring Action; When Action May Be Brought]

(a) A child, his natural mother, or a man presumed to be his father under Paragraph (1), (2), or (3) of Section 4(a), may bring an action

(1) at any time for the purpose of declaring the existence of the father and child relationship presumed under Paragraph (1), (2), or (3) of Section 4(a); or

(2) for the purpose of declaring the non-existence of the father and child relationship presumed under Paragraph (1), (2), or (3) of Section 4(a) only if the action is brought within a reasonable time after obtaining knowledge of relevant facts, but in no event later than [five] years after the child's birth. After the presumption has been rebutted, paternity of the child by another man may be determined in the same action, if he has been made a party.

(b) Any interested party may bring an action at any time for the purpose of determining the existence or non-existence of the father and child relationship presumed under Paragraph (4) or (5) of Section 4(a).

(c) An action to determine the existence of the father and child relationship with respect to a child who has no presumed father under Section 4 may be brought by the child, the mother or personal representative of the child, the [appropriate state agency], the personal representative or a parent of the mother if the mother has died, a man alleged or alleging himself to be the father, or the personal representative or a parent of the alleged father if the alleged father has died or is a minor.

(d) Regardless of its terms, an agreement, other than an agreement approved by the court in accordance with Section 13(b), between an alleged or presumed father and the mother or child, does not bar an action under this section.

(e) If an action under this section is brought before the birth of the child, all proceedings shall be stayed until after the birth, except service of process and the taking of depositions to perpetuate testimony.

§ 7. [Statute of Limitations]

An action to determine the existence of the father and child relationship as to a child who has no presumed father under Section 4 may not be brought later than [three] years after the birth of the child, or later than [three] years after the effective date of this Act, whichever is later. However, an action brought by or on behalf of a child whose paternity has not been determined is not barred until [three] years after the child reaches the age of majority. Sections 6 and 7 do not extend the time within which a right of inheritance or a right to a succession may be asserted beyond the time provided by law relating to distribution and closing of decedents' estates or to the determination of heirship, or otherwise.

§ 8. [Jurisdiction; Venue]

(a) [Without limiting the jurisdiction of any other court,] [The] [appropriate] court has jurisdiction of an action brought under this Act. [The action may be joined with an action for divorce, annulment, separate maintenance, or support.]

(b) A person who has sexual intercourse in this State thereby submits to the jurisdiction of the courts of this State as to an action brought under this Act with respect to a child who may have been conceived by that act of intercourse. In addition to any other method provided by [rule or] statute, including [cross reference to "long arm statute"], personal jurisdiction may be acquired by [personal service of summons outside this State or by registered mail with proof of actual receipt] [service in accordance with (citation to "long arm statute")].

(c) The action may be brought in the county in which the child or the alleged father resides or is found or, if the father is deceased, in which proceedings for probate of his estate have been or could be commenced.

§ 9. [Parties]

The child shall be made a party to the action. If he is a minor he shall be represented by his general guardian or a guardian ad litem appointed by the court. The child's mother or father may not represent the child as guardian or otherwise. The court may appoint the [appropriate state agency] as guardian ad litem for the child. The natural mother, each man presumed to be the father under Section 4, and each man alleged to be the natural father, shall be made parties or, if not subject to the jurisdiction of the court, shall be given notice of the action in a manner prescribed by the court and an opportunity to be heard. The court may align the parties.

§ 10. [Pre-Trial Proceedings]

(a) As soon as practicable after an action to declare the existence or nonexistence of the father and child relationship has been brought, an informal hearing shall be held. [The court may order that the hearing be held before a referee.] The public shall be barred from the hearing. A record of the proceeding or any portion thereof shall be kept if any party requests, or the court orders. Rules of evidence need not be observed.

(b) Upon refusal of any witness, including a party, to testify under oath or produce evidence, the court may order him to testify under oath and produce evidence concerning all relevant facts. If the refusal is upon the ground that his testimony or evidence might tend to incriminate him, the court may grant him immunity from all criminal liability on account of the testimony or evidence he is required to produce. An order granting immunity bars prosecution of the witness for any offense shown in whole or in part by testimony or evidence he is required to produce, except for perjury committed in his testimony. The refusal of a witness, who has been granted immunity, to obey an order to testify or produce evidence is a civil contempt of the court.

(c) Testimony of a physician concerning the medical circumstances of the pregnancy and the condition and characteristics of the child upon birth is not privileged.

§ 11. [Blood Tests]

(a) The court may, and upon request of a party shall, require the child, mother, or alleged father to submit to blood tests. The tests shall be performed by an expert qualified as an examiner of blood types, appointed by the court.

(b) The court, upon reasonable request by a party, shall order that independent tests be performed by other experts qualified as examiner of blood types.

(c) In all cases, the court shall determine the number and qualifications of the experts.

§ 12.   [Evidence Relating to Paternity]

Evidence relating to paternity may include:

(1) evidence of sexual intercourse between the mother and alleged father at any possible time of conception;

(2) an expert's opinion concerning the statistical probability of the alleged father's paternity based upon the duration of the mother's pregnancy;

(3) blood test results, weighed in accordance with evidence, if available, of the statistical probability of the alleged father's paternity;

(4) medical or anthropological evidence relating to the alleged father's paternity of the child based on tests performed by experts. If a man has been identified as a possible father of the child, the court may, and upon request of a party shall, require the child, the mother, the man to submit to appropriate tests; and

(5) all other evidence relevant to the issue of paternity of the child.

§ 13.   [Pre-Trial Recommendations]

(a) On the basis of the information produced at the pretrial hearing, the judge [or referee] conducting the hearing shall evaluate the probability of determining the existence or nonexistence of the father and child relationship in a trial and whether a judicial declaration of the relationship would be in the best interest of the child. On the basis of the evaluation, an appropriate recommendation for settlement shall be made to the parties, which may include any of the following:

(1) that the action be dismissed with or without prejudice;

(2) that the matter be compromised by an agreement among the alleged father, the mother, and the child, in which the father and child relationship is not determined but in which a defined economic obligation is undertaken by the alleged father in favor of the child and, if appropriate, in favor of the mother, subject to approval by the judge [or referee] conducting the hearing. In reviewing the obligation undertaken by the alleged father in a compromise agreement, the judge [or referee] conducting the hearing shall consider the best interest of the child, in the light of the factors enumerated in Section 15(e), discounted by the improbability, as it appears to him, of

establishing the alleged father's paternity or nonpaternity of the child in a trial of the action. In the best interest of the child, the court may order that the alleged father's identity be kept confidential. In that case, the court may designate a person or agency to receive from the alleged father and disburse on behalf of the child all amounts paid by the alleged father in fulfillment of obligations imposed on him; and

(3) that the alleged father voluntarily acknowledge his paternity of the child.

(b) If the parties accept a recommendaton made in accordance with Subsection (a), judgment shall be entered accordingly.

(c) If a party refuses to accept a recommendation made under Subsection (a) and blood tests have not been taken, the court shall require the parties to submit to blood tests, if practicable. Thereafter the judge [or referee] shall make an appropriate final recommendation. If a party refuses to accept the final recommendation, the action shall be set for trial.

(d) The guardian ad litem may accept or refuse to accept a recommendation under this Section.

(e) The informal hearing may be terminated and the action set for trial if the judge [or referee] conducting the hearing finds unlikely that all parties would accept a recommendation he might make under Subsection (a) or (c).

§ 14. [Civil Action; Jury]

(a) An action under this Act is a civil action governed by the rules of civil procedure. The mother of the child and the alleged father are competent to testify and may be compelled to testify. Subsections (b) and (c) of Section 10 and Sections 11 and 12 apply.

(b) Testimony relating to sexual access to the mother by an unidentified man at any time or by an identified man at a time other than the probable time of conception of the child is inadmissible in evidence, unless offered by the mother.

(c) In an action against an alleged father, evidence offered by him with respect to a man who is not subject to the jurisdiction of the court concerning his sexual intercourse with the mother at or about the probable time of conception of the child is admissible in evidence only if he has undergone and made available to the court blood tests the results of which do not exclude the possibility of his paternity of the child. A man who is identified and is subject to the jurisdiction of the court shall be made a defendant in the action.

[(d) The trial shall be by the court without a jury.]

§ 15. [Judgment or Order]

(a) The judgment or order of the court determining the existence or nonexistence of the parent and child relationship is determinative for all purposes.

(b) If the judgment or order of the court is at variance with the child's birth certificate, the court shall order that [an amended birth registration be made] [a new birth certificate be issued] under Section 23.

(c) The judgment or order may contain any other provision directed against the appropriate party to the proceeding, concerning the duty of support, the custody and guardianship of the child, visitation privileges with the child, the furnishing of bond or other security for the payment of the judgment, or any other matter in the best interest of the child. The judgment or order may direct the father to pay the reasonable expenses of the mother's pregnancy and confinement.

(d) Support judgments or orders ordinarily shall be for periodic payments which may vary in amount. In the best interest of the child, a lump sum payment or the purchase of an annuity may be ordered in lieu of periodic payments of support. The court may limit the father's liability for past support of the child to the proportion of the expenses already incurred that the court deems just.

(e) In determining the amount to be paid by a parent for support of the child and the period during which the duty of support is owed, a court enforcing the obligation of support shall consider all relevant facts, including

(1) the needs of the child;

(2) the standard of living and circumstances of the parents;

(3) the relative financial means of the parents;

(4) the earning ability of the parents;

(5) the need and capacity of the child for education, including higher education;

(6) the age of the child;

(7) the financial resources and the earning ability of the child;

(8) the responsibility of the parents for the support of others; and

(9) the value of services contributed by the custodial parent.

§ 16. [Costs]

The court may order reasonable fees of counsel, experts, and the child's guardian ad litem, and other costs of the action and pre-trial proceedings, including blood tests, to be paid by the parties in proportions and at times determined by the court. The court may order the proportion of any indigent party to be paid by [appropriate public authority].

§ 17. [Enforcement of Judgment or Order]

(a) If existence of the father and child relationship is declared, or paternity or a duty of support has been acknowledged or adjudicated under this Act or under prior law, the obligation of the father may be enforced in the same or other proceedings by the mother, the child, the public authority that has furnished or may furnish the reasonable expenses of pregnancy, confinement, education, support, or funeral, or by any other person, including a private agency, to the extent he has furnished or is furnishing these expenses.

(b) The court may order support payments to be made to the mother, the clerk of the court, or a person, corporation, or agency designated to administer them for the benefit of the child under the supervision of the court.

(c) Willful failure to obey the judgment or order of the court is a civil contempt of the court. All remedies for the enforcement of judgments apply.

§ 18. [Modification of Judgment or Order]

The court has continuing jurisdiction to modify or revoke a judgment or order

(1) for future education and support, and

(2) with respect to matters listed in Subsections (c) and (d) of Section 15 and Section 17(b), except that a court entering a judgment or order for the payment of a lump sum or the purchase of an annuity under Section

15(d) may specify that the judgment or order may not be modified or revoked.

§ 19. [Right to Counsel; Free Transcript on Appeal]

(a) At the pre-trial hearing and in further proceedings, any party may be represented by counsel. The court shall appoint counsel for a party who is financially unable to obtain counsel.

(b) If a party is financially unable to pay the cost of a transcript, the court shall furnish on request a transcript for purposes of appeal.

§ 20. [Hearings and Records; Confidentiality]

Notwithstanding any other law concerning public hearings and records, any hearing or trial held under this Act shall be held in closed court without admittance of any person other than those necessary to the action or proceeding. All papers and records, other than the final judgment, pertaining to the action or proceeding, whether part of the permanent record of the court or of a file in the [appropriate state agency] or elsewhere, are subject to inspection only upon consent of the court and all interested persons, or in exceptional cases only upon an order of the court for good cause shown.

§ 21. [Action to Declare Mother and Child Relationship]

Any interested party may bring an action to determine the existence or nonexistence of a mother and child relationship. Insofar as practicable, the provisions of this Act applicable to the father and child relationship apply.

§ 22. [Promise to Render Support]

(a) Any promise in writing to furnish support for a child, growing out of a supposed or alleged father and child relationship, does not require consideration and is enforceable according to its terms, subject to Section 6(d).

(b) In the best interest of the child or the mother, the court may, and upon the promisor's request shall, order the promise to be kept in confidence and designate a person or agency to receive and disburse on behalf of the child all amounts paid in performance of the promise.

§ 23. [Birth Records]

(a) Upon order of a court of this State or upon request of a court of another state, the [registrar of births] shall prepare [an amended birth registration] [a new certificate of birth] consistent with the findings of the court [and shall substitute the new certificate for the original certificate of birth].

(b) The fact that the father and child relationship was declared after the child's birth shall not be ascertainable from the [amended birth registration] [new certificate] but the actual place and date of birth shall be shown.

(c) The evidence upon which the [amended birth registration] [new certificate] was made and the original birth certificate shall be kept in a sealed and confidential file and be subject to inspection only upon consent of the court and all interested persons, or in exceptional cases only upon an order of the court for good cause shown.

§ 24. [Custodial Proceedings]

(a) If a mother relinquishes or proposes to relinquish for adoption a child who has (1) a presumed father under Section 4(a), (2) a father whose relationship to the child has been determined by a court, or (3) a father as to whom the child is a legitimate child under prior law of this State or under the law of another jurisdiction, the father shall be given notice of the adoption proceeding and have the rights provided under [the appropriate State statute] [the Revised Uniform Adoption Act], unless the father's relationship to the child has been previously terminated or determined by a court not to exist.

(b) If a mother relinquishes or proposes to relinquish for adoption a child who does not have (1) a presumed father under Section 4(a), (2) a father whose relationship to the child has been determined by a court, or (3) a father as to whom the child is a legitimate child under prior law of this State or under the law of another jurisdiction, or if a child otherwise becomes the subject of an adoption proceeding, the agency or person to whom the child has been or is to be relinquished, or the mother or the person having custody of the child, shall file a petition in the [   ] court to terminate the parental rights of the father, unless the father's relationship to the child has been previously terminated or determined not to exist by a court.

(c) In an effort to identify the natural father, the court shall cause inquiry to be made of the mother and any other appropriate person. The inquiry shall include the following: whether the mother was married at the time of conception of the child or at any time thereafter; whether the mother was cohabiting with a man at the time of conception or birth of the child; whether the mother has received support payments or promises of support with respect to the child or in connection with her pregnancy; or whether any man has formally or informally acknowledged or declared his possible paternity of the child.

(d) If, after the inquiry, the natural father is identified to the satisfaction of the court, or if more than one man is identified as a possible father, each shall be given notice of the proceeding in accordance with Subsection (f). If any of them fails to appear or, if appearing, fails to claim custodial rights, his parental rights with reference to the child shall be terminated. If the natural father or a man representing himself to be the natural father, claims custodial rights, the court shall proceed to determine custodial rights.

(e) If, after the inquiry, the court is unable to identify the natural father or any possible natural father and no person has appeared claiming to be the natural father and claiming custodial rights, the court shall enter an order terminating the unknown natural father's parental rights with reference to the child. Subject to the disposition of an appeal, upon the expiration of [6 months] after an order terminating parental rights is issued under this subsection, the order cannot be questioned by any person, in any manner, or upon any ground, including fraud, misrepresentation, failure to give any required notice, or lack of jurisdiction of the parties or of the subject matter.

(f) Notice of the proceeding shall be given to every person identified as the natural father or a possible natural father [in the manner appropriate under rules of civil procedure for the service of process in a civil action in this state, or] in any manner the court directs. Proof of giving the notice shall be filed with the court before the petition is heard. [If no person has been identified as the natural father or a possible father, the court, on the basis of all information available, shall determine whether publication or public posting of notice of the proceeding is likely to lead to identification and, if so, shall order publication or public posting at times and in places and manner it deems appropriate.]

§ 25. [Uniformity of Application and Construction]

This Act shall be applied and construed to effectuate its general purpose to make uniform the law with respect to the subject of this Act among states enacting it.

The following states have enacted this Law as of August 1, 1979.

California
Colorado
Hawaii
Montana
North Dakota
Washington
Wyoming